JAN – – 2010

Jossey–Bass Teacher

DISCARD

Jossey-Bass Teacher provides educators with practical knowledge and tools to create a positive and lifelong impact on student learning. We offer classroom-tested and research-based teaching resources for a variety of grade levels and subject areas. Whether you are an aspiring, new, or veteran teacher, we want to help you make every teaching day your best.

From ready-to-use classroom activities to the latest teaching framework, our value-packed books provide insightful, practical, and comprehensive materials on the topics that matter most to K–12 teachers. We hope to become your trusted source for the best ideas from the most experienced and respected experts in the field.

PEABODY INSTITUTE LIBRARY
PEABODY, MASS.

Social Skills Activities for Special Children

Second Edition

Darlene Mannix

JOSSEY-BASS
A Wiley Imprint
www.josseybass.com

Copyright © 2009 by John Wiley & Sons, Inc. All rights reserved.

Published by Jossey-Bass
A Wiley Imprint
989 Market Street, San Francisco, CA 94103-1741—www.josseybass.com

No part of this publication may be reproduced, stored in a retrieval system, or transmitted in any form or by any means, electronic, mechanical, photocopying, recording, scanning, or otherwise, except as permitted under Section 107 or 108 of the 1976 United States Copyright Act, without either the prior written permission of the publisher, or authorization through payment of the appropriate per-copy fee to the Copyright Clearance Center, Inc., 222 Rosewood Drive, Danvers, MA 01923, 978-750-8400, fax 978-646-8600, or on the Web at www.copyright.com. Requests to the publisher for permission should be addressed to the Permissions Department, John Wiley & Sons, Inc., 111 River Street, Hoboken, NJ 07030, 201-748-6011, fax 201-748-6008, or online at www.wiley.com/go/permissions.

Permission is given for individual classroom teachers to reproduce the pages and illustrations for classroom use. Reproduction of these materials for an entire school system is strictly forbidden.

Limit of Liability/Disclaimer of Warranty: While the publisher and author have used their best efforts in preparing this book, they make no representations or warranties with respect to the accuracy or completeness of the contents of this book and specifically disclaim any implied warranties of merchantability or fitness for a particular purpose. No warranty may be created or extended by sales representatives or written sales materials. The advice and strategies contained herein may not be suitable for your situation. You should consult with a professional where appropriate. Neither the publisher nor author shall be liable for any loss of profit or any other commercial damages, including but not limited to special, incidental, consequential, or other damages.

Jossey-Bass books and products are available through most bookstores. To contact Jossey-Bass directly call our Customer Care Department within the U.S. at 800-956-7739, outside the U.S. at 317-572-3986, or fax 317-572-4002.

Jossey-Bass also publishes its books in a variety of electronic formats. Some content that appears in print may not be available in electronic books.

ISBN 978-0-470-25935-1

Printed in the United States of America

SECOND EDITION

PB Printing   10 9 8 7 6 5 4 3 2 1

About This Book

The idea for this book originated many years ago when I found myself teaching in a rural school with few materials. I was hired as the teacher of ten children considered "emotionally disturbed." Ten children seemed like a comfortable class size to me, and I liked the idea of teaching in a self-contained classroom. I had taught learning disabled students in a resource room prior to this point and had enjoyed my time there, but I couldn't resist the opportunity to take on this new challenge offered to me. (The superintendent of schools let out a visible sigh of relief when I accepted the job, as did the other teacher who was being considered for the position.) I pulled out my undergraduate textbooks, looked through my predecessor's notes on the class, paged through educational catalogues daydreaming of all the supplies I would order, and thought I was prepared for my new assignment. How hard could it be?

Then reality hit. My classroom was in a tiny trailer with no air-conditioning. The textbooks were outdated, and there was no budget for anything. I had bus duty in the morning; had to eat with my students; and was responsible for coming up with activities for physical education, art, and music. My only break each week was thirty minutes of library time. My first weeks were rocky. Pencils were used as weapons, desks were overturned, and crumpled-up assignments were hurled around the room. Tempers were short, and voices were loud. One student even threw a brick through the window. When we gathered for community circle time every day, students would have to leave the group one by one to take a time-out for displaying rude and inappropriate behavior. The kids could not take turns talking, quiet down to listen, handle any sort of criticism, or pay attention to me for more than one minute.

Little by little, I realized that I had to draw on whatever strengths I had as a teacher to reach these children. I did not have the military background of the previous teacher, and I was not as physically imposing (I was probably half his size). But I discovered something about the children: they loved to listen to stories, and they were quiet while I was reading. *Quiet!* I began writing stories for them. I wove their problems and issues and concerns into the stories. I used their names in the stories and drew funny pictures to illustrate them. The children began looking forward to social skills time because it had become interesting and even a little meaningful to them. I had students memorize definitions of sitting still, lining up, and active listening. I let the artist in each child draw pictures to indicate how they might solve a problem. We acted out appropriate and inappropriate ways to handle a typical situation. We practiced having conversations, lining up at the door, raising hands to talk, and other behaviors that seemed to be natural for other students. On top of all that, we had to address learning problems, family issues, suspensions, attitudes, and puberty.

The job ended up being one of my favorite teaching assignments. The writer and artist in me exploded with opportunity. I was able to provide exactly what my students needed because I wrote each worksheet for them the night before. Over the first year, the students and I bonded and came to realize what expectations we had for each other. The second year was even better. The students were experiencing success academically and socially. We used peer tutors to help practice conversational skills. We produced a play. We took field trips. Gradually I began to feel that the students really wanted to be socially accepted, and they began to exert some control over the way they behaved. I don't think I worked any miracles, but I sincerely believe we touched on something important to them. With patience, humor, and much perseverance I gradually developed the materials for teaching basic social skills that appeared in the first edition of *Social Skills Activities for Special Children.* As I revised the book for this second edition, I was amazed that so many of the skills I initially covered remain relevant. Kids now have their own cell phones and MP3 players, and computers are commonplace, and classrooms have interactive whiteboards, computer labs, and DVD players. But kids are still kids, and they still need and want to be accepted by others. For special-needs children, these are skills that need to be intentionally addressed. They still need to understand how authority works. They need friends. They need to know how to behave in various settings to be accepted.

Some things never change.

Contents

This book is divided into three main parts with 164 topics. The topics in Part One address accepting rules and authority at school, those in Part Two are about relating to peers, and those in Part Three are devoted to developing positive social skills. Each part contains sample parent letters, a story that relates to the general social skill for each part, and chapters full of ready-to-use activities as well as classroom tips.

Within each activity is a teacher page that provides:

- A learning objective
- A rationale for the skill
- Several thinking questions for discussion that can be used with a group
- Follow-up activities that can be used after completion of the worksheet
- Answers to the worksheet

The reproducible student worksheet for each activity is generally focused on one skill. It asks the student to read, listen to, and respond in some way to questions or situations that are typical for the school, home, or community environment. If you have a designated social skills time or community circle, you may want to select a chapter or common theme to address during the week. The lessons can be done in any order and adjusted for time by including or omitting follow-up activities. The classroom tips at the end of each part focus on further skill building. The thinking questions for each lesson will also help build social skills as students learn to think before answering, listen to the opinions of others, and try to focus on coming to conclusions. The first three chapters in Part One, "Accepting Rules and Authority at School," focus on the student's relationship with the teacher, rules and responsibilities within the classroom, and relating appropriately to other school personnel. It also contains a chapter on what to do if problems come up. There are sixty-six lessons in Part One. The story for this part, "Mrs. Tryit's Ideas," is about a teacher who becomes frustrated with her class's inability to walk down the hall in an orderly manner and comes up with some unusual training techniques to help them. The skills imparted in Part Two, "Relating to Peers," address learning and working with others, making friends, and being a good friend. There are thirty-two lessons. The story for this part is "Ralph and His Purple Face," about a boy who finds teasing hard to ignore.

Part Three, "Developing Positive Social Skills," is general in nature and targets skills such as having a clear understanding of the social situation, being positive, getting along with others at home, and learning to use everyday good manners. There are sixty-six lessons in this part. The story for this part is "The Accident," about two girls who collide on swings at school and exchange personalities for a few days.

I hope that you will find this book helpful and timely.

Darlene Mannix

About the Author

Darlene Mannix has worked as an educator for more than twenty years and has taught a wide range of children, including learning disabled, emotionally disturbed, language-disordered, and multiply disabled students. She received her bachelor of science degree from Taylor University and her master's degree in learning disabilities from Indiana University. A past presenter at numerous educational conferences, including the Council for Exceptional Children, she has authored many books, including *Life Skills Activities for Special Children* (Jossey-Bass, 1991), *Social Skills Activities for Secondary Students with Special Needs* (Jossey-Bass, 2001), and *Writing Skills Activities for Special Children* (Jossey-Bass, 2001). She currently works as a Title 1 reading teacher at Indian Trail Elementary School in La Porte, Indiana.

Contents

Contents xiii

Accepting Rules and Authority at School

I was walking down the hall one afternoon when I noticed David, a kindergartner. He was in a line with other kindergartners who were standing next to the wall after they had finished at the water fountain. "Hey David," I called to him.

He looked at me sadly and waved.

"What's the matter?" I asked him, bending down to look him in the face. He shook his head and shrugged and then said, "I just learned the lining-up protocol, and they changed it AGAIN." He shook his head. "Kindergarten is kind of hard." And, yes, he actually used the word *protocol*.

One change that I have noticed over the past few years is that of the terminology we use. Instead of "rules," we now have "procedures." (There is a lining-up procedure. A fire drill procedure. A coming-into-the room procedure.) Substitute teachers are now "guest teachers." We have "benchmarks" for every-thing. We have "conflict resolution coaches." But no matter what words are used, the underlying goal for students in the classroom remains the same: understand and accept your environment, and things will go much more smoothly for everyone. It is important not only to teach students the rules or procedures, but also to help them understand why these rules are in place.

Some students from a very young age have difficulty respecting authority. When a five-year-old declares: "I don't have to do what you say!" we wonder what set of expectations accompanied him to school. We sigh and begin the task of teaching obedience, because at some point he or she will need to trust an adult who has safety or efficiency or cooperation in mind for the student's own good. And we as adults continue to model our philosophy of accepting rules and authority in front of our little observers every time we have to submit to authority ourselves. (A humbling moment comes to mind: On my way to work one morning I was pulled over for speeding and had to admit to the officer that I was a teacher on my way to teach rule-following to eager young students. And now I was late and would have to explain why.)

Part One is devoted to helping students learn about and deal with authority at school. The lessons in this part help the student identify and learn how to accept authority from the classroom teacher, other adults, or older peers who are there to help. The lessons also help the student deal with rules and problems they might encounter. To this end, it is divided into these sections:

- Parent letters
- Story: "Mrs. Tryit's Ideas"
- Chapter One: Understanding the Teacher's Role
- Chapter Two: Classroom Rules and Responsibilities
- Chapter Three: Relating Appropriately to Other School People
- Chapter Four: When You Have Problems

PARENT LETTER #1

RE: Accepting Rules and Authority at School—Understanding the Teacher's Role

Dear Parents,

We will be starting a course of study about learning social skills. The first part deals with lessons involving rules and authority at school.

The first set of lessons addresses understanding the teacher's role. Your child's teacher spends many hours each day as a significant voice in your child's life. He or she is more than just a person who engineers the learning of a lot of content and skills; he or she cares about the needs and interests of your child and every other student in the class. Although your child may encounter teachers through the school years who are more or less to his or her liking, the teacher is a very important individual. These lessons acquaint the student with some of the aspects of being a teacher.

Here are some ways that you can help reinforce these ideas at home:

- Ask your child to tell you about the rules at school. Why are they necessary?

- Find out some of the personal interests of your child's teacher. Does he enjoy running? Is she a gourmet cook? Spend a few minutes finding out about the teacher's life outside the classroom.

- Handle conflicts with the teacher in an up-front, positive manner—and never in front of your child. Remember that there are two sides to every story. Before you become upset, call the school and find out what's going on if you are concerned. Information can be misrepresented. Find out the facts.

- Reinforce respect for the teacher. Our lessons will focus on treating the teacher politely, being trustworthy, and allowing the teacher to do his or her job as smoothly as possible.

Sincerely,

_____

Teacher

Copyright © 2009 by John Wiley & Sons, Inc.

PARENT LETTER #2

RE: Accepting Rules and Authority at School—Classroom Rules and Responsibilities

Dear Parents,

Our next unit of study for social skills is about following classroom rules and taking seriously the responsibility of being a student—and all that that implies—while at school. Rules are a necessary part of life for efficient functioning. The rules will make sense and contribute to a good learning environment.

Some of the lessons include working independently, entering and leaving the classroom quietly and in a mannerly way, following instructions, being a good listener, bringing homework to school, and completing assignments.

You can help your child with these skills by:

- Discussing specific classroom rules. What is important in your child's classroom? Does the child know the rules?

- Watching out for homework or other assignments that come home each day. Is your child prepared to finish the work independently? If you don't dig through the backpack or pockets, would the homework be shown to you? Have a routine established so that parent and teacher notes are not missed.

- Making sure that your child is not absent or tardy unless absolutely necessary. The first few minutes of the classroom day often set the tone and agenda for the rest of the day. A child who is late or absent misses something. Make arriving on time a priority.

Sincerely,

_____

Teacher

Copyright © 2009 by John Wiley & Sons. Inc.

PARENT LETTER #3

RE: Accepting Rules and Authority at School—Relating Appropriately to Other School People

Dear Parents,

Besides the classroom teacher, other individuals are at school to help your child learn and help keep school a safe place. Other people who will be [or are] authority figures at school include the principal, other teachers, the bus driver, the counselor, and substitute teachers. We hope that our children will be respectful to these adults as well.

Here are some ideas to keep in mind:

- When you know there will be a substitute teacher in class, do not write off the day as baby-sitting. Go over your expectations for good behavior with your child, and inform your child to be as cooperative and helpful as possible.

- If you are upset with the principal or other administrators, discuss your concerns with them—not your children.

- You may not agree with the decisions made for your child by the adults in school, but first try to understand. You can negotiate better by understanding the position of the other side. Sometimes mistakes are made. No one is perfect.

- The bus driver does not have an easy job. He or she must have control to ensure a safe ride for the children. If your child becomes unruly or uncooperative on the bus, discuss the consequences with him or her. If your child has a long bus ride, send something enjoyable for him or her to do (a special book or word puzzles, for example).

- Be a good role model yourself. Show respect for people who have authority over you: your boss, city officials, the police department. Your attitude toward them conveys your respect.

Sincerely,

_____

Teacher

Copyright © 2009 by John Wiley & Sons, Inc.

PARENT LETTER #4

RE: Accepting Rules and Authority at School—When You Have Problems

Dear Parents,

Everyone experiences difficulties at some time. One of the coping strategies we want our children to understand is that there are resources and techniques available to them to help them get through their difficulties.

The lessons in this unit of study include defining the problem, asking for help, looking harder at the problem, avoiding excuses, using a peer tutor, keeping track of assignments, doing homework, and seeking out adults or friends who can help.

You are a resource for your child when he or she is facing a problem. Keep these points in mind:

- Talk to your child every day. Find out what's bugging him or her. What happened at school? Are things going okay? Even though you may be busy, do not be too busy to stop, look in your child's eyes, and really listen.

- Let your child know that you care about him or her. Spend time together, even if it is just by washing the dishes together or waxing the car.

- Listen. Can you let your child talk for one entire minute without interrupting?

- Encourage your child to talk to the school counselor, his or her teacher, a respected adult, or an older student you trust. It may be difficult for a child to open up to you, but it might be easier after bouncing some ideas off other people. Maybe you are too close to the problem. Don't shut off other avenues for your child to get needed help.

Sincerely,

_____

Teacher

Copyright © 2009 by John Wiley & Sons, Inc.

Story: Mrs. Tryit's Ideas

Mrs. Tryit's class just could not walk down the hall in a line. Oh, they started out pretty well, but soon the students had all kinds of problems. No matter how often they started looking like this . . .

. . . it was only a matter of minutes until the line looked like this:

Copyright © 2009 by John Wiley & Sons, Inc.

Sometimes somebody would walk a little too fast and would step on the heels of the person in front of him or her.

Or somebody would walk too slowly, and everyone behind would pile up like a traffic jam.

One or two people always got out of line and had to fight to get back in.

And little Sheldon Shufflesnout just could not stop looking in every classroom that they passed along the way and give a friendly wave to the people inside.

The teacher, Mrs. Tryit, always had an idea or two to try.

Copyright © 2009 by John Wiley & Sons. Inc.

Copyright © 2009 by John Wiley & Sons, Inc.

First, she went to the supply room, got some black paint and a brush, and painted footsteps all the way down the hall for the students to follow. This way, she thought, they wouldn't walk all over the hall, but would go exactly where they were supposed to go.

So five minutes before they had to go down the hall, the students had to take off their shoes so they wouldn't scrape the paint off the floor.

But there were still problems. The students kept switching places while they were walking. No one could remember where they were supposed to be.

But Mrs. Tryit had another idea: she gave every child a number that was to be taped on his or her back as the students left the room.

"No changing places," she said. "You have to stay in this order."

So ten minutes before it was time to go down the hall, the class took off their shoes and got their number cards.

But there were still problems. Some people in the class walked fast and were always bumping into other people.

But Mrs. Tryit had yet another idea.

Accepting Rules and Authority at School

Copyright © 2009 by John Wiley & Sons. Inc.

Copyright © 2009 by John Wiley & Sons. Inc.

She went to a used car lot on her lunch break and got some old tires. Each student wore one so that if someone behind him or her walked too fast, the jolt would not be too hard.

So fifteen minutes before it was time to go down the hall, the class took off their shoes, got their number cards, and put on their tires.

But there were still problems. Some people walked too slowly and couldn't keep up with others.

But Mrs. Tryit had an idea.

She had a friend who used to work in a circus, training elephants. She borrowed the leg chains that they used to keep the elephants together. When all of the chains were in place, the students could stay together.

So twenty minutes before it was time to go down the hall, the students took off their shoes, got their number cards, put on their tires, and waited for Mrs. Tryit to attach the leg chains.

But there was one more problem. As the class walked down the hall, they kept looking into classrooms, restrooms, and any kind of can, box, or desk that they passed.

But Mrs. Tryit had an idea.

Copyright © 2009 by John Wiley & Sons. Inc.

Accepting Rules and Authority at School

She lived next door to Farmer Fred who had some draft horses that pulled a big cart at the county fair. He put big black blinders on the horses' heads so they could only look straight ahead—not to the right or to the left. Mrs. Tryit asked if she could borrow some.

So twenty-five minutes before it was time to go down the hall, the students took off their shoes, got their number cards, put on their tires, waited for Mrs. Tryit to attach the leg chains, and put on their blinders.

Now, finally, the class was able to walk down the hall with no problems.

Copyright © 2009 by John Wiley & Sons, Inc.

Did I say no problems?

It took the class so long to get ready to go anywhere that by the time they got to where they were going, they had to turn right around and go back.

Some days they had to eat lunch while they were still walking in the hall.

And the day of the fire drill, it took them so long to get their things together that Mrs. Tryit just told them to jump out of the window and not tell anyone.

Finally, the students had had enough. They looked at Mrs. Tryit, got down on their knees, and begged: "Mrs. Tryit—this is all just too much trouble! We'll walk right from now on! Give us a chance!"

Mrs. Tryit smiled. "I think we're all ready to give it a try," she said. "Open the back closet and let's toss everything in.

Copyright © 2009 by John Wiley & Sons, Inc.

Accepting Rules and Authority at School

Copyright © 2009 by John Wiley & Sons, Inc.

Now the class has no problems at all walking down the hall. No one has missed lunch in a long time and fire drills are back to normal. In fact, once someone commented that Mrs. Tryit's class was the fastest and quietest as they walked down the hall!

If the class ever forgets and starts to push or shove or walk a little too fast or too slowly, all Mrs. Tryit has to do is go to the back closet and start to stir up the black paint a little bit.

THE END

Chapter 1

Understanding the Teacher's Role

1.1 My Teacher Is a Person!

Objective

The student will summarize three to five characteristics of a favorite teacher after conducting an informal interview with him or her.

Rationale

Students will have lots of experiences with lots of different teachers in their school career. Some teachers will be favorites; others may not. However, all teachers are people. They have good days and bad days; different interests, hobbies, family members, pets, and so on. By interviewing a favorite teacher, the student can learn about this person's interests and thoughts as a person, not solely as a teacher.

Thinking Questions

1. Who are some teachers you have had? *(ask for names)*

2. What are some things that you remember about these teachers? *(activities that they did in class, funny things that happened, what kind of car they drove)*

3. Why do you think people want to become teachers? *(they like kids, they enjoy helping others, they like the summers off)*

4. Think about a teacher you really liked. Why did you like this person? *(he or she listened, had good games, explained things clearly)*

5. Would you ever like to become a teacher? Why or why not? *(answers will vary)*

6. If you were a teacher, what would you teach? *(answers will vary)*

Activity

Directions: Arrange for students to conduct an interview with a teacher who is willing to participate. It might be a teacher at your school or a teacher the student knows from another place. Help the students arrange a time and place for the interview. Encourage the student to think of additional questions.

Answers: Answers will vary.

Follow-up: Have students share their interviews with the class. What interesting things did they discover about the teacher? What were some things that the teachers liked or disliked about teaching?

Name _____ Date _____

My Teacher Is a Person!

Find out some interesting things about a teacher!

Teacher: _____ Subject or Class: _____

1. How long have you been a teacher? _____

2. What is your favorite thing about teaching? _____

   _____

3. What is the funniest thing that happened to you while teaching? _____

   _____

4. What is something you don't like about teaching? _____

   _____

5. What made you decide to be a teacher? _____

   _____

6. What do you like to do when you are not at school? _____

   _____

7. If you could buy anything for your class, what would you buy? _____

   _____

8. Do you have any children? Pets? _____

   _____

   _____

On the back of this sheet, write any other questions you can think of.

Copyright © 2009 by John Wiley & Sons, Inc.

Understanding the Teacher's Role

1.2 School Rules Are Different from Home Rules

Objective

The student will recognize examples of rules as being appropriate for school, home, or either place.

Rationale

Sometimes what is acceptable behavior at home (eating while you're reading, getting out of your chair whenever you want to) is not appropriate for school, and vice versa. It is important for students to understand the importance of school rules and to follow them when at school, even when the same situation in a different environment (home) might be completely acceptable.

Thinking Questions

1. What are some rules that you have to follow at home? *(take out the garbage, don't talk with your mouth full, make your bed every morning)*
2. What are some rules that you have to follow at school? *(clean off your desk, don't drink too long at the water fountain)*
3. Can you think of some rules that are the same for both home and school? *(don't fight, clean up your mess, don't use bad words)*
4. Why do you think each place has some different rules? *(school has a lot of people, home has just family members)*
5. Why do you think we need so many rules at school? *(to keep things running smoothly, so everyone does things the same way)*
6. What school rules are hardest for you to follow? *(no talking to your neighbor, keep your desk clean)*
7. What school rules do you think are the most important? *(don't talk during a fire drill, no fighting)*

Activity

Directions: Have students complete the worksheet about home and school rules. Write down H (home), S (school), or H and S (both) to indicate where the rule would most likely be needed.

Answers: 1. H   2. S   3. S   4. H, S   5. H, S   6. H   7. S   8. H   9. S   10. H, S

Follow-up: Have students make a list of ten school rules and ten home rules. Compare their answers. Discuss why the rules are important.

1.2   School Rules Are Different from Home Rules

Write H if this sounds like a home rule; write S if this sounds like a school rule. Some rules might be both H and S, so think carefully!

1. Make your bed. _____

2. Put your name at the top of the paper. _____

3. Raise your hand to talk. _____

4. Don't interrupt when someone else is talking. _____

5. Take off your coat and hang it up when you come in. _____

6. Ask before you invite your friends to play. _____

7. Keep your feet under your desk. _____

8. Don't tease your brother or sister. _____

9. Don't take pencils off the teacher's desk. _____

10. Don't throw food at other people. _____

Copyright © 2009 by John Wiley & Sons, Inc.

Understanding the Teacher's Role   **21**

1.3 Different Ways of Learning

Objective

The student will identify several ways that people can learn.

Rationale

Although students may be in a classroom together, they are individuals and learn in different ways. Some students are primarily visual learners; others learn best by moving around, touching, repeating, hearing, or other unique methods. It can be helpful for a student to recognize ways that he or she learns best.

Thinking Questions

1. What is something that you learned how to do in the past few weeks? *(write in cursive, learn to multiply by 5s)*
2. How did you learn to do this? *(repetition, someone showed me how to do it, memory tricks)*
3. Do you think that everyone learns how to do things the same way? *(no)*
4. How could a blind person learn to operate a computer? *(learn where the keys are, have someone assist him or her)*
5. How could someone in a wheelchair play basketball? *(specialized wheelchairs)*
6. Can you think of three different ways that you could learn how to spell some new words? *(copy them ten times, say them out loud, look at the word for ten seconds)*
7. Does everyone learn best in exactly the same way? *(no; there are lots of different ways)*
8. What ways do you learn to do things the best? *(someone shows me, I learn by making mistakes)*

Activity

Directions: Your students are to match each student on the worksheet with the drawing showing the way that he or she learns best.

Answers: 1. Dana   2. John   3. Max   4. Carol

Follow-up: Have students discuss other tasks that can be learned in different ways *(reading, memorizing facts, drawing animals, playing a computer game).* Discuss how individual students think that they learn best.

Name _____ Date _____

1.3   Different Ways of Learning

Each of these students is trying to learn how to bake a cake, but they are learning in different ways. See if you can match the name of each student with the picture by using these clues. Write the student's name on the line below each picture.

JOHN is learning to make a cake by reading a recipe.

CAROL is learning by listening to a friend tell her what to do.

MIGUEL already knows how to bake a cake, so he is using his memory.

DANA is watching a friend make a cake and is doing what the friend does.

Copyright © 2009 by John Wiley & Sons, Inc.

_____

_____

_____

_____

Understanding the Teacher's Role

1.4 Showing Respect for Your Teacher

Objective

The student will identify examples of children who are showing respect for a teacher.

Rationale

"Respect" means treating someone as a valued person. Students should show respect for their teacher and other adults by using words and actions that demonstrate this. It is acceptable to state an opinion, but respect implies that a student uses words or comments that treat the teacher as a valued person. Good manners are always expected.

Thinking Questions

1. How would you feel if I slammed the door in your face? *(mad, upset)*
2. How would you feel if you were standing in a long line, and I let you go ahead of me? *(thankful, pleased)*
3. Which of those examples shows having respect for someone? *(the second)*
4. Can we come up with a good definition for *respect*? *(treating someone as valued)*
5. What are some ways that you can show respect for a teacher? *(being polite, being quiet, not saying nasty things about him or her)*
6. How do you think a teacher feels when the students show respect? *(good, proud, wants to help the students more)*

Activity

Directions: Have the students look at each of the nine examples on the worksheet to determine whether the children are showing respect for their teacher. They are to circle those showing respect and put an X through those who are not.

Answers: 1. circle   2. X   3. circle   4. circle   5. circle   6. X   7. X   8. X   9. circle

Follow-up: Have students take turns explaining their responses to the examples and discuss how the children were or were not showing respect. What could the children who were not behaving respectfully have done differently to express their feelings and still show respect? *(explain why they were mad at the teacher, use a polite voice, discuss the problem calmly with a friend)*

1.4   **Showing Respect for Your Teacher**

Some of these students are showing respect for their teacher. Some are not. Circle the respectful students. Put an X on those who are not showing respect.

Copyright © 2009 by John Wiley & Sons, Inc.

1.5 Doing What the Teacher Asks

Objective

The student will select examples of children who are doing what the teacher asks them to do.

Rationale

Teachers give instructions all day long. When students hear, understand, and then follow the instructions, they can accomplish a lot. This lesson focuses on identifying which children are following the teacher's instructions.

Thinking Questions

1. What are some things that your teacher might ask you to do during the day? (*get out your homework, hang up your coat, put papers in your homework folder*)
2. Why do you think the teacher asks you to do so many things? (*to help us learn, to show us good ways to do things*)
3. What are some reasons that it is hard sometimes to not follow the teacher's directions? (*you might not understand, you might get distracted, you might forget what you're supposed to do*)
4. Why is it a good idea to do what the teacher asks? (*you won't get in trouble, she has a good reason for asking you to do something, you will learn better if everyone follows the directions*)

Activity

Directions: Students read the example of a teacher giving directions and pick out the children who are following the teacher's instructions.

Answers: 1. Albert, yes 2. David, no 3. Sally, no 4. Ed, no

Follow-up: Discuss with students why David, Sally, and Ed did not follow the teacher's instructions. What could they have done instead? What might happen because they did not follow the instructions?

Understanding the Teacher's Role

Copyright © 2009 by John Wiley & Sons, Inc.

Name _____ Date _____

1.5   Doing What the Teacher Asks

Mr. Green asked each of these students to do something. Which of them did what the teacher asked? Circle YES or NO.

1. "Albert, please take this list to the office. The lunch people need to know how many students want pizza today." Albert went to the office, turned in the list, and came right back.

YES   NO

2. "David, would you please take this book to Mrs. Pink down the hall?" David took the book to Mrs. Pink's room, but on the way back he stopped by Mrs. White's class to see if he could wave to his little sister.

YES   NO

3. "Sally, I'm sorry, but you will have to stay in for recess since you didn't get your math done. Please work on it right now." Sally opened her math book and got out her paper, but then she drew horses all over the paper and the table.

YES   NO

4. "Ed, I am glad you brought your library book back. Don't forget to write down the name of the book before you return it to the library." Ed returned the book to the library.

YES   NO

1.6 When the Teacher Leaves the Room

Objective

The student will identify appropriate and inappropriate behaviors for students when the teacher is not in the room.

Rationale

There's nothing more embarrassing than walking down the hall toward your room, hearing an awful commotion, and finding out that it's coming from your room. Students need to learn that even when an authority figure is not physically in the room, good behavior is still expected.

Thinking Questions

1. What would happen if the teacher left this room for a few minutes? (*students would continue working, some would play*)

2. What do you think students should do when their teacher is gone for a little while? (*continue doing what they were told to do*)

3. Before your teacher leaves the room, what does he or she tell you or ask you to do? (*continue working, sit quietly*)

4. Why do you think it's important for things not to get out of control while the teacher is gone? (*someone might get hurt, it wastes time*)

Activity

Directions: Students are to look at the characters who are alone in the classroom. They are to circle or put an X through the children according to their behavior. Make sure that students understand what the children on the worksheet are doing if it is not clear.

Answers: Circle: Mike, Kathy, Dave, John, Kevin, Ellen. X: Pete, Chou, Sue, Rick, Sandy, Jane

Follow-up: What are some possible consequences of the behavior of the students who were not following directions while the teacher was gone r? (*get behind on work, disturb other students*)

Name _____ Date _____

1.6   # When the Teacher Leaves the Room

Mrs. O'Brien got an emergency phone call in the office and had to leave the classroom. She said:

Circle the children she could trust to behave in the room. Put an X through those she could not trust.

Copyright © 2009 by John Wiley & Sons, Inc.

1.7 Getting the Teacher's Attention

Objective

The student will identify several appropriate ways to get the teacher's attention.

Rationale

Students need the attention of their teacher from time to time—to clarify things, get some extra help, or maybe just to tell the teacher something. They need to know how to make that contact with the teacher. Can you be interrupted while you're working with someone else? How can a student reach you? This lesson offers items for discussion about how to get the teacher's attention in an appropriate way.

Thinking Questions

1. What do you think the teacher thinks when you raise your hand? (*you know the answer, you want something*)
2. Why is raising your hand a good signal to let the teacher know you want some attention? (*it's quiet, easy, fairly noticeable in class*)
3. What are some other good ways to let the teacher know you need some attention? (*go up to the desk, call his or her name quietly, put a question mark card on your desk*)
4. What are some ways that don't work very well in a classroom? (*making noises, yelling out*)
5. What system works well in your classroom? (*classrooms may vary as to their method of connecting teacher with student—ask students for their experiences in other classrooms*)

Activity

Directions: Students are to think about the ten suggestions for getting the teacher's attention and put a check mark next to the best ones.

Answers: Check marks by 3, 6, 7, 9.

Follow-up: Discuss why the unchecked answers were inappropriate. Although some may result in getting the teacher's attention (*throwing a book at him or her*), what kind of attention would it get? (*probably a reprimand*)

Copyright © 2009 by John Wiley & Sons, Inc.

Name _____ Date _____

1.7   Getting the Teacher's Attention

Which of these are good ways to get the teacher's attention? Put a check mark next to each good answer.

1. Yelling as loudly as you can: "Hey, you!" _____

2. Throwing a book at the teacher. _____

3. Raising your hand. _____

4. Pulling on the teacher's sleeve while she is working with a small group. _____

5. Standing on your chair. _____

6. Going up to the teacher's desk and waiting quietly. _____

7. Looking at the teacher's face. _____

8. Telling your friend to go get the teacher and make him come over to your desk. _____

9. Using the teacher's name to call him over. _____

10. Yelling the teacher's name as loudly as you can. _____

Understanding the Teacher's Role

1.8 Complaining About Work

Objective

The student will identify characters who are making noncomplaining remarks about work.

Rationale

Complaining leads to arguing and noncompliance. Although it would be nice if all students enjoyed doing their assigned work, many do not—and some are quick to voice their displeasure. This lesson compares complaining statements with noncomplaining statements and puts the student in the position of having to decide which he or she would rather listen to.

Thinking Questions

1. How do you feel when you're given an assignment you don't really want to do? (*in a bad mood, frustrated, tired*)
2. What are some comments that students might make about doing something they don't want to do? (*"Do we have to?" "I don't like this"*)
3. Do you think that complaining about work changes things? (*probably not, might aggravate the teacher*)
4. What are most of the complaints that you hear about? (*work is too hard/long/boring*)
5. If complaints don't get you anywhere, what could you do instead? (*just do it, talk to the teacher about legitimate reasons that you're having trouble, commiserate with your friends after class*)

Activity

Directions: A teacher has given a class some work to do. There are two characters shown for each assignment. The student is to circle the one in each pair who is not complaining.

Answers: 1. second   2. first   3. second   4. second

Follow-up: Discuss ways that students can voice their frustration or problems with work. Is it a problem of not wanting to do the work or simply wanting to complain about it? Is the first character in number 3 really in pain or making a big deal about nothing? What does it feel like to hear constant complaining?

1.8   Complaining About Work

Which of these students would you rather listen to? Circle the student in each pair who is *not* complaining.

Copyright © 2009 by John Wiley & Sons, Inc.

1.9 Arguing with the Teacher

Objective

The student will state comments that are argumentative and then give reasons that the comments are impolite, unhelpful, or unnecessary.

Rationale

The step after complaining seems to be all-out arguing. Some students feel that they have to find something negative about every situation, no matter how neutral that situation may be. This lesson gives the student a chance to think of argumentative comments and then decide whether the arguing is helpful or unnecessary.

Thinking Questions

1. What does it mean to argue with someone? (*try to tell your point of view, which is probably different from the other person's*)
2. What are some bad things that come from arguing? (*hurt feelings, loud voices, nothing solved*)
3. Can good things come from arguing? (*possibly—if one side really listens to the other*)
4. Can you change someone's mind in another way other than arguing with him or her? How? (*be logical, be polite when talking about how you feel*)
5. If you disagree with your teacher about something, is arguing about it going to help? What would help? (*arguing probably wouldn't help; ideas from question 4 might*)

Activity

Directions: The students are to fill in each balloon with words that the arguing student might say to the teacher. Remind students not to go overboard (not to use bad language or gestures!) but to think like an arguer.

Answer examples: 1. "It is not."   2. "They lined up first yesterday! It's not their turn!"   3. "I don't want to use a pencil."   4. "I don't want to read it out loud."   5. "That's too much work! I don't want to!"   6. "Ten pages are too much! Why can't we do one? I don't like that assignment."

Follow-up: Have students volunteer their answers. Then talk about similarities among the answers that students have come up with for Arthur's arguments. How many times do the words *don't*, *won't*, and *not* appear? Students may want to role-play the situations and keep the argument going back and forth a few times. Have them think about the bottom line: Did anything change because Arthur argued? If you were Arthur's friend, what would you advise him to do? How could Arthur change his words to get his point across without (1) complaining and (2) arguing?

Understanding the Teacher's Role

1.9   # Arguing with the Teacher

Meet Arthur Q. Arguer. He likes to argue with teachers about everything and anything. Write in the balloon what you think Arthur might be saying in each situation below.

1.

Your handwriting is very hard to read, Arthur.

2.

It's the girls' turn to line up first.

3.

Don't do your math in markers – use a pencil.

Copyright © 2009 by John Wiley & Sons. Inc.

Understanding the Teacher's Role

4.

5.

6.

Copyright © 2009 by John Wiley & Sons. Inc.

Understanding the Teacher's Role

1.10 Notes Have to Make It Home

Objective

The student will give a reason that it is important to take a note from the teacher home to a parent or guardian.

Rationale

Many items on paper are very important to a school. Behavioral notes, school menus, returned forms that lead to extra services for the school, report card information, and information about class activities are just some examples of notes or messages that need to make it from the school to the student's home. It is a waste of time to have to rewrite, recopy, and relocate notes that should have made it the first time.

Thinking Questions

1. What are some messages or notes that you take home from the school? *(lunch menus, weekly announcements, report cards)*

2. Why do you think it is important for your parents to know what's going on at school? *(so they can come to plays and programs, so they know when to schedule appointments)*

3. What are some ways that notes might get lost? *(drop them, use them to write other things on and then forget about them)*

4. What are some ways that you can make sure a note gets home? *(put it in my homework folder, give it to my mom right away)*

5. How does it help the teacher when you take these notes home? *(important information gets home, the teacher doesn't have to rewrite the note or call home)*

6. How does it help your parents when notes get home? *(they know what's going on, they can send in supplies)*

Activity

Directions: The students are given examples of notes or papers that need to go home. Students should write one reason that it is important for the note to make it home.

Answer examples: 1. permission slip: so I can go on a field trip   2. behavior note: so I can get my reward   3. lunch menu: so I know that I want to order pizza on Friday   4. parent conference: so my parents can come to school and talk to the teacher

Follow-up: Collect examples of notes, messages, and other papers that occasionally go home. Discuss ways that students can remember to take these notes home.

1.10   # Notes Have to Make It Home

Here are some notes or messages from your teacher that need to go home. Write down why it is important that this note makes it home.

1. **Permission slip:** "We are taking a class field trip to the zoo on Friday. Please make sure your child brings $2.00 and a sack lunch."

   _____

   _____

2. **Behavior note:** "Vincente had an excellent day today! He got all of his work done with no complaints."

   _____

   _____

3. **Lunch menu:** "Pizza will be served on Friday instead of on Wednesday next week."

   _____

   _____

4. **Parent conference form:** "Sign up for your conference time with your teacher. First come, first served!"

   _____

   _____

Copyright © 2009 by John Wiley & Sons. Inc.

Understanding the Teacher's Role

1.11 When the Teacher Is Talking . . .

Objective

The student will state the rule: "When the teacher is talking, be quiet and listen."

Rationale

When the teacher is addressing the class, students need to be quiet and listen. Not only is this respectful to the teacher, but it also enables the students to hear what is being said and reminds them to pay attention.

Thinking Questions

1. Are there times when the teacher is talking that you don't need to listen? *(if the teacher is talking to an individual)*
2. How do you know when you are supposed to be listening to what the teacher says? *(when it's in class, during a lesson)*
3. What are some distractions to hearing the teacher's words? *(noises in the classroom, other conversations, something going on outside)*
4. If the teacher is saying something really important, what do you think students should do? *(listen, be quiet)*
5. How does this show respect for the teacher? *(shows that you value the teacher's words and actions)*

Activity

Directions: The characters on this worksheet have a word below them. Students are to find the characters who are quiet when the teacher is talking and write the word that goes with him or her *in order* in the boxes below the drawing.

Answer: Be quiet and listen.

Follow-up: Discuss why the rude students are not listening to the teacher while she is talking. What are they doing instead? *(talking, yelling for help, whistling)* Why is it important not only to follow the rule but to show manners and respect by being quiet?

1.11   # When the Teacher Is Talking . . .

See if you can finish the rule. Underneath each student is a word. Find those students who are listening to the teacher. Put the words together in the boxes below the drawing in order to finish the rule.

be   good   loud   quiet

to   from   and   bad

hear   see   listen   help

Copyright © 2009 by John Wiley & Sons, Inc.

1.12 Teacher-Pleasing Behaviors

Objective

The student will be able to give examples of behaviors that are teacher pleasing in various school settings.

Rationale

Some students may have problems getting along with certain teachers, especially teachers whom they perceive are not "their" teacher. Others have a chip on their shoulder, and they anticipate the negative possibilities of every behavior. By learning to identify and use a few simple teacher-pleasing behaviors, students get off on the right foot with a teacher and may be able to change negative attitudes that unfortunately some teachers might develop from contact with difficult students.

Thinking Questions

1. In the "olden days," students used to bring in an apple for their teachers. Why do you think they did this? (*so the teachers would like them, maybe the teacher didn't have a big enough lunch*)

2. If you were going to bring something to school to give your teacher, what might it be? (*depends on the teacher: perhaps a magnet for the board, computer game, a drawing*)

3. Let's think about one teacher in particular. Let's say the P.E. teacher. What is something that you could do or say that would make him or her say, "Wow! What a nice class" or "You are a thoughtful person!" (*being polite, picking up the equipment at the end of class*)

4. When you wake up in the morning, would you rather hear your mom or dad say, "Get up and get your shoes on! Hurry up"! or "Good morning! Let's have a good day!" (*the second*)

5. Can you think of some things you could say to a teacher to make him or her smile? (*"Good morning. May I help you with your books?" "I'm going to have a great day!"*)

Activity

Directions: After reading the examples on the worksheet, students should circle the child in each pair who is demonstrating a teacher-pleasing behavior. Discuss why the behavior is pleasing to a teacher.

Answers: 1. second child: saying something polite   2. first child: anticipating something the teacher might need   3. first child: looking at the teacher while he is giving directions   4. second child: complimenting the teacher

Follow-up: Have students think about ways that they can do things that will please their various teachers. Discuss the difference between trying to manipulate the situation with false flattery versus trying to anticipate something that the other person might find nice or pleasing.

1.12   **Teacher-Pleasing Behaviors**

Which student in each pair is showing a teacher-pleasing behavior? Circle your choice.

1.

2.

Copyright © 2009 by John Wiley & Sons, Inc.

3.

Copyright © 2009 by John Wiley & Sons, Inc.

4.

1.13 When Your Teacher Has a Bad Day

Objective

The student will identify appropriate responses to a teacher who might be having a bad day.

Rationale

We all have them: the days when you get to school late, can't find your answer key, the computer lab is filled with another class, and you have a long and difficult parent conference to look forward to after school. It is important for students to realize that even their teachers might have an off day and that they need to rise to the occasion to be mature and caring.

Thinking Questions

1. What do you think might make a teacher have a bad day? (*something going wrong at home, being late, having a headache*)

2. Sometimes even teachers get grouchy or make mistakes. Can you think of any examples? (*a teacher spelled a word wrong on the board, had a headache, came in very tired from staying up with a sick child*)

3. Do you think that when a teacher has a bad day, it would be a good time to ask for special favors or extra recess or to make a lot of noise? Why or why not? (*no, because the teacher is already dealing with other issues*)

4. What are things that you could do to help your teacher if he or she is having a bad day? (*be quiet, help each other instead of bothering the teacher with something trivial, draw a card*)

Activity

Directions: Have students read the scenario on the left side of the worksheet, which shows a situation in which a teacher is struggling with something. Students should draw a picture on the right side that shows something they could do for or say to the teacher.

Answer example: 1. headache: play soft music   2. yelled at by a parent: "You are a good teacher." 3.   late for work: "We know what to do and already took the lunch count for you." 4. art class was can-celled—"That's okay. We can just draw in the room."

Follow-up: Have students share their drawings and responses. The next time you have a bad day, maybe you can hang up the pictures for a reminder!

Understanding the Teacher's Role

1.13   # When Your Teacher Has a Bad Day

The teachers on the left side are having a bad day for various reasons. Draw a picture on the right that shows something you or your classmates could do to help the teacher have a better day.

1.

2.

Copyright © 2009 by John Wiley & Sons, Inc.

3.

4.

Copyright © 2009 by John Wiley & Sons, Inc.

Understanding the Teacher's Role

1.14 Having Fun, But Knowing When to Stop

Objective

The students will recognize situations in which having fun can go too far, continue on too long, or become inappropriate.

Rationale

Even teachers like to joke around sometimes! It is fun to tell some jokes, tease someone, toss a ball around the room, and engage in other playful behaviors. Students, however, need to recognize the limits of when and how to be playful in the classroom.

Thinking Questions

1. What would you do if I told you that I can imitate the sound of an elephant? *(we'd ask you to demonstrate!)*

2. What if everyone in the class made an animal noise at the same time? What would happen? *(it would be funny, it would get loud in here)*

3. Would it be funny if I had a soft foam ball and bounced it off of Tommy's head? *(yes)*

4. What if I had twenty balls and everyone starting throwing them around? *(it would be great, it would be really funny)*

5. Would it be funny if we kept throwing the balls for a couple of hours and didn't get anything else done? *(we might get tired of throwing the balls around, we would get behind in our work)*

6. What if I said we can have three people each tell a joke? *(that would be good, fun)*

7. What if I said that everyone in the whole class can tell ten jokes? *(it would take a long time and some of the jokes might not be funny)*

8. Do you think it's okay to have fun in the classroom like telling jokes and teasing and playing around sometimes? *(yes)*

9. When do you think it's too much? *(if it hurts someone, if it takes too long, if we get tired of it)*

10. What would be a good signal to let everyone know that the fun time is over for now and we have to get back to work? *(ringing a bell, flashing the lights)*

Activity

Directions: These teachers like to have fun in class and have fun with their students. But in some of the examples, the students are going too far and not calming down from the fun. Circle OKAY or NOT OKAY to show whether the students are behaving appropriately.

Answers: 1. NOT OKAY (all of the students wanted to turn the chairs backward and they tossed the book) 2. OKAY (everyone laughed at the joke, then went back to work) 3. NOT OKAY (the students were laughing so loudly that the teacher next door came to see what was going on) 4. OKAY (the students know that she is "the assistant" only for a little while and for fun) 5. NOT OKAY (all of the students wanted to jump up and touch Mr. Hall's hair)

Follow-up: Discuss with the students why it is great to be able to laugh and have fun together in a class, much like in their own family. Discuss why it is important to stay within appropriate limits so that you can have fun often without fear of it turning into trouble.

1.14   Having Fun, But Knowing When to Stop

All of these teachers like their students and like to have fun. But in some of these examples, the kids in the class don't know when to stop. Read each example, and circle OKAY or NOT OKAY to show if the students are behaving appropriately.

1. On April Fool's Day, Mrs. Young turned Vincente's desk backward, and put his chair on top of his desk. She told him that he was going to be the teacher for the day and gave him the teacher's edition of the reading book. The students laughed at the desk and started to turn their desks around too. Then they came up to Vincente and tried to grab the answer book out of his hand. They began passing the book around and tossing it over their heads trying to play keep-away with it!

   OKAY   NOT OKAY

2. Mr. Kona heard a good joke on the radio on his way to school, so he asked everyone to listen very carefully to something really, really important! He was going to tell them something that was extremely important and would be on their big test on Friday! Then he told a knock-knock joke that was really silly. The students groaned at the joke and told him he needed to learn some better jokes.

   OKAY   NOT OKAY

3. Mr. Wildhair showed the class a picture of himself as a chubby baby in a baby pool putting a rubber duck in his mouth. The class began laughing louder and louder until the teacher from the class next door stopped in to see what was going on.

   OKAY   NOT OKAY

4. Mrs. Zip picked the new student who is very shy to be her assistant for the day. She let the new girl take lunch count, assign computers to everyone, and pass out papers. At first one of the kids in the class said that it wasn't fair, but the other students said that she was a new girl and it was just for a day and just for fun, so everyone pretended that the new girl was their teacher.

   OKAY   NOT OKAY

5. Mr. Hall got a spiky new hair cut and asked Denny if he wanted to touch a spike to see how sharp it was. Denny touched the spike and yelled, "OWWW!" Then all of the kids ran up to touch Mr. Hall's hair and began yelling, "OWWW! OWWWW! That hurts!!!"

   OKAY   NOT OKAY

Copyright © 2009 by John Wiley & Sons, Inc.

Classroom Tips for Understanding the Teacher's Role

- For a writing assignment, give students these titles: "If I Were the Teacher for a Day . . . ," "School Rules I Could Live Without," or "When I Become a Parent, I'm Going to . . ."

- Allow volunteer students to teach a fairly easy task or short lesson to the class. Afterward, discuss with the class how the lesson was hard, or easy, or fun and what things made it clear. Do they think it's easier to learn if there are visual aids or by hands-on experiences?

- Have students write instructions for making or doing something (but without revealing the answer). Ask various students to read their instructions out loud, and see if the rest of the class can figure out what the task is.

- Leave the room periodically, allowing students a chance to control their own behavior. Have students take turns being "in charge" to handle questions or greet visitors. Sometimes the most disruptive child does a complete turnaround when empowered to be the one with the responsibility.

- Have students role-play ways to get the teacher's attention.

- For constant complainers or arguers, pretend to put on "earmuffs." Take them "off" when the student is ready to discuss the matter calmly.

- Have a signal for the class to know when you need everyone to listen. It may be tapping something with a pencil, clearing your throat, or simply saying, "Time to listen." Be consistent with your cue. No one can be in a state of perpetual listening, so let students know when you need their undivided attention.

- If it is one of those days when things are not going well, model for students how to reset the attitude for the day. You might declare a cookie break, take an extra recess, skip a science lesson in order to read a story to students, or do some other activity as a opportunity to calm things down and mentally regroup.

Chapter 2

Classroom Rules and Responsibilities

2.1 Entering the Classroom

Objective

The student will state or demonstrate appropriate ways to enter a classroom.

Rationale

It is very disturbing to have a lesson interrupted by a noisy entrant or to lose the attention of the class to students who bring outside aggravations, arguments, or moods into the class. It is an important classroom skill for students to walk into a classroom (ongoing or not) in a quiet, mannerly fashion.

Thinking Questions

1. When you walk down a hallway, what is usually going on in the classrooms you pass? *(teachers teaching, students working, perhaps singing or talking)*

2. Who are some of the people who come into your room from time to time? *(guests, parents, other teachers, school nurse)* What is their purpose? *(to pick up students, to talk to the teacher)*

3. When you have interruptions, what usually happens in class? *(students stop what they're doing to watch)*

4. When you walk into a class that has already started, what are some ways you can go in without interrupting too much? *(tiptoe in quietly, go to the back of the room)*

5. How can the whole class enter a classroom peacefully? *(go in a few at a time, go in quietly, lower voices, stop talking about what went on in the hall)*

Activity

Directions: The worksheet shows examples of students entering a classroom in various loud ways. Students write at least one way the students could improve this aspect of their behavior.

Answer examples: 1. Ellen could stop tattling about what went on during the bus ride. 2. John could leave the paper airplane in the restroom. 3. Andy and Frank could finish their lunches in the cafeteria. 4. Sandy could talk to Ashley about her dress later.

Follow-up: Have students pay attention to the kinds of conversations that go on as students enter the classroom. Do students bring outside problems (fights, arguments, bad moods) into the class? You may want to have students role-play alternatives to coming into the classroom noisily and seeking attention.

2.1 # Entering the Classroom

These students are entering the classroom, but they are not coming in quietly. What can each student do to improve his or her behavior?

1. Ellen is coming in first thing in the morning.

   Ellen could _____

   _____

   _____

   _____

   _____

2. John is coming into the room after going to the restroom.

   John could _____

   _____

   _____

   _____

   _____

Copyright © 2009 by John Wiley & Sons. Inc.

Classroom Rules and Responsibilities

2.1 Entering the Classroom (continued)

3. Andy and Frank are coming into the room after lunch.

The boys could _____

_____

_____

_____

_____

4. Sandy is coming into the room while the teacher is leading a discussion in the front.

Sandy could _____

_____

_____

_____

_____

Copyright © 2009 by John Wiley & Sons. Inc.

Classroom Rules and Responsibilities

2.2 Morning Agenda

Objective

The student will identify expected activities that will take place on a daily basis in a classroom.

Rationale

Students and teachers benefit from routine and organization. Being able to anticipate events is helpful for planning, organizing, and making predictions for needs and expectations, as well as helping to give the big picture for what will be happening that day. Of course, both teachers and students need to be flexible, but in general it is helpful to have an agenda.

Thinking Questions

1. What day is it today? What are some things that will probably happen in class today? *(recess, art, go to lunch)*

2. How did you know what would be happening today? *(agenda on the board, routine every week, special notices)*

3. Why do you think it is helpful to know ahead of time what's going to happen? *(you know whether to get out your gym shoes, you know how much time to plan for getting your work done)*

4. How does having a daily agenda help both the teacher and the class to have a better day? *(kids won't be asking, "What are we doing today?" all the time; if something good is going to happen, you can look forward to that; everyone will know when a test is coming up)*

5. What are some things that you would like to know about for each day? *(what's for lunch, special activities, tests, guest speakers, indoor or outdoor recess)*

Activity

Directions: The worksheet shows a sample agenda for a class. Students are to look at the agenda and answer questions related to it. Students can either give their answers orally or write them on the back of the worksheet.

Answers: 1. Gym is at 9:30. 2. There is a spelling test on Friday. 3. Robbie's father is coming to talk about bike safety. 4. Fire drill at 1:00. 5. Reading Buddies with kindergartners is today, so bring a book. 6. Recess is indoors today. 7. We will need our subtraction facts flash cards.

Follow-up: Discuss ways that the class can help get the agenda ready each day. What information is helpful? What information could you add to the agenda? (perhaps a weather report?) Are there ways to enliven the agenda board? Would it help to have students take turns going over the agenda with the rest of the class each day?

2.2   **Morning Agenda**

GOOD MORNING STUDENTS!! TODAY IS THURSDAY!!
• Who is not here today?
• Lunch choices are: pizza, peanut butter & jelly, sandwiches
• 9:00   Morning Seat Work
• 9:30   Gym
• 10:00 Spelling—Don't forget TEST tomorrow!
• 10:30 Reading—Poetry Section
• 11:30 Reading Buddies today with Kindergarten Friends
• 12:00 Lunch
• 1:00   Fire Drill!
• 1:30   Special Guest: Robbie's Dad—bike safety
• 2:00   Math Practice—Subtraction Flash Cards
• 2:30   Indoor Recess
• 3:00   Clean Up

Copyright © 2009 by John Wiley & Sons. Inc.

Look at the illustration and answer the following questions:

1. What is happening at 9:30 today?
2. What do you need to know about spelling for tomorrow?
3. Who is the special guest? What will he talk about?
4. What time is the fire drill?
5. What do you need for your Reading Buddy today?
6. Should you plan to go outside for recess today?
7. What should you get for math today?

2.3 Paying Attention to the Task

Objective

The student will identify characters who are paying attention to a given task.

Rationale

Part of the responsibility of being a good student is to be able to pay attention to the task at hand. Paying attention might involve eye contact, taking notes, or tuning out other distractions and really listening. The purpose of this lesson is for students to focus on thinking about what paying attention to a task involves.

Thinking Questions

1. What does it mean when someone tells you to "pay attention"? *(listen, be quiet)*
2. How could you tell just by looking if someone is paying attention? *(the person might be quiet, look interested)*
3. Why is it easier to pay attention to some tasks than others? *(might be more interesting, easier to understand)*
4. Why do you think it is important to pay attention to whatever job you are supposed to be working on? *(do a better job, get better grade, won't have to do over)*
5. If you're working on a task you don't like, could paying attention to what you're doing make it any easier? *(possibly—understanding it better might make it easier to perform)*

Activity

Directions: On this worksheet, students are to select the student in each pair who is paying attention to the task. Students are to circle the correct student. Make sure students understand each task.

Answers: 1. student on right   2. student on right   3. student on left   4. student on right   5. student on right

Follow-up: Discuss the tasks on the worksheet with the class. When a teacher accuses someone of "not paying attention," what might the teacher be seeing? *(a student doing something else, not doing anything at all)* How does a student look and act when he or she is paying attention?

2.3   **Paying Attention to the Task**

These students are supposed to be working on different tasks at school. Circle the student in each pair who is paying attention to the job.

1. Writing spelling words on a piece of paper:

2. Making a cat out of modeling clay:

Classroom Rules and Responsibilities

Copyright © 2009 by John Wiley & Sons. Inc.

2.3 Paying Attention to the Task (continued)

3. Copying the sentence off the board:

4. Reading the story in the book:

5. Putting books away:

Copyright © 2009 by John Wiley & Sons, Inc.

2.4 Talking to Your Neighbor

Objective

The student will identify appropriate and inappropriate times to talk with nearby students in class.

Rationale

Some students just love to talk! This is particularly annoying when the teacher is trying to give instructions and a student is not listening and is preventing another student from hearing as well. Students have a responsibility to refrain from talking under certain circumstances.

Thinking Questions

1. Why do you think there are rules like "No talking in class"? *(so people can hear the teacher, keep the room quiet)*
2. What if you sat right next to your best friend and had something important to tell him or her? Should you talk then? *(depends on what the teacher is doing, can you say it quickly?)*
3. Why might it bother other people if you were talking? *(they couldn't hear what the teacher is saying)*
4. What are some times during the school day when you can talk to your friends? *(lunch, recess, in the bathroom)*

Activity

Directions: Students are to decide whether each situation is a good time for talking to friends. After thinking about each situation, they are to write YES or NO on the line next to each problem.

Answers: 1. no   2. yes   3. no   4. no   5. no   6. yes, but quietly

Follow-up: Discuss the problems that accompany inappropriate talking in each of the "no" situations. If you already know how to do something, why wouldn't it be okay to talk? *(disturb others)* Discuss what times are acceptable for talking in your classroom.

2.4   # Talking to Your Neighbor

Is this a good time to talk to your neighbor? Write YES or NO on the line next to each situation.

1. The bell just rang at the start of class, and you want to tell your friend all about the birthday presents you got over the weekend. _____

2. It's lunch and you are sitting by your best friend, who wants to talk about what you'll do when you spend the weekend together. _____

3. You are in P.E. class, and the teacher is explaining how to play kickball. You already know how to play kickball, so you want to tell the boy next to you about what you watched on TV last night.

   _____

4. The teacher is giving the answers to your math worksheet. You got a lot of problems wrong, so you ask your neighbor to show you how to do them correctly. _____

5. Fire drill! While you are lining up, you want to tell your friend about the time you rode in a fire truck. _____

6. All of your work for the day is done, so the teacher lets you go to the back table and work on an art project with a friend. You have a great idea for a poster and want to ask your partner what he or she thinks. _____

Copyright © 2009 by John Wiley & Sons, Inc.

2.5 Oops, Wrong Assignment

Objective

The student will identify whether an assignment shown on the worksheet is the one the teacher assigned.

Rationale

How many times have you looked at papers that were laboriously completed—but the assignment was the wrong one? A student needs to be sure that he or she understands what the assignment is and does it according to the directions. This lesson gives students practice in identifying whether the assignments were the specified ones.

Thinking Questions

1. How do you know what assignments you are supposed to do? *(teacher says something, written on the board)*
2. What might happen if you weren't listening when the teacher gave the assignment? *(might do the wrong one)*
3. How could you make sure that you are doing what the teacher asked you to do? *(listen, write it down, check with a friend)*
4. What happens in some classes if you do the wrong assignment? *(you still have to do the right one)*
5. Why do you think the teacher chooses certain assignments for you to do? *to practice what we've been doing in class, the teacher knows we are able to do them)*

Activity

Directions: Students are to look at the assignments given to characters by a teacher and then decide whether the student did the given assignment. Students must use picture cues to determine what the characters did. Tell students not to make assumptions (for example, there might be more math problems on the *back* of the paper), but just to use what's obvious from the picture.

Answers: 1. no (she only did three)   2. yes   3. yes   4. no   5. no (the book is open to page 24, so we assume that the student didn't even see the sentences on page 26)

Follow-up: Discuss with students why some of the characters did the wrong assignment and what they could have done not to have made the mistake. Have students tell about experiences in which they may have done the wrong assignment and what happened as a result.

2.5   # Oops, Wrong Assignment

Here are some assignments given to the class by the teacher. But not all of the students did the correct assignment! Check each drawing carefully to decide whether the assignment is the right one. Then write YES or NO on the line.

1. Do math problems 1 through 10. _____

2. Do the reading game on the computer. Use the thumb-drive that is on the right side of the

   computer. _____

Copyright © 2009 by John Wiley & Sons, Inc.

Classroom Rules and Responsibilities   **63**

3. Run to the far side of the field, touch the tree,

    and run back. _____

4. Cut out five pictures of things that begin with the

    letter M. _____

5. Copy all of the sentences in the spelling book on

    page 26. _____

Copyright © 2009 by John Wiley & Sons, Inc.

Classroom Rules and Responsibilities

2.6 Complying with Instructions Right Away

Objective

The student will identify examples of characters who are complying right away with the teacher's directions.

Rationale

When a student is given a task to do, even something as simple as "sit down" or "come over here," we expect him or her to comply right away. Many students, however, comply at their leisure (if at all), as if their slowness to respond might cause the teacher to forget the command. This lesson focuses on having students identify characters who respond right away.

Thinking Questions

1. When a teacher (or parent) asks you to do something, what do you usually do? *(do it)*
2. How long does it take before you actually get started doing something that you might not want to do? *(a few minutes, after I get a drink, a very long time)*
3. Does it make the job any easier to put it off? *(usually no)*
4. Why do you think people put things off or procrastinate? *(hope it will go away)*
5. What do you think a teacher expects when he or she asks you to do something? *(to do it right away)*

Activity

Directions: This activity involves having students read about characters who have been asked to do something. They must decide whether the character complies quickly.

Answers: 1. no   2. no   3. yes   4. no   5. no   6. yes

Follow-up: Discuss the character's responses to the teachers' requests. What do students think that the characters might say to defend their actions? *("I was going to do it . . . ")* Is there anything wrong with looking out the window or cleaning out a desk? *(No, but wrong timing)*

2.6　　**Complying with Instructions Right Away**

Is the student doing what the teacher asked him or her to do right away? Circle YES or NO.

1. Mrs. Brown asked Tommy to come up to her desk. Tommy walked over to the window.　**YES　NO**

2. Mrs. Smith asked Susan to put away her math book. Susan did four more math problems.　**YES　NO**

3. Mrs. Green asked Mike to hang up his coat. Mike got up and hung it up.　**YES　NO**

4. Mr. Peters asked the class to line up for lunch. George started to clean out his desk.　**YES　NO**

5. Mr. James asked Joan to put her pencil down. Joan put it in her ear.　**YES　NO**

6. Miss Clark asked Mark to take a note to the office. Mark said, "Who does it go to?" Miss Clark said, "It goes to Mrs. Jones." Mark took the note and went to the office.　**YES　NO**

Copyright © 2009 by John Wiley & Sons, Inc.

2.7 Saying "I Can't"

Objective

The student will offer alternative statements to express "I can't" in several different school situations.

Rationale

"I can't!" can be a cry for help, a refusal to persevere, a demonstration of frustration, and sometimes giving up too soon. Although a student will face many seemingly difficult tasks at school, the "I can't" attitude is a block to figuring out how to solve the problem in a positive way.

Thinking Questions

1. What is something that was really hard for you to do when you were in kindergarten [or several years ago or when you were little]? *(tie a shoe, do addition problems, read)*

2. Did you ever use the words "I can't"? Why? *(it seemed really hard, I was frustrated)*

3. How did you ever learn to do the task? *(someone taught me, I got older, I tried until I got it)*

4. What are some things that are hard for you to do now? *(write in cursive, solve division problems, do well on tests)*

5. Do you think that sometime you will be able to do those tasks? How? *(work harder, get some help)*

6. Instead of saying "I can't," what are some other things you could say? *("I need help." "This is hard for me.")*

Activity

Directions: The children on the worksheet are saying "I can't" about something that they are supposed to do. Select the answer that shows a more positive way to express how they feel.

Answers: 1. a 2. b 3. a 4. a 5. b

Follow-up: Make a bulletin board of alternative phrases to "I can't" that students can use when they are frustrated. Remind students that there are always ways to solve a problem, but giving up shuts down the path to finding the answers.

2.7
Saying "I Can't"

These students are having some trouble. Instead of saying "I can't!" circle the letter of the answer that they could say to show they need help.

1. Belinda is supposed to copy her spelling words, but her pencil broke.
   a. "My pencil broke! I need to get another one so I can finish this."
   b. "My pencil broke! I can't do this assignment."

2. Marcus is having trouble putting his books neatly in his desk.
   a. "This desk is too small! There are too many books!"
   b. "Could someone help me put the books away?"

3. Ethan is having trouble painting a picture of a house that he likes.
   a. "Ms. Albright, my paint keeps dripping. What should I do?"
   b. "I hate this paper! This paint is too watery!"

4. Alison is getting frustrated trying to put a jigsaw puzzle together.
   a. "I'll keep trying different pieces until I find the right ones."
   b. "This puzzle is too hard."

5. Jayden is supposed to write his sentences in cursive.
   a. "I don't want to learn to write in cursive. It takes too long."
   b. "If I look at the chart, I can remember how the letters go."

Copyright © 2009 by John Wiley & Sons, Inc.

2.8 Appropriate and Inappropriate Language

Objective

The student will determine whether certain language and certain topics are appropriate for use at school.

Rationale

Some forms of language are definitely not appropriate for school: swearing, derogatory words toward others, mean-spirited teasing, insulting comments, and so on. Furthermore, some topics are not appropriate for school either. Students should think through what is okay for the situation they are in at the time.

Thinking Questions

1. We know that we should always try to be polite to each other, but sometimes you might hear words that are unkind or mean. Can you give an example of something that would be mean to say to someone? *(you are ugly, you are fat, you smell)*

2. There are some types of words that you should not use at school, and probably your parents don't want you to use at home either. Don't say the words out loud, but what kinds of words am I talking about? *(swear words, gang words, lyrics from some hip-hop songs)*

3. Your parents probably have told you that you can't go to certain movies. Why not? *(they have bad words, they are for grown-ups)*

4. Why do you think someone your age is not supposed to see things like that? *(it will give us nightmares, make us think bad thoughts)*

5. I bet some of you have played some video games that have some violence and killing in them. I am not your parent, but why do you think I am going to tell you that you aren't going to talk about how great the game is in my classroom? *(others will want to play it too and their parents might not allow it; maybe it's really for older kids; the class is for learning, not for talking about scary things that might hurt others)*

6. Some words can hurt people, and some words show disrespect. How can you figure out which words are okay? *(think about how they would make you feel if someone said it to you)*

7. Sometimes there are things that are funny to talk about, but you have to pick the right time. What is something you would not want to hear about while you are eating? *(something disgusting)*

8. Remember that the words you use are what people use to make an impression of you. What kind of impression do you want to make on others? What do you want them to say about you? *(polite, nice to others, knows how to act)*

Activity

Directions: Students are to read the situation and circle YES or NO to determine whether the child is using appropriate language at the appropriate time.

    Answers: 1. no 2. no 3. yes 4. no 5. no 6. yes

Follow-up: Using good language and recognizing appropriate times for the discussion of controversial topics is an ongoing process. Whenever teachable moments arise, have students focus on recognizing good examples of appropriate language.

2.8   Appropriate and Inappropriate Language

Copyright © 2009 by John Wiley & Sons, Inc.

Is this language appropriate for the classroom in these situations? Circle YES or NO.

1. The class is having a birthday party. Anthony wants to tell about a violent video game that he got for his birthday. **YES   NO**

2. Christopher accidentally got hit in the head by an eraser that someone threw toward him. Christopher called the boy a bad word. **YES   NO**

3. Alexandria and Sally are working on flash cards together. Sally got an answer wrong and said, "I must be crazy! I know that answer!" **YES   NO**

4. William didn't get picked to give his answer, so he began to swear at the teacher. **YES   NO**

5. Friday is movie day! Alyssa wanted to bring in a movie that her older sister really likes, but it is rated R. **YES   NO**

6. The counselor is talking to the class about not talking to strangers because children need to stay safe. Carlos told about a time when he was at a wedding and a man was drinking too much. He told his parents, and they made sure that Carlos was safe with them. **YES   NO**

    Classroom Rules and Responsibilities

2.9 What Do I Need for This Job?

Objective

The student will identify what items, tools, or materials are necessary for a given task.

Rationale

It may seem obvious, but certain tasks at school require certain tools. For example, a spelling test will probably require a pencil and a sheet of paper. Teaching a student to think ahead will help him or her gather the necessary items and maybe leave the unnecessary items behind.

Thinking Questions

1. I am going to give you a job or task to think about. You tell me what you need for the job. Ready? Spelling test [or math flash card practice, reading groups, P.E., or outside recess]. *(students should offer appropriate items)*

2. Tell me if you think these things are helpful for doing your work at school: stuffed animals, key chains, cell phone, plastic knife, a picture of your grandmother. *(answers will vary)*

3. Some things can get in the way of getting a job done. Would you find it distracting if someone was listening to music on headphones if you could hear a little bit of the music? Why would that disturb you? *(you would want to hear the music too)*

4. Why would it be okay to bring in some personal things during free time or community circle? *(that's the time to talk about other things, share fun things)*

5. Why is it important to have only what you really need on your desk while you are working? *(focus better, have more work space)*

Activity

Directions: Students should read the job description and circle all of the items that might be helpful to get the job done.

Answers: 1. Math test: pencil, eraser   2. Story: crayons, paper, pencil   3. Computer work: nothing   4. Show and tell: pictures from home, stuffed animal   5. Calendar: numbers, month

Follow-up: Discuss how it can be a time-saver to stop for a moment and think about what is needed before tackling a job. Also discuss how having your materials well organized can save some time because everything will be exactly where it is needed You might start to use a classroom phrase to let students know it's time to stop, think, and get what they need.

2.9   # What Do I Need for This Job?

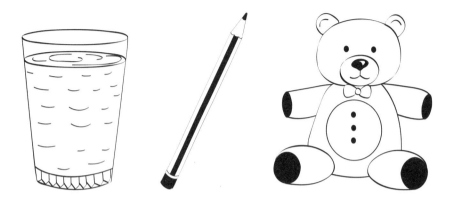

Here are some jobs. Think about what is needed for each task in the first column, and circle every item that is useful for it.

Copyright © 2009 by John Wiley & Sons, Inc.

1. **Math test**   pencil   geoboard   marker   eraser   reading book

2. **Writing and illustrating a story**   basketball   crayons   candy   paper   pencil

3. **Reading a story on the computer**   gum   glass of water   calculator   toy car

4. **Show and tell**   pictures from home   kitchen table   rotten eggs   stuffed animal

5. **Making a calendar**   spoon   number cards   month card   baseball cards

2.10 Good Choices for Free Time

Objective

The student will identify appropriate activities for free time at school.

Rationale

Sometimes you have to deal with indoor recess. If students are aware of what choices are available to them during free time or even moments when they have finished their work and need something to do, they will be more likely to use that time in a constructive manner. Sometimes students need to know what they can or can't do when they are in this situation. Other times they may have to think a little bit to come up with something they can do on their own.

Thinking Questions

1. Have you ever said, "I'm bored!"? *(probably)*
2. There should never be a time when you can't think of something to do with your time. What are some things that you can do at home when you are bored? *(read a book, go for a walk, call a friend)*
3. When you are at school, it's a little different, but you still have choices. What are some things that you know you are always able to do if you have free time? *(work on a puzzle, draw a picture, read a book)*
4. Before you give yourself free time, what should you make sure you have done? *(all of my work, any homework, any missed assignments)*
5. Why should you be careful to choose activities that won't bother someone who does not have free time? *(they will be distracted)*
6. What are some free time activities that might bother other people who are still working? *(singing, playing with loud games, moving around a lot)*
7. What are some of your free time activities? *(seven-up game, drawing, looking at the ant farm)*

Activity

Directions: Students should examine a list of possible free time activities, and check the ones that they think are appropriate for school.

Answers: Activities with an X: 1, 2, 4, 8, 10

Follow-up: Discuss the list of activities, and determine why these were selected as appropriate. Have the class brainstorm, and put together an ongoing list of twenty different activities that are good free time activities. You may want to qualify if these are okay for the individual, for the whole class, for a few minutes versus extended time, and other constraints.

2.10   **Good Choices for Free Time**

Copyright © 2009 by John Wiley & Sons. Inc.

Which of these would make good activities for class free time? Put an X in front of each one.

_____ 1. working on a jigsaw puzzle

_____ 2. drawing cartoons

_____ 3. blowing up and popping balloons

_____ 4. sitting in a beanbag chair and reading

_____ 5. jumping off of the table

_____ 6. drawing a tattoo on your arm

_____ 7. playing catch with a football

_____ 8. playing a game on the computer with headphones

_____ 9. letting the class guinea pig run loose

_____ 10. taking turns reading a play with a friend

2.11 Leaving the Classroom

Objective

The student will state or demonstrate appropriate ways to leave a classroom.

Rationale

As with entering a room, leaving a room is a time when some students enjoy grandstanding or making noises or long farewells with friends. Students should be taught to leave the room quietly, quickly, and without fanfare.

Thinking Questions

1. What are some reasons that you might have to leave the classroom while the rest of the class stayed? *(special reading, go to the bathroom, go to the office, run an errand)*

2. Why might it bother other people if someone left loudly? *(they might be trying to finish their work)*

3. How could it be a problem if someone wanted to touch and pat people on their way out the door? *(it's like "tag"—the touched person will want to touch back, patting is invading someone's space)*

4. What are ways that people shut the door that are bothersome? *(slamming the door, making the door creak, taking a long time to go out the door)*

5. What is a good way for people to leave the classroom when they have to go out? *(go quietly and quickly without trying to get attention)*

Activity

Directions: Students are to consider several examples of characters leaving a classroom and write YES or NO in the box next to each example to indicate if the character is leaving appropriately.

Answers: 1. no   2. yes   3. yes   4. no   5. no

Follow-up: Discuss why the characters who got a "no" were not leaving appropriately. *(1—did lots of talking, interrupting; 4—slammed the door; 5—touched people on his way out)* Discuss what method the teacher wants to use for people who want to leave to use the restroom. Should they raise their hands? Interrupt the teacher during reading groups? Convey your preferences to students so they will know at what times they are allowed to disturb you to go out.

2.11   # Leaving the Classroom

These students need to leave the classroom. Do you think they are leaving appropriately? Write YES or NO in each box.

Classroom Rules and Responsibilities

Copyright © 2009 by John Wiley & Sons, Inc.

2.12 Moving Around in Class

Objective

The student will identify characters who are moving about the classroom in an acceptable way.

Rationale

Students need to be able to move around the class not only to gather materials and go to different groups, but to change their positions and remain active learners. It is important for students to move around the class without bothering others or wasting time. It is also important to realize that students need to move around!

Thinking Questions

1. What are some of the reasons you need to move around in class? *(move around to get things, change groups, go outside, catch the bus, sharpen pencil)*

2. What is the shortest path to the pencil sharpener [closet, window, and so forth]? *(answers will vary)*

3. If the shortest way to get somewhere takes you past someone who wants you to stop and talk, or walk across a table in the middle of the room, why should you think twice before going that way? *(might get in trouble for talking, shouldn't walk on a table)*

4. What are some good things to keep in mind when moving around the class so you don't bother others? *(be quiet, don't stop and talk)*

5. If you feel that you need to get up and move around, what are some things you can do or areas of the room you can go to? *(varies—might stretch, stroll by the window, look at the aquarium)*

Activity

Directions: Students read short paragraphs about students who have to move around the class and pick the one in each pair who is moving appropriately. They write the name of the student on the line.

Answers: 1. Denny 2. Sally 3. Doug

Follow-up: Discuss why Rick, Maria, and Ben were not the best movers. *(Rick jumps across desks; Maria disturbs others, wastes time; Ben makes four trips instead of one)* What could Rick, Maria, and Ben do differently? What is the best time or place to jump or to show people something new? How could Ben plan his project better? *(organize himself first, then make one trip)*

2.12   # Moving Around in Class

These students need to move around in the classroom. One in each set of sentences is doing a better job than the other. Write the name of the student who is moving around the classroom appropriately.

1. Rick and Denny need to sharpen their pencils on the other side of the room.

   Rick jumps across the desks to get to the other side quickly.

   Denny walks quietly around the back of the room and doesn't touch anyone.

   _____

2. Sally and Maria need to get some books from the bookcase on the side of the room by a large window.

   Sally walks quietly over to the bookcase and takes the books she needs.

   Maria stops to show everyone her new watch on the way to the bookcase.

   _____

3. Ben and Doug are supposed to work on a science poster at the table in the back of the room.

   Ben takes his pencils, then has to return to his desk to get a ruler. Then he goes back again to get some glue. Now he needs to get his science book and get some ideas.

   Doug thinks about what he needs, then gathers everything up and makes one trip.

   _____

Copyright © 2009 by John Wiley & Sons, Inc.

2.13 Moving as a Group

Objective

The student will indicate characters who are moving in a line without running, touching each other, talking, or otherwise stopping the progress of the group.

Rationale

Movement between classrooms is often a monumental task in itself. It's hard to watch everyone, and it's a time when students are close together and may want to talk or goof around. Moving from place to place in an organized manner is a skill that requires practice and clear directions. In this lesson, students are instructed to stay together, not change places, be quiet, and not touch each other.

Thinking Questions

1. What are some times or places where the entire class has to move together to get somewhere else? *(lunchtime, P.E. time, going to the buses)*

2. Why would it cause problems if everyone wanted to be first in line? *(only one person can be first, others might shove or be angry)*

3. What would happen if people wanted to keep changing places while the class was moving down the hall? *(would make others behind stop, might be noisy, others would want to change places too)*

4. Why would this be a bad time to stop and tie your shoe, wave to a friend in another class, or play tag? *(it would stop the whole group)*

5. What are some good rules to remember about walking as a group? *(stay together, don't change places, be quiet, don't touch)*

Activity

Directions: Students are to read (or listen to) the story about students walking to the library. Using the clues, they are to label each character in the story and count how many children were moving as a group correctly.

Answers: 1. Richard   2. Ron   3. Ellen   4. Ben   5. Steve   6. Mike   7. Tom   8. Maria

Four students were walking correctly.

Follow-up: Discuss the problems that each character had and made for others. Discuss which part of the rule was violated.

2.13   **Moving as a Group**

Read the story below and use the clues to write the name of each student in the boxes.

Mrs. Jones's class was on its way to the library. On the way, Steve and Mike were throwing a softball back and forth. This made it hard for Tom and Maria to keep walking in line, but they did. Ron was walking behind Richard, who was walking at a good rate. Ben was upset, however, that Ellen was walking too slowly, so he decided to give her a push.

How many students were walking correctly?

_____

Classroom Rules and Responsibilities

Copyright © 2009 by John Wiley & Sons. Inc.

2.14 Thinking About Consequences

Objective

The student will identify at least one possible consequence for a given situation.

Rationale

Wouldn't it be nice if students thought through what might happen before they did something? This lesson provides students with a few situations to consider and to identify one consequence (or "thing that might happen") if they didn't stop and think first.

Thinking Questions

1. What might happen if you stayed up all night and then remembered you were supposed to study for a test the next day at school? *(might be frantic with worry, might give up on the test, try to cram)*
2. What could avoid a problem like that? *(planning ahead, thinking)*
3. What do we mean by "consequences"? *(something that happens because of something you do)*
4. What would be a possible consequence of studying hard for a test? *(do well)*
5. Think about some things that you do at school. Can you give examples of good consequences and then bad consequences? (**good:** *getting a good grade for working hard, getting recess because you finished your work;* **bad:** *having to stay in because you aren't done, not being invited to a party because you teased someone at school)*

Activity

Directions: Students are to draw or write down a possible consequence for each situation on the worksheet. Make sure students understand that not all consequences are bad, but that these students were in situations where they didn't think it through first and ended up with a possible bad situation.

Answer examples: 1. might do poorly on test   2. might get beaten up   3. might forget to do it 4. might give Sharon something that she won't return

Follow-up: Discuss how each character on the worksheet could end up with a totally different consequence by changing his or her own behavior to a more positive action.

2.14   # Thinking About Consequences

What might happen as a consequence if you didn't think through a situation? Draw or write a possible consequence for each student's situation below.

1.

> I think I'll skip my homework tonight and go to a movie with my friends instead.

2.

> I know that kid is a lot bigger than I am, but I'm going to tell him that he's fat and ugly.

3.

> That list of vocabulary words is so long—I think I'll just copy it tomorrow instead of today.

4.

> Every time Sharon comes up to me, she wants to borrow something and she never gives it back. Oh, oh—here she comes!

Copyright © 2009 by John Wiley & Sons. Inc.

2.15 Doing It Right the First Time

Objective

The student will identify consequences of not doing a task properly the first time.

Rationale

A task isn't done until it is done correctly. This lesson gives students examples of jobs that are "done" but not "done correctly."

Thinking Questions

1. What would happen if you did the wrong assignment in a class, but everything you did was right? *(might still have to do the correct assignment)*

2. Do you think it is more important to be the first one done with a job or to do it correctly? *(to do it correctly)* Why? *(because even if you're done first, it wouldn't matter)*

3. What about people who take a long time to get things done? Should they try to speed up to get finished or stay slow and get it done right? *(eventually a balance would be nice, but probably most teachers would strive for accuracy first)*

4. Why do you think it's important or better to do things right the first time? *(don't have to do it over, faster in the long run)*

5. What are some ways that you can help yourself remember to do something right the first time? *(slow down at first, make sure you understand the directions, check your work over before turning it in)*

Activity

Directions: Students are going to read about characters who turned in work but did not do it right. They are to write suggestions for how the character could have avoided the problem.

Answer examples:

1. slow down, write clearly
2. take time to understand the directions
3. read the directions
4. make sure you have the right assignment; write down the assignment at the top of the page
5. listen to all of the directions; ask if you don't understand

Follow-up: Everyone makes mistakes, but some mistakes can be avoided by listening and thinking. Have students tell about some mistakes that they may have made in class and how they learned to do it right. Be sure to display examples of good student work in your room or in the hallway.

2.15   # Doing It Right the First Time

Here are some students who are ready to turn in some work, but there are some problems because they didn't do it right the first time. How could these students have done it right the first time?

1. John was the first one done, but no one can read his work because he wrote so fast.

2. Hailey finally finished her math worksheet. All of the answers are wrong because she put down any number to make it look as if she was done.

3. Daniel finished his reading assignment, but he didn't read the directions. He wrote *opposites* for each word instead of words that mean the *same*.

4. Martha did the math problems on page 35 instead of page 36.

5. Benjamin wrote a long story on the computer, but he wasn't listening when the teacher told the class how to save their work. He just turned off the computer and lost everything he had done.

Copyright © 2009 by John Wiley & Sons. Inc.

2.16 Sitting Appropriately

Objective

The student will state, demonstrate, or identify proper sitting posture.

Rationale

Some students have creative ways of positioning their bodies in a chair, on the carpet, or other items of furniture that are intended for housing a student. If students are given a clear definition of "sitting appropriately," it is easier to enforce the request to "sit down" or "sit still." "Sitting appropriately" is defined as having one's bottom on the chair or floor with arms and legs kept to oneself.

Thinking Questions

1. How many ways can you sit on a chair? *(forward, backward, sideways)*
2. Why do you think your teachers care how you sit? *(looks more orderly to all sit facing forward, if you stretch out too much you're in someone else's way, you might hurt yourself if you fall)*
3. Where are some other places around school that you might have to sit? *(auditorium, cafeteria, bleachers)*
4. Why do you think it's important to sit still sometimes? *(so you don't touch others, so you don't disturb others with wiggling)*
5. What would be a good definition for "sitting appropriately"? *(bottom down, arms and legs to yourself)*

Activity

Directions: Students are to circle the characters on the worksheet who are sitting appropriately. They are to put an X through the ones who are not. Be sure students understand your expectations for sitting appropriately. (student 11 might fit the definition, but if sitting backward bothers you, this would be an X'd person.)

Answers: Circle 2, 5, 7, 9, 12.

Follow-up: Discuss why the other students received an X. What were they doing that did not satisfy the definition? *(student 1 wasn't in his seat at all, student 6 had his knees on the seat)* Discuss proper sitting positions for other areas of the school. How should the students sit at the computer lab? The art room? On the floor in the gym?

2.16   **Sitting Appropriately**

Look at this class of students. Circle the ones who are sitting appropriately. Put an X on the ones who are not.

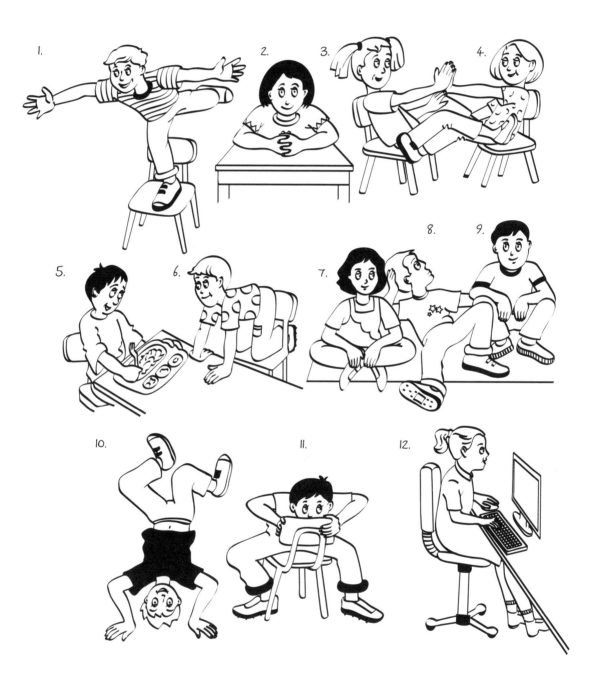

Classroom Rules and Responsibilities

Copyright © 2009 by John Wiley & Sons, Inc.

2-17 Doing Homework

Objective

The student will identify characters who are or are not completing a specified homework task.

Rationale

What good is it to send home homework if it doesn't get done? This lesson focuses on identifying whether someone is actually doing the homework. Most teachers use homework as extra practice or for unfinished classroom assignments, so students should not have too many excuses for not getting it done.

Thinking Questions

1. What are some kinds of homework assignments that you have had? (*finish something, read a story, bring in something*)

2. Why do you think students have homework sometimes? (*extra practice, punishment [inevitably someone will say this]*)

3. Sometimes people try to avoid doing something they don't really want to do. What are some ways students might try to avoid doing homework? (*play with friends, lose their papers, forget to bring books home*)

4. Are there any good consequences for not doing homework? (*probably not*)

5. What are some good ways to help you get homework done? (*do it right away, do it correctly, have a friend help you study, put it where you will remember to do it*)

Activity

Directions: Students are to select the one character from each pair who is doing the assigned homework and write the name on the line.

Answers: 1. Maria   2. Rob   3. David   4. Sarah   5. Beth

Follow-up: There are lots of excuses for not doing homework. What excuses will Ann, Mark, Pedro, Jerry, and Randy give at school the next day? Discuss with students that there is a proper time to play in leaves, watch television, or do other things—and that time, in most cases, is probably after the homework is done.

2.17   **Doing Homework**

Mrs. Wright gave all of her students homework. Write the name of each student from the pair who is doing his or her homework.

1. Find five different kinds of leaves. _____

     Ann   Maria

2. Have someone call your spelling words to you at home for practice. _____

     Rob   Mark

3. Read a story by yourself. _____

David   Pedro

Classroom Rules and Responsibilities

Copyright © 2009 by John Wiley & Sons, Inc.

4. Finish your art collage. _____

Jerry   Sarah

5. Answer all of the questions on the science worksheet. _____

Beth   Randy

Copyright © 2009 by John Wiley & Sons. Inc.

2.18 Bringing Homework to School

Objective

The student will give at least two reasons that it is important to bring homework to school.

Rationale

How many times have you heard, "I did my homework! I just left it at home!" Even the most conscientious student at times forgets to bring something in. But the habitual offender is the one who loses out because the homework never shows up. This results in sorting through an even bigger mess. Should he or she redo it? Call Mom to bring it in? It would be so much easier on everyone if students would accept the responsibility to finish the homework task by bringing it in!

Thinking Questions

1. Have you ever forgotten to bring something to school? What? *(homework, note, lunch, extra pencils)*

2. Why is it hard to remember to bring things in sometimes? *(lots on your mind, busy evening, in a hurry in the morning and rush out without thinking)*

3. Everyone forgets sometimes. Why is it so important to remember to bring in your homework? *(so you'll get points or a grade, so you won't have to remember it for the next day, so you'll be caught up on assignments)*

4. Whose responsibility is it for bringing in homework? Is it your teacher's job? Parent's job? *(the student's)*

5. What are some ways that you could help yourself remember to bring your homework to school? *(put it in your backpack the night before, put it by the front door)*

Activity

Directions: Students are peeking into Fred's room—a real mess!—to locate his homework. They are to circle the items among the mess.

Follow-up: Discuss why Fred probably has trouble bringing things to school. Would it help Fred if his mother cleaned his room? *(He might not know where things are anymore.)* How could Fred be more organized?

2.18   # Bringing Homework to School

Poor Fred! He did his homework—but then forgot to bring it to school. Find and circle the following items in Fred's room:

science book   ruler   poster of a truck
colored pencils   math sheet   note to Mom from teacher

Copyright © 2009 by John Wiley & Sons, Inc.

2.19 Finishing the Job

Objective

The student will assist cartoon characters in completion of a given task.

Rationale

One of the most aggravating conditions teachers deal with is unfinished work. How can we evaluate a paper if it's only half done? What if the half is not enough to tell us whether the student understands the concept of the lesson? Students may come up with lots of excuses for not finishing (*I didn't understand; it was too long; I couldn't think of anything*), but for most appropriate tasks that have been well taught and serve a purpose, the excuses are not good enough. Being able to finish the job is a skill that will follow students through their life.

Thinking Questions

1. Why is it important to finish what you start? (*otherwise it doesn't count, it looks better to have something all the way done*)

2. What are some things that you have to finish in order to win something or to get a prize? (*a race, a contest, papers at school for a sticker*)

3. What would happen if you painted a room only halfway? Or the bus driver wanted to stop in the middle of the route? Or your chicken dinner was cooked only a little bit? (*answers will vary, but you'd have a mess*)

4. Can you think of other jobs that are important to complete all the way? (*vacuuming a room, building a swing set, reading a book*)

5. What happens if a job needs to be done and the person who is supposed to do it doesn't finish? (*someone else may have to complete it, he or she won't get full credit for the job*)

Activity

Directions: Students are to examine the assignments of the characters on the worksheet and complete the task. Assume that the characters either had excuses for not finishing or just did not want to finish. Provide whatever materials are necessary for your students to complete the job (markers, crayons, rules for letter writing).

Answer examples: 1. Draw another Native American and a horse or two. 2. Finish coloring in the numbers. 3. Match the rest of the words with the pictures. 4. Add a few lines such as: " . . . you? I'm fine. I'm playing baseball these days. Write back. Your friend, Tim."

Follow-up: If your students interviewed the characters from the worksheet, what excuses might they hear? (*I can't draw, I was tired, I don't like to write*) How hard were the tasks for them to finish? (*not hard*) Discuss ways in which jobs that aren't as fun to do could be done to make them easier. (*don't stop until you're finished, work with a friend, think about it first*)

2.19   **Finishing the Job**

Help these students finish their assignments.

Copyright © 2009 by John Wiley & Sons, Inc.

1. Carrie is supposed to draw a picture of Native Americans and horses.

2. George is coloring a math worksheet.

2.19 Finishing the Job (continued)

3. Phyllis is matching words and pictures.

4. Tim is writing a letter to his pen-pal.

Copyright © 2009 by John Wiley & Sons. Inc.

2.20 Independent versus Group Assignments

Objective

The student will identify appropriate behavior for independent assignments contrasted with appropriate behavior for work on group tasks.

Rationale

Different behaviors are expected and needed for tasks that students are to do on their own compared to tasks that can be done with a partner, a small group, or the whole class. It is important for students to be able to identify the type of task (independent, small group, or large group) and the corresponding behaviors to complete that task. Students need to consider factors such as noise level, sharing, taking turns, and dividing the jobs.

Thinking Questions

1. What are some assignments or jobs that you do at school that you are supposed to do all by yourself? (*study spelling, take a test, pass out papers, complete worksheets, organize your desk*)

2. What are some jobs that you might do with a partner? (*quiz each other on vocabulary words, partner reading, hang up a bulletin board*)

3. What are some things that the whole class works on together? (*indoor games, community circle time, cleaning up the room*)

4. Why do you think some things have to be done on your own? Why can't we do everything together? (*students have to acquire skills, learn to work independently*)

5. Some people prefer to work one way or another: alone or in groups. Which way do you prefer to get your work done? (*students will have various opinions*)

6. What are some advantages to working together? (*share the work, get more done*)

7. What are some advantages to working alone? (*work at your own pace, get credit for the whole project*)

Activity

Directions: Students are given a list of typical classroom activities. They are to indicate which are most likely done independently, which can be done with a partner, and which are probably group activities.

Answers: 1. partner   2. group   3. independently   4. independently   5. group   6. partner

Follow-up: Make a chart on the board with these headings: "Alone," "Partner," "Group." Have students give examples of appropriate behaviors for each situation.

2.20   **Independent versus Group Assignments**

How would these school activities probably be done? After each, write I (independently), P (with a partner), or G (or in a group).

Copyright © 2009 by John Wiley & Sons, Inc.

1. The assignment is to read a play with two main parts. _____

2. The assignment is to read a play with a lot of parts. _____

3. The assignment is to read a story and answer questions at the end of it. _____

4. The assignment is to write about your favorite summer vacation. _____

5. The assignment is to discuss ways that the class can decorate the room for Grandparents' Day.

    _____

6. The assignment is to practice giving the definitions for vocabulary words. _____

2.21 Fire Drills and Other Interruptions

Objective

The student will state the appropriate procedures for behavior during a safety drill or other unexpected interruptions in the classroom.

Rationale

Although routine drills are usually scheduled, it is important for both the teacher and student to know exactly what needs to be done and how to follow the school procedures without hesitation. Occasionally there are other interruptions, such as an unexpected bus delay, early dismissals for weather, and changes in the routine schedule. The more comfortable the students are with handling change, the smoother transitions will be.

Thinking Questions

1. What would you do if the fire drill sounded right now? *(line up at the door in single file, turn off the lights, no talking)*
2. How did you know what to do? *(the teacher told us, we practice drills)*
3. Why is it important to practice drills? *(so if the real thing ever happens, we would be safe)*
4. What are some other drills that we practice? *(storm drill, lockdown drill)*
5. Although we always hope for a normal day, sometimes there are other unexpected things that change the schedule. Can you think of some of them? *(early closing due to snow, special speakers, bus delay, P.E. teacher absent)*
6. Why is it important to handle changes without getting upset about them? *(usually they are temporary, things will be back to normal again later, getting upset won't make anything better, could be unsafe)*

Activity

Directions: Students are to read over the list of possible interruptions of a typical day and choose one that they would like to focus on. With a partner or in a small group, have the students show the wrong way that this procedure could be handled, and then the right way. Be sure that your students know the specific school policy for your class and community.

Answers: Will vary according to the school.

Follow-up: Have students perform their skits in front of the class. You may want to have students make posters with the procedures written and illustrated. Display the posters around the room, and remind students to read them occasionally.

2.21   # Fire Drills and Other Interruptions

Here is a list of some possible safety drills and other interruptions that might change the normal day. Check the one you want to focus on. With a partner or small group, write and perform a skit that shows (1) the WRONG way to handle this and (2) the RIGHT way.

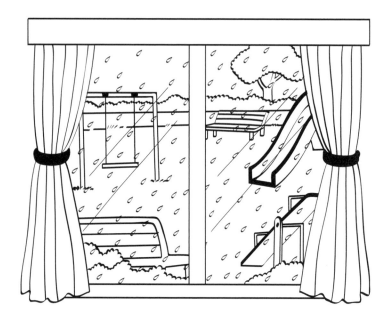

❑ Fire drill

❑ Storm/bad weather drill

❑ Lockdown drill

❑ Bus delay

❑ Early dismissal

❑ Power out at school

❑ Computer lab closed

❑ Change in lunch schedule

❑ Indoor recess

❑ Assembly with special speaker

❑ (other) _____

❑ (other) _____

Copyright © 2009 by John Wiley & Sons, Inc.

2.22 Behaving at a Special Program

Objective

The student will identify appropriate and inappropriate behaviors for attending a school assembly or other special program involving multiple classes.

Rationale

There is something about being in a huge mass of people that triggers the "The teacher can't watch all of us at the same time!" response. Students need to learn how to enter the assembly area, be respectful of the speaker and others in the audience, and leave in an orderly manner.

Thinking Questions

1. What are some assemblies or special programs that you have attended at school? (*guest author, awards assembly, Service League play, reading skits performed by other classes*)

2. Have you ever been a performer in a special program? What did you do? (*sang, got an award, recited a poem from memory*)

3. Let's say you are at the movies. What are some annoying things that can happen when you are there? (*people talking during the movie, kicking seats, getting up and down, talking on a cell phone or texting on it*)

4. Why is it important to be a good listener at an assembly or play? (*the people are trying hard to perform for the audience, should be respectful*)

5. Why is it important not to bother others in the audience? (*they want to hear what's going on*)

Activity

Directions: Look at the students who are sitting in the audience for a special program. Circle the students who are behaving appropriately. Put an X on the ones who are not.

Answers: Circle 1, 2, 3, 4, 6

Follow-up: Discuss what the X'd students are doing that is inappropriate for a special program. Have students suggest alternative behaviors for the children who could be redirected to more appropriate behavior.

2.22 # Behaving at a Special Program

These students are attending a special program in the school gym. The special speaker is talking about teaching dogs to do some tricks. Circle the students who are showing good audience behavior. Put an X on the ones who are not.

1.

2.

3.

4.

Copyright © 2009 by John Wiley & Sons, Inc.

5.

6.

7.

8.

Copyright © 2009 by John Wiley & Sons. Inc.

2.23 Welcoming a New Student

Objective

The student will identify several welcoming behaviors when there is a new student in their class.

Rationale

It is often hard for a new student at the school to break into friendship groups. It can also be frightening to face new faces everywhere, new schedules, new books, and the uncertainty of finding one's place. If students intentionally make efforts to include a new student in their class, they will help foster a smooth transition and perhaps make a new friend.

Thinking Questions

1. Have you ever moved and gone to a new school? What was it like? *(scary, didn't know where things were, no one to eat with at lunch)*

2. What are some things that you could do to welcome someone who is new? *(ask their name, ask what they like to do, include them at lunch)*

3. What if a friend tells you that there are enough of you in your group and there isn't room for anyone else? *(you can still be friendly, maybe find new activities that involve more people)*

4. How would you feel if there was a birthday party for someone in your class and you were not invited? *(very excluded if you were the only one left out)*

5. What are some things that our class could do whenever we get a new student? *(let them be Student for the Day, make sure they always have someone to help them with class procedures, write welcome notes to them)*

Activity

Directions: Which of the following behaviors help welcome new students?

Answers: 2, 3, 6, 8, 9, 10

Follow-up: Have the class come up with a procedure for welcoming new students. Perhaps they want to make a special gift bag or box with pictures of students in the class, a student-drawn map of the school, special name tags, and other personal touches to make the student feel welcome.

Classroom Rules and Responsibilities

2.23   **Welcoming New Students**

Which of the following behaviors would help welcome a new student to your class, school, or community? Put a check mark in front of each one.

_____ 1. Tell the new student that he can't sit at the front table because that's where you and your friends sit.

_____ 2. Show the new student where to hang up his jacket and book bag.

_____ 3. Invite the new student to go roller skating with you and your friends.

_____ 4. Tell the new student that she'll get in trouble if she tattles on anybody.

_____ 5. Talk about things that the new student doesn't know anything about.

_____ 6. Ask the new student to tell you about his family and his old school.

_____ 7. Make sure you get the good playground equipment before the new student does.

_____ 8. Ask the new student to sit with you at lunch.

_____ 9. Pick the new student to be on your team when you choose sides for kickball.

_____ 10. Let the new student borrow your markers if he didn't bring any to school yet.

Copyright © 2009 by John Wiley & Sons, Inc.

Classroom Rules and Responsibilities   **103**

2.24 Sharing in Community Circle

Objective

The student will participate in community circle activities displaying appropriate behavior and topics of conversation.

Rationale

A community circle time can serve many classroom purposes: to go over the daily agenda or calendar, assign tasks, bond as a group, practice expressing opinions, and set the tone for the rest of the day. The basic rules for circle time need to be clear and simple, and students must follow them. The goal is to arrange a comfortable setting in which students feel free to talk but not dominate the whole group discussion.

Thinking Questions

1. We are in a discussion group or circle time right now! What other times do we gather together as a group to do things? *(story time, calendar time, briefing at the end of the day)*

2. What would happen if our group time didn't have any rules about whose turn it is to talk? *(everyone would talk at once and no one would listen; it would get too loud)*

3. How do we know whose turn it is to talk in our group? *(depends on class procedure: passing around a beanbag, one student calling on another)*

4. What are some topics that are good to discuss at school? *(any problems you are having, show and tell ideas, things that are coming up)*

5. Why do you think it is good to share ideas? *(someone might know a better way to do something; we can help each other; it helps us get to know each other)*

Activity

Directions: Students are to look at the examples of children who are supposed to be participating in a community circle but are not using good judgment. What is inappropriate or not the best idea in each case?

Answers: 1. monopolizing the conversation   2. bringing up a personal argument   3. telling something personal about another person   4. ignoring who is talking   5. interrupting

Follow-up: Discuss the answers. Have students come up with alternative behaviors for the problems. If you have a topic of the day to discuss, it can be an opportunity for students to practice focusing on staying on the topic or staying on task.

2.24   # Sharing in Community Circle

1.

_____

_____

_____

Copyright © 2009 by John Wiley & Sons, Inc.

2.24 Sharing in Community Circle (continued)

2.

_____

3.

Classroom Rules and Responsibilities

Copyright © 2009 by John Wiley & Sons, Inc.

4.

_____

5.

_____

Copyright © 2009 by John Wiley & Sons, Inc.

2.25 Using the Class Computers

Objective

The student will state and then follow classroom procedures for using the computers.

Rationale

Students need to understand the procedures for using the computers in all of their school settings.

Thinking Questions

1. What kinds of electronics do you have at home? [This includes things like video games, cell phones, portable music players, video players, or computers.]

2. Has someone ever picked up one of your games and broken it or messed it up in some way? What happened? *(younger brother, friends who were careless; it broke, the settings got messed up)*

3. How did you feel when something you were working on got messed up, erased, or broken? *(pretty mad!)*

4. Why do you think we have to have rules or procedures for working with equipment at school? *(computers are expensive, lots of different people use them)*

5. Why do you think you have to listen to instructions for how to use computers and things like that when you already have one at home? *(it might be a little different from the one at home)*

6. Why is it a good idea to take good care of the equipment we have at school? *(so it will last a long time, so it will be easy for others to use when it is their turn)*

Activity

Directions: Students should look at the list of instructions or procedures for each piece of equipment and underline the ones that they think are important for each.

Answers: computer: 1, 3; digital camera: 2, 3; CD player: 1, 3

Follow-up: Spend some time going over the expected behaviors and procedures for student use of computers, audiovisual equipment, and any other tools that students will be entrusted with at school. It is helpful to have one student explain the procedures and use of the equipment to another student. ("I teach and I understand.")

2.25   # Using the Class Computers

Here are some instructions for using the class computer and other tools for learning. Underline the instructions that you think are important for handling each tool.

Computer

1. If you are playing a game, make sure your headphones are on before you start the game.
2. If you have a problem, jump up and wave your hand so the teacher will come over to help you.
3. Touch the keys on the keyboard carefully.
4. Shut down the computer by pulling the plug out of the power strip.

Digital Camera

1. Touch all of the buttons until you see what you want.
2. Make sure you understand how to delete the pictures you don't want.
3. Put the camera in a safe place when you aren't using it.
4. Don't turn the camera off until the battery is dead.

CD Player

1. Hold the CD by the edges, not the flat part.
2. If the CD doesn't go in the slot, push harder until it does.
3. Know where the Eject button is so you can get the CD out.
4. If it doesn't start right away, shake it to get it going.

Copyright © 2009 by John Wiley & Sons, Inc.

Classroom Rules and Responsibilities

2.26 Attendance Is Important

Objective

The student will be able to explain why school attendance is important.

Rationale

A student who is not in school misses the instruction, discussion, nuances of being in a classroom, and social skill building. The activities can be made up, but the time to do that has to come from omitting something else. We all have days when we don't feel well or wish we could be somewhere else, but if at all possible, the student should be in attendance so every opportunity to learn is taken advantage of.

Thinking Questions

1. Why do you think it is important to come to school every day? *(so you can keep up with your assignments, so you can learn something)*

2. What are some reasons that a person might be absent? *(sick, head lice, traveling with family, miss the bus, oversleep and don't bother to come)*

3. Some reasons for being absent are things like a dentist appointment or having to go somewhere with your family. Can you think of some reasons that people are absent that are not very good? *(forgot to come to school, wanted to watch something on TV, stayed up too late the night before)*

4. Why is it important to get to school on time? *(so you start when everyone else does, so you get your lunch count in on time, so the teacher doesn't have to say things all over again when somebody comes in late)*

Activity

Directions: These students all have reasons that they were not at school yesterday. Circle the ones who had good reasons for being absent.

Answers: 1: throwing up   3: had to go to the doctor   6: The whole family was delayed by the weather.

Follow-up: Since teachers don't always know what is truly going on at home (and many of us are parents as well), it's hard to be too judgmental for reasons that a student may not be in attendance and on time. However, encourage students to make every effort to come to school—and that might include greeting them with a kind word of welcome at the door each morning.

Classroom Rules and Responsibilities

2.26   # Attendance Is Important

Read the reasons that these students were absent from school yesterday. Circle the students who you think had acceptable excuses.

1.

2.

Copyright © 2009 by John Wiley & Sons, Inc.

2.26 Attendance Is Important (continued)

3.

4.

Copyright © 2009 by John Wiley & Sons, Inc.

Classroom Rules and Responsibilities

2.26 Attendance Is Important (continued)

5.

6.

Speech bubble (5): My mom told me to get up but then she went back to sleep, so I thought I would go back to sleep too.

Speech bubble (6): My family was coming back from Ohio and we got caught in a blizzard and had to spend the night in a hotel so we didn't get home until late last night.

Copyright © 2009 by John Wiley & Sons, Inc.

Classroom Tips for Classroom Rules and Responsibilities

- Decide how your morning agenda will be organized. Do you have a life skill for the day? Weather report? Class news? This meeting may set the tone for the remainder of the day. Inform students what to expect that day, and remind them that they are appreciated and welcomed.

- Allow the students time to talk. Perhaps you can sandwich these breaks in between quiet activities or before they go outside for recess. Knowing that they can expect five minutes at a certain time each day might help them store up those conversations that they desire for the right time.

- For students who have to leave in the middle of class (for special classes or whatever else), develop a quiet signal acknowledging permission to leave. If possible, let these students have a seat close to the door so leaving is convenient.

- Change line leaders periodically so everyone has a turn and everyone knows his or her turn will come. Avoid fighting over who gets to go first.

- If your line spreads out and you have stragglers, designate certain stopping points throughout your journey. The line leader must stop at the point and wait for everyone to catch up before continuing.

- Display students' best papers, tests, and projects prominently in the classroom. Explain the difference between a first draft or rough planning and the final product.

- Reward students who have been faithful at bringing in homework by a special homework-free night. Or assign a silly homework assignment for that night, such as eating an ice cream cone or watching a television show.

- Have a class goodwill ambassador team that will be responsible for welcoming new students who join the class throughout the year.

Chapter 3

Relating Appropriately to Other School People

3.1 It's a Substitute!

Objective

The student will identify appropriate behaviors for when a substitute teacher is in charge of the classroom.

Rationale

When the regular teacher is gone, some students feel that they can take advantage of the substitute. Often the classroom teacher is horrified to find out how the class behaved in his or her absence. This lesson focuses on how students should behave for a substitute.

Thinking Questions

1. Has your regular teacher ever missed a day of teaching? Why? *(conferences, illness, personal days)*
2. Who usually fills in when the regular teacher is gone? *(a substitute, another classroom teacher, sometimes the principal)*
3. What do you think the job of a substitute teacher is like? What situations might he or she run into during the day? *(job might be confusing at first; knowing who everyone is, how the class routine is conducted, unusual situations, bad behavior of the class clowns)*
4. How does your regular teacher expect you to behave with a substitute? *(the same, some expect better behavior)*
5. Why do you think some students show their worst behavior when there is a substitute? *(the substitute might be meek, students might think they won't be punished for anything they do that day)*
6. How should students act when a substitute is in charge of the room? *(follow the instructions as if he or she were the regular teacher)*

Activity

Directions: Students are to consider the list of behaviors on the worksheet and put a check mark next to the ones that are respectful to a substitute teacher.

Answers: 2 (if it is a sincere greeting), 4 (if the substitute seems to need help), 5, 8, 9

Follow-up: Discuss your expectations for the class in your absence. Explain that you will deal with discipline problems, that you expect the students' best behavior, and that you will be in contact with the substitute about the day's events. Perhaps you could offer a special reward or incentive for "good helpers." Don't overload the substitute with complicated instructions for managing the day.

Relating Appropriately to Other School People

3.1   # It's a Substitute!

There is a substitute in your classroom today. Put a check mark next to each behavior that shows respect for the substitute.

❑ 1. Switch seats so she doesn't know who anyone is.

❑ 2. Say "hello" when you walk into the room.

❑ 3. Pretend that you are sick and have to go to the nurse.

❑ 4. Show her where the reading workbooks are kept.

❑ 5. Follow all of her instructions right away.

❑ 6. Tell her that you aren't supposed to have any homework, even if you really do.

❑ 7. Walk into class late.

❑ 8. Raise your hand to answer questions.

❑ 9. Be quiet when she is talking to the class.

❑ 10. Argue about who goes to lunch first.

Copyright © 2009 by John Wiley & Sons, Inc.

Relating Appropriately to Other School People

3.2 The Classroom Assistant (Aide)

Objective

The student will identify at least ten common activities that the classroom assistant helps the teacher or class with each day.

Rationale

The classroom assistant (if you are lucky enough to have one) works alongside the teacher by helping, reinforcing, reteaching, cutting, pasting, drilling, caring, and working hard in the classroom. Students sometimes act as though the assistant does not deserve the respect their teacher does. This lesson strives to create an awareness of the many tasks an assistant helps out with in the classroom.

Thinking Questions

1. Why do some classrooms have assistants? (*many children, younger children, need extra help*)
2. Is an assistant the same as a teacher? What is the difference? (*some assistants do have degrees in education; however, the role in the classroom is for the assistant to help carry out the teacher's plans and instructions*)
3. What are some activities that the assistant helps out with? (*listening to students read, running off worksheets*)
4. How do you think a classroom assistant should be treated? (*with respect, just like any other adult*)
5. What would happen if you didn't like the assistant? (*still be cooperative, try to follow the directions, respect him or her as you would the teacher*)

Activity

Directions: Students are to list at least six different tasks or responsibilities of an assistant with whom they are familiar. These could be daily tasks (listening to reading) or tasks that occur occasionally (helping with a fun fair, helping with a birthday party).

Answers: Answers will vary, but may include handing out stickers, helping check papers, watching in the lunchroom, calling spelling words.

Follow-up: Discuss how important an assistant is to you—allowing you as the teacher to get more accomplished in class. By conveying your appreciation of the assistant in front of the class, you will provide a good example to follow.

Relating Appropriately to Other School People

Name _____ Date _____

3.2 # The Classroom Assistant (Aide)

Your classroom assistant does many things. Make a list of at least six different activities that the assistant helps your class with during the day.

1. _____
   _____

2. _____
   _____

3. _____
   _____

4. _____
   _____

5. _____
   _____

6. _____
   _____

Copyright © 2009 by John Wiley & Sons. Inc.

3.3 The Principal

Objective

The student will identify ways to show respect to the principal of the school.

Rationale

The principal is the leader of the school who often has time to get to know many of the students on a personal level. The principal is a menacing threat only to those students who do not choose to follow the school's rules. It is wonderful to see students who seek out the school's leader to share a special moment or to seek a compliment. The principal is not a police officer, but should be shown absolute respect as one who has to enforce policy.

Thinking Questions

1. What do you think a principal does all day? *(you'll probably get all kinds of surprising answers!)*
2. Do you think the principal has the power to do away with or make any rules he or she wants to? *(realistically, no)*
3. What are some school rules that the principal has to enforce or make sure that everyone does? *(no fighting at school, don't skip out, take notes home to your parents)*
4. How do those school rules help everybody at school? *(for protection, to give students a chance to learn at school by being at school, to communicate with parents)*
5. What are some nice things or fun things that your principal has done? *(maybe helped with a field trip, sat in a "dunk" booth at the fair, gave prizes for good readers)*

Activity

Directions: Students are pretending that they are the school's principal and see six faces outside their office. They are to circle the students who are being respectful.

Answers: 3, 4, 6

Follow-up: Although the principal may see lots of students like numbers 1, 2, and 5, why are those situations unpleasant to the principal? *(show defiance, apathy)* Discuss how students can convey their problems in a respectful manner.

Relating Appropriately to Other School People

3·3

The Principal

You are the principal! Which of these students would you like to have in your office? Circle the students who are being respectful and pleasant to the principal.

Copyright © 2009 by John Wiley & Sons. Inc.

Relating Appropriately to Other School People

3.4 The School Secretary

Objective

The student will write polite or respectful requests for something needed from the school secretary.

Rationale

At many schools, the secretary is the catch-all person—handling everything from minor emergencies on the playground to screening problems for the principal, not to mention shuffling daily paperwork, counts, and other records. Though this is a very important position, students may view the secretary as their own personal servant. ("Call my mom." "I need that book." "Run this off for me.") Students should be respectful to this very important person.

Thinking Questions

1. What are some of the responsibilities of a school secretary? *(keep attendance records, type, answer the phone, schedule meetings)*

2. Do you think the secretary knows a lot about what's going on at the school? *(probably)* Why? *(she's at the center of activity, probably is near the principal's office, sees kids coming and going)*

3. What might be hard about being a secretary? What might be fun? *(hard: handling many problems at once, answering to angry parents; fun: talking to all the kids, answering the phone)*

4. What kinds of things do you think people ask the secretary to do for them? *(run off materials, find certain things, make phone calls)*

5. What are some ways that you could show respect to the secretary if you needed something? *(ask politely, be sure to thank her, be patient when waiting your turn)*

Activity

Directions: Students are to help the characters on the worksheet ask for something from the school secretary in a polite manner. They are to write what the character might say.

Answer examples: 1. May I please use the telephone?   2. I would like some supplies, please.   3. Mrs. George sent me for the menu.   4. Hello, this is for you. I have to leave early.   5. May I wait here for my parents, please?

Follow-up: The secretary may be a liaison between the principal and the parent, the teacher and the parent, or the principal and the teacher. Explain that when someone is in the middle, as this job may put someone, extra patience is required while both sides connect through her. Ask students to think about what parties are connected through the secretary in worksheet situations. (*1: student and parent; 2: student and supplies; 3: teacher and cafeteria; 4: parent/dentist and school; and 5: teacher and parent*)

3.4   # The School Secretary

Each of these students is talking to the school secretary. Write something that each might say to the secretary that is respectful.

1. Molly needs to use the telephone to call home.

   _____

   _____

2. Luis wants to buy a pad of paper and two pencils.

   _____

   _____

3. Benjamin's teacher sent him to the office to pick up lunch menus for the month.

   _____

   _____

4. Jennifer is supposed to give the secretary a note telling that she has to go to the dentist and must leave early.

   _____

   _____

5. Nicholas got in trouble at recess and is supposed to ask if he can wait in the office for his parents to come and get him.

   _____

   _____

Copyright © 2009 by John Wiley & Sons. Inc.

Relating Appropriately to Other School People   **123**

3.5 You're Not My Classroom Teacher!

Objective

The student will identify instances in which a person who is not the classroom teacher should be obeyed.

Rationale

Although students may be obedient and have won the respect of their classroom teacher, those same students may not feel that they have to listen to any other teachers or other adults in the school. This lesson gives the student opportunities to think through situations in which any teacher (coach, and so on) is his or her teacher.

Thinking Questions

1. How many teachers have you had since you started school? *(numbers will vary)*
2. When you went on to the next grade, was the teacher you had before still your teacher? *(yes in a way since there was a relationship, but not directly anymore)*
3. Would you still be expected to do what those teachers asked you to do if you were in their classroom? *(yes)*
4. Would you be expected to follow their instructions if you weren't in their classroom? *(yes—there would be a reason for whatever instruction was given)*
5. What about teachers on the playground, in art and music, or teachers walking down the hall? Are they teachers for your school even though they may not be your teacher in class? *(yes—should still be respected)*
6. Who are some teachers at school who give instructions to you even though they aren't your teacher? *(teachers of other grades, coaches, music and art teachers, lunchroom supervisors)* Why do they give you instructions? *(they give instructions because they were needed in the situation)*

Activity

Directions: This worksheet follows Pete through part of his day at school and his encounters with several teachers who each give Pete something to do or an order to follow. Students are to circle the teachers who give Pete instructions.

Answers: 1, 2, 4, 6, 7, 8, 9

Follow-up: Discuss why the teachers on the worksheet were or were not giving Pete instructions. Why were the instructions given important? *(for example, 1: the floor was slippery and it could have caused an accident; 2: probably other people wanted to use the restroom too)*

3·5   You're Not My Classroom Teacher!

Circle every example you can find of someone who is not Pete's classroom teacher but who is giving him instructions. How many can you find?

Copyright © 2009 by John Wiley & Sons, Inc.

Relating Appropriately to Other School People

3.6 The Bus Driver

Objective

The student will identify situations regarding the bus and bus driver that require student compliance.

Rationale

The bus driver is an authority figure who is an extension of the school. Without this driver, parents would have more work to do getting their children to school. Thus, it is extremely important for students to get along on the bus, especially so that they do not interfere with the driver's need to concentrate on driving safely. Everyone will be safer with the bus driver able to concentrate on driving, not disciplining.

Thinking Questions

1. How do students get to and from school each day? *(enumerate ways: walking, bike, parents, car-pooling, bus)*

2. How does a bus driver help make getting to school easier—or even possible—for some students? *(parents can get to work on time, saves a long walk for some students)*

3. What do you think a bus driver has to think about when he or she is operating the bus? *(other cars, remembering to stop at the right places, watching out for children who are walking)*

4. What are some problems that a bus driver might have if the students on the bus weren't cooperative? *(lack of concentration, might have an accident, longer bus ride)*

5. What are some good rules for riding the bus safely? *(sit down, be quiet, don't change seats, don't throw things)*

Activity

Directions: Students are to evaluate four situations to decide whether the characters are being respectful to the bus driver by following his or her instructions. They are to write YES or NO.

Answers: 1. no   2. yes   3. no   4. yes

Follow-up: Discuss how the students in numbers 1 and 3 could resolve their problems without involving the bus driver. What are safe, quiet activities that could be done on the bus?

3.6   **The Bus Driver**

Next to each picture, write YES if the students are being respectful to the bus driver; write NO if they are not.

Copyright © 2009 by John Wiley & Sons, Inc.

Relating Appropriately to Other School People   **127**

3.7 Specials Teachers

Objective

The student will give several reasons why it is important to follow classroom procedures for specials (art, music, P.E.).

Rationale

Students often have many different teachers to answer to throughout the week. Specials teachers might include art, music, P.E., library, special help teachers, and computer helpers. Although specific classroom rules may differ, these teachers all need to be respected.

Thinking Questions

1. Who are some of the teachers that you see during the week for specials? *(art, music)*
2. Why would there be different rules for these classes? *(these classes are different from the regular class; they have musical instruments, art supplies, get to go outside for P.E., some classes are a lot smaller)*
3. What should your behavior be like with specials teachers? *(should always be respectful and do your work)*
4. What is a rule or procedure that you would have in music class but not art class? *(don't bang on the piano, open your mouth when you sing, stand in the same place on the stage)*
5. What is a rule or procedure that you would have in P.E. but no other class? *(wear your gym shoes, be quiet when you hear the whistle)*
6. Which of your specials do you like the best, and why? *(answers will vary)*

Activity

Directions: Students are to match each rule with its class.

Answers: 1. art   2. music   3. P.E.   4. library   5. special reading   6. computer lab

Follow-up: Discuss the students' responses. How did they know which rule went with which class? Discuss which rules are hardest to follow, and why.

Relating Appropriately to Other School People

3.7   **Specials Teachers**

Which of the following rules go with a special class? Draw a line from each rule to its correct specials class.

1. Put the caps on the markers when you are finished so the markers don't dry out.

   Library

2. Sing the words clearly so the audience will be able to understand what they hear.

   Computer lab

3. All of the equipment from outside has to be put away before you can go back inside the building.

   Music

4. If you take a book off the shelf, be sure to put it back in the same spot.

   P.E.

5. Take this book home to practice reading; then bring it back tomorrow.

   Special reading

6. Don't click on the icon until I tell you to.

   Art

Copyright © 2009 by John Wiley & Sons, Inc.

Relating Appropriately to Other School People

3.8 The Custodian

Objective

The student will identify several jobs that the school custodian is responsible for.

Rationale

Many students have no idea what the school custodian does. Yet this is the person who single-handedly can make your life easier, as he or she often helps with the little things that you need to make your class run more smoothly. Getting a bigger desk, an extra desk, fixing a broken window, and moving a television and VCR are important. The custodian is a valued member of the school staff. Convey this to your students.

Thinking Questions

1. What happens if there is a burned-out lightbulb in the room? *(the custodian replaces it)*
2. What are some of the jobs that a custodian does? *(fixes things, finds things, cleans things)*
3. Why are these jobs important? *(someone needs to know where everything is kept, how to keep things running properly, make the school property look nice)*
4. Why is it important for the school building to look nice? *(we want to work in a nice environment, shows pride in the school)*
5. How does the custodian help make the teacher's job easier? *(teacher doesn't have to take class time to find materials, keeps things working properly so the teacher can use them in class)*

Activity

Directions: Students are to color in all of the jobs on the worksheet that a school custodian is probably responsible for. Discuss the activities that your custodian does for your school. You may have somewhat different job descriptions from the ones on the worksheet.

Answers: (possible answers—depends on the individual school) 1, 2, 3, 5, 7, 9, 10, 12, 14

Follow-up: Discuss who might be responsible for the activities that were not selected (4, 6, 8, 11, 13). Are there other jobs that you could add to the custodian's list?

Relating Appropriately to Other School People

3.8   The Custodian

Color all of the jobs that your school custodian might do.

1. Bring another desk to your classroom.

2. Fix a broken window.

3. Clean the floor in the restroom.

4. Drive the principal to school.

5. Put in a new blackboard.

6. Cook the lunch in the cafeteria.

7. Repair a broken overhead projector.

8. Help students with their homework.

9. Empty the trash after lunch.

10. Cut the lawn in front of the school.

11. Coach the track team.

12. Paint parking lines in the teachers' parking lot.

13. Type a letter for the principal.

14. Polish the floors in the hallway.

Copyright © 2009 by John Wiley & Sons, Inc.

Relating Appropriately to Other School People

3.9 Field Trip Helpers

Objective

The student will identify ways to behave with a field trip helper during a field trip with the class.

Rationale

Field trips can be a lot of fun—or a nightmare. When there are helpers to go along, they can make things run more smoothly for the class, allowing everyone to get the most out of the trip. Prepare children for field trips by going over expectations before the trip. Name tags, emergency procedures, objectives for the trip, and restroom and lunch procedures should all be covered with the helpers so everyone knows what to do.

Thinking Questions

1. What are some field trips that you have taken with your class? (*museums, zoos, picnics, special events*)

2. Who goes along on the trips to help out? (*parents, bus driver, older siblings, other teachers*)

3. What are some things that could go wrong on a field trip if it wasn't planned carefully? (*leave someone behind, not have enough lunches, forget medication*)

4. How do field trip helpers make a field trip easier and more fun? (*let you have smaller groups, get around easier, some parents are really fun, don't have to wait as long*)

5. What are some ways that you or our class could help a field trip helper have an easier time? (*wear name tags; go over the class rules; make sure they have maps, money, special instructions*)

Activity

Directions: Students are to match each picture with the description of how the students are being helpful to the field trip helper.

Answers: 1. d   2. b   3. c   4. a   5. e

Follow-up: Make a class list of field trip procedures. What could go wrong? What will the emergency procedures consist of? What are good rules to have in effect for field trip safety?

3·9   # Field Trip Helpers

How are these students behaving correctly with the field trip helpers? Match each picture with the description.

1. wearing a name tag _____

2. staying with the group _____

3. following instructions to go to the restroom _____

4. obeying the helper's request to wait _____

5. sitting quietly through the movie _____

a.

b.

c.

d.

e.

Copyright © 2009 by John Wiley & Sons, Inc.

Relating Appropriately to Other School People   **133**

3.10 The School Counselor

Objective

The student will identify several reasons for visiting the school counselor.

Rationale

Depending on your school, the counselor may be responsible for scheduling, handling discipline, some teaching, and even counseling needy students. This is a wonderful resource for all students. Make sure that your students know that this person is available to all of them.

Thinking Questions

1. Who could you go to if you were having problems with schoolwork? *(teacher, principal)*
2. Who could help if you had problems that were bigger, like problems getting along with other kids or problems at home? *(school counselor, teachers)*
3. Counselors are people who are specially trained to help students. What might a counselor do that a teacher doesn't? *(work with small groups instead of large class, be able to talk about personal things, doesn't give homework)*
4. What are some reasons that someone might see the counselor? *(problems at home, problems at school, just want someone to talk to, scheduling, excused from school)*
5. Do you have to have a problem to see the counselor? *(ideally a counselor should interact with all of the students on some level—teaching study skills and problem-solving skills, for example)*

Activity

Directions: Students are to read about the seven students on the worksheet and decide which students could see the counselor.

Answers: Any of these students should be able to see the counselor.

Follow-up: Discuss how a counselor could fit into your classroom needs. What activities is he or she responsible for in your school?

Relating Appropriately to Other School People

3.10   **The School Counselor**

Which of these students would be welcome to see the school counselor? Circle each student you choose.

Copyright © 2009 by John Wiley & Sons. Inc.

1. ABBY is very worried because her parents are getting a divorce. She wishes she had someone to talk to about this.

2. TYLER got an A on his science project and is so excited that he wants to tell someone.

3. KAYLA has been getting bad grades in math. She doesn't know how to study very well.

4. ALEX is new in the school and doesn't have many friends. He feels scared and lonely.

5. CHLOE wants to know if she can take an art class for free choice period instead of going to volleyball.

6. ANDY can't get his locker open.

7. PRIYA has a note that says she has to leave school early to go to the hospital. She will miss three days of school.

Relating Appropriately to Other School People   **135**

3.11 Peer Tutors

Objective

The student will identify excuses that prevent an effective tutoring session with a peer tutor.

Rationale

Having older students work with younger students can benefit both. Older students enjoy helping younger children and can often relate well to them. However, because of a close age difference, sometimes the children who are being tutored can find interesting excuses to try to manipulate their helper or take advantage of a person who is "not quite their teacher."

Thinking Questions

1. What is a peer tutor? *(someone close to your age who helps with something, someone who comes to our class and reads with us)*

2. Do you think it is easier to learn from someone who has already learned what you are learning right now? *(probably—they remember how it felt to be our age, they are not as strict as a teacher)*

3. What might be fun about having a peer tutor? *(it could be someone you already know, they are like an older friend, they probably have good study habits)*

4. How is a peer tutor like a teacher? *(helps you learn things, is older)*

5. How is a peer tutor different from a teacher? *(younger, might be a friend of your older brother or sister)*

Activity

Directions: Have students read the comments that the character is making while working with a peer tutor. Is the child showing respect to the peer tutor?

Answers: 1. no   2. no   3. yes   4. no   5. no   6. no   7. no   8. yes   9. no   10. yes

Follow-up: Discuss the answers. Why are the "no" responses showing disrespect? Talk about what kind of excuse the child is giving *(trying to distract the tutor, trying to get out of work, not telling the truth about an assignment, making up excuses for not trying)*

3.11   **Peer Tutors**

Which children are showing respect to their peer tutor? Write YES or NO on the line before each item.

Copyright © 2009 by John Wiley & Sons. Inc.

_____ 1. "You have weird hair!"

_____ 2. "You look like my cousin. My cousin is really fat."

_____ 3. "Thank you for helping me with this."

_____ 4. "I don't have to do all the questions on the paper—just the ones I want to do."

_____ 5. "I forgot how to read. Will you read the story to me?"

_____ 6. "My teacher always gives me candy when we're done with our work. I hope you brought some for me."

_____ 7. "I don't have to do what you say!"

_____ 8. "I like it when you help me read."

_____ 9. "I have to go to the bathroom again."

_____ 10. "I think I can figure out that big word, so don't tell me the answer yet, okay?"

Relating Appropriately to Other School People   **137**

3.12 Community Helpers

Objective

The student will identify ways that community helpers and volunteers can help at school.

Rationale

Often parent or grandparent volunteers and other community helpers (librarian, police officer, career speakers, partners-in-education businesses) visit the school and can lend a hand in many ways. Some give presentations, others spend time with the students, and others may simply help out with specific projects (gardening, building a set for the play). At all times, these special people should be shown appreciation and respect.

Thinking Questions

1. Who are some adults who have visited our school? *(vision screening people, grandparents on Grandparents' Day, a friend's mother for a class party)*

2. Why do you think these people come to school to help, even when they might have jobs or don't get paid to come? *(they want to see what their kids are doing, they are interested in the school, they have skills that the teachers need)*

3. What are some projects that you have seen some of these adults working on? *(building a puppet show theater, helping with a class play, reading stories, giving a talk about bike safety)*

4. How do you think we could help these special helpers feel appreciated when they come to our school? *(be sure to say thank you, be especially nice to them, don't pretend that you don't know what you're doing)*

Activity

Directions: Students are to read a list of special helpers and their interests. They should then write at least one activity that the helper might do in the classroom.

Answer examples: 1. read a story to the class 2. help design a set for a play 3. talk about what it's like to fly a plane 4. make a bulletin board for the class 5. help play games at a class party 6. go on a field trip 7. plant flowers around the school 8. show students how to draw cartoons

Follow-up: Throughout the year, keep a list of the visitors and special helpers who help out in your class. Assign several students to make a personal thank-you card to send to the helpers. You may want to have a class or school appreciation breakfast at which these helpers are given special thanks for volunteering.

3.12   **Community Helpers**

Here are some community helpers. Read about them, and think of something that they might be interested in doing at your school or for your classroom. Write your answer on the lines.

1. Mr. Alexander is a retired reading teacher, but he still loves to read. He has a very good voice and can change his voice to make different characters sound different.

       _____

       _____

2. Ms. Bokland likes to act in plays. She has been in several community theater plays and has built some of the sets too.

       _____

       _____

3. Steven's grandpa has a small plane and takes Steven and his brothers for rides on weekends.

       _____

       _____

4. Mrs. Smith likes to come to the classroom to help with any jobs that the teacher has for her.

       _____

       _____

5. Sally's aunt loves parties! She knows all kinds of good party games for kids.

       _____

       _____

6. Josh's dad enjoys going to museums. There is a chance that your class might get to visit a museum in the spring.

       _____

       _____

7. Amanda's grandmother loves plants. She can grow anything!

       _____

       _____

8. Mr. Keller draws illustrations for children's books. He likes to visit schools.

       _____

       _____

Copyright © 2009 by John Wiley & Sons, Inc.

3.13 Cafeteria Helpers

Objective

Students will identify comments that are pleasant and helpful to cafeteria workers.

Rationale

Who doesn't like someone who serves food every day? Cafeteria workers (the "lunch ladies") work hard to make sure that students are given food that is well prepared and on time. It takes only a moment to show courtesy to these workers.

Thinking Questions

1. Do you know the names of any of the helpers who work in the lunch line or in the cafeteria? (*hopefully yes!*)

2. Why do you think it is important for your class to be on time for lunch? (*many children need to get through the line each day*)

3. What is the procedure for hot lunches or cold lunches? (*have students state the lunchroom procedures*)

4. What are some comments that you think the lunch people like to hear? (*"I love the food," "Thank you for serving us"*)

5. What are some comments that you think they don't like to hear? (*"That looks gross," "I forgot my lunch ticket," "I have to charge again"*)

6. Why do you think the helpers in the lunchroom want children to eat their food slowly? (*so students don't choke*)

7. What are some things that you have noticed about the cafeteria or lunchroom that the helpers have done to make it a nice place for you? (*maybe decorate the walls, put flowers on the tables, play soft music*)

Activity

Directions: Students are to look at the children on the worksheet who are in the lunchroom. They should circle the children who are showing good lunchroom behavior.

Answers: 1, 3, 4, 6

Follow-up: Have one of the cafeteria workers come to your class to talk about nutrition, what it's like to order food for an entire school, how they prepare the food, and any other information that might be interesting for the students. Perhaps she could even give the class a tour of the facilities. She might tell how it makes her feel when one of the students compliments the workers on a good job.

Relating Appropriately to Other School People

3.13   # Cafeteria Helpers

These children are in the lunchroom. Circle the ones who are showing good lunchroom behavior.

Copyright © 2009 by John Wiley & Sons, Inc.

Relating Appropriately to Other School People   **141**

3.14 Playground Supervisors

Objective

The student will identify which children on the worksheet are following the playground rules.

Rationale

Students need time to run off their energy, play, socialize with others, and just enjoy being outside. The playground can offer great opportunities for all of these experiences. It can also be a dangerous place if students aren't careful on the monkey bars, push each other, or jump off swings that are too high in the air. It can be a sad place for students who don't fit in and are reminded that they don't have friends. By following playground rules, students can learn social skills in a natural setting.

Thinking Questions

1. What is your favorite way to spend time on the playground? (*swings, monkey bars, tires, basketball*)

2. Why do most kids love recess or playground time? (*they can do whatever they want, it's fun to move around, fun to be with friends*)

3. What are some rules that you have for outdoor recess? (*line up when the whistle blows, stay inside the fence*)

4. How do those rules keep you safe? (*you won't get hurt if you are careful, not too many people at one time on the tires*)

5. Do you think most kids like to play with others on the playground, or do some kids like to be alone? (*most kids probably like to be with others*)

6. What would be a nice way to include someone who might not have a lot of friends? (*get off the swing and let someone else have it, ask them to play ball or tag*)

7. What do you think is the hardest part about being a playground supervisor? (*watching so many kids at the same time, being outside when it's really hot or cold*)

Activity

Directions: The playground supervisor has given the class a lot of rules to follow. Which of the students is following the procedures?

Answers: 1. first student   2. second student   3. first student   4. first student   5. first student

Follow-up: Discuss the need for playground rules at your school. Have students make a list of twenty activities that they could play on the playground (*for example, tag, catch, follow-the-leader*). Perhaps the playground supervisor could select the best-behaved class each week and reward them with an extra five minutes of recess time.

3.14 Playground Supervisors

The playground supervisor has reminded the children of the rules. Circle the child in each group who is following the directions.

Copyright © 2009 by John Wiley & Sons, Inc.

4.

5.

Relating Appropriately to Other School People

Copyright © 2009 by John Wiley & Sons. Inc.

Classroom Tips for Relating Appropriately to Other School People

- Have a special box, game, or surprise for the students that only a substitute is allowed to distribute. Make sure students know that at a certain time during the day, they will have a treat if their behavior has been appropriate.

- When it is your assistant's birthday, arrange a surprise party. The students will enjoy planning and carrying out the event. Make sure all students sign a card, perhaps including nice comments or funny remarks.

- Get to know your principal. Invite him or her to the classroom for a special activity, or if time allows, have him or her listen to your students read a story. Some classes enjoy having lunch with the principal (either in the cafeteria or a "feast" in the classroom).

- Invite the school secretary as a special guest speaker to share some anecdotes about what it's like to work in the office. What are the funniest excuses he or she has heard? What were the wildest moments?

- Make a bulletin board featuring other teachers in your school. Include a display showing their interests, hobbies, awards, and other jobs they have had. Have some leading questions on the board, such as: Which teacher tried skydiving? Who has four dogs?

- Before going on a field trip, go over the do's and don'ts of what to expect from the field trip helpers. For example, students DO NOT beg for money; DO NOT wander off alone; DO stay where you can see your leader at all times. Field trips can be fun, or they can be exasperating. If you're lucky enough to have volunteer helpers, make sure that students realize how important they are to ensure future trips.

- Invite your school counselor if you have one (the principal may do double-duty) to visit your class and explain what services are available for students. Some schools have groups that meet to discuss various topics—for example, divorce, homework help, peer tutoring, and how to improve grades.

Chapter 4

When You Have Problems

4.1 Having a Problem

Objective

The student will identify common problems that children might experience in school or at home.

Rationale

The first step in problem solving is identifying what the problem is—the nature of what the student is dealing with. Everyone has problems at some time, and solving those problems can be a challenge as well as a chore. This lesson centers around deciding what the basic problem is in several situations.

Thinking Questions

1. When you think of problems that you may have at home or school, what do you think of? (*getting along with the teacher or students, keeping up with work, remembering things*)

2. What are some problems that may come up on the playground or after school? (*fighting over equipment, chasing others, trying to fight when the teacher isn't around*)

3. What are some problems that most kids have to deal with in the classroom? (*doing work, understanding the work, finishing the work, remembering homework*)

4. What are some ways that people try to blame others for the problem? (*saying that it's someone else's responsibility, giving up and letting someone else finish*)

5. Do you think there is an answer or solution for every problem? (*answers may vary; the hope is that the students will decide that there are solutions to their problems*)

Activity

Directions: Students are to decide what the problem is in each of the situations on the worksheet and then write their answer on the lines.

Answer examples: 1. boy can't tie his shoe   2. girl needs a new pen   3. boy is bothered by the other boy   4. boy is having trouble understanding something   5. boy can't reach the books

Follow-up: Have students discuss what each character might try in order to begin solving the problem. Discuss the seriousness of each situation. Is each problem worth getting upset about? Which are not as crucial or important?

Copyright © 2009 by John Wiley & Sons, Inc.

Name _____ Date _____

4.1   Having a Problem

Each of these students is having some difficulty. What is the problem that each student below is bothered by? Write your answer on the lines next to each student.

1. *I can't get this stupid shoe tied! I'm going to trip and fall!*

    _____
    _____
    _____

2. *This pen isn't working! How can I get my story finished?*

    _____
    _____
    _____

3. *If you give me that look one more time, I'm going to POUND you!*

    _____
    _____
    _____

4. *I just can't figure this out. It doesn't make any sense!*

    _____
    _____
    _____

5. *I---can't- --quite---reach- ---this---*

    _____
    _____
    _____

When You Have Problems   **149**

4.2 Asking for Help Politely

Objective

The student will identify polite ways to request help from others.

Rationale

Simply asking for help on something may get a response, but asking politely gets a better response. Most requests can be delivered in a clear, appropriate manner and still get results. Students should focus on requesting rather than demanding.

Thinking Questions

1. When you want something from someone, what do you do? *(ask the person for it)*
2. Do you think it makes a difference in how you ask someone for something? *(most people prefer to be asked nicely)*
3. What are some things you would ask for help on at school? *(questions about schoolwork, the teacher's time)*
4. What are some things you might ask for help on at home? *(homework, chores, running errands)*
5. Do you think there is a way to ask for help politely rather than demanding it? *(yes)*
6. What could you do to make a request for help sound polite and more pleasant? *(add "please," be patient with request, don't be pushy)*

Activity

Directions: Students are to circle the students on the worksheet who are asking for help politely. They are to put an X through those who are not.

Answers: Circle: 2, 3, 5; X: 1, 4, 6

Follow-up: Discuss how the X'd students could have asked for help politely. Discuss why "You!" and "Hey!" are impolite. Explain that asking for help is not a bad thing; in fact, it is necessary for lots of problem-solving situations. But adding a polite touch will make a difference in how others respond to you.

When You Have Problems

4.2

Asking for Help Politely

Which of these students are asking for help in a polite way? Circle the students who are being polite, and put an X through those who are not being polite or respectful.

Copyright © 2009 by John Wiley & Sons, Inc.

4.3 Taking Another Look

Objective

The student will identify ways to solve problems by looking at the situation carefully.

Rationale

Some problems can be solved simply by taking a good look at the situation at hand. Minor things can be overlooked, such as the location of materials, glancing at a page without really "seeing" it, or assuming that something is in place when it actually isn't. Teach students to carefully assess the problem situation before getting upset.

Thinking Questions

1. Have you ever looked all over for something and eventually found it—right under your nose? (*probably someone will have an anecdote*)
2. Why do you think people make mistakes like that? (*they are in a hurry, looking in the wrong spot*)
3. Have you ever made mistakes in school where you just didn't look hard enough at something? (*ask for anecdotes*)
4. What's a way to help get out of that problem of just not seeing something? (*double-check your work, slow down*)
5. How can another person help you take another look? (*ask a friend to check it over for you or with you, different perspective*)

Activity

Directions: Students are to go through Tom's day, finding clues that he overlooked—resulting in his having a very bad day. They are to circle the clues that Tom should have noticed.

Answers: 1. math book in desk   2. problem was $2 + 3$ 3. directions asked for complete sentences   4. no name on paper   5. the clock shows that it's past eleven o'clock—the class is at recess   6. the door was shut but came open again

Follow-up: Discuss with your class the idea of saying, "Take another look," if you notice a problem that the student should be able to solve simply by looking again at the situation.

Name _____ Date _____

4.3

Taking Another Look

Tom is having a very bad day: nothing is going right for him. Help him get through his problems by taking another look at each situation. Circle something that Tom should look at carefully in each picture below.

Copyright © 2009 by John Wiley & Sons, Inc.

4.4 Thinking Harder

Objective

The student will identify multiple solutions to problems by spending time thinking about alternatives.

Rationale

We often want students to spit forth quick answers to many problems or situations rather than allowing them to mull things over before answering. Requiring students to think through possible solutions before giving an answer is a good skill for thinking (on the part of the student) and waiting (on the part of the teacher).

Thinking Questions

1. When someone asks you a question, how soon does the person want the answer? *(usually right away)*

2. When you stop and think about something for awhile, do you sometimes change your mind about how you feel about it or what you think of it? *(ask for anecdotes)*

3. If you had a problem situation, why might it be important to think about it for awhile rather than just do something quickly? *(you might not know the whole situation, time might change things somewhat)*

4. When someone tells you to "stop and think about it," is it hard to do? *(probably)* Why or why not? *(we're used to quick answers)*

5. Do you think there are several answers to some problems? Why? *(yes, especially when many factors are involved)*

Activity

Directions: Students are to generate several possible (and plausible) solutions for the situations given. Encourage them to "stop and think" before putting down only one answer.

Answer examples:

1. Invite both friends over to your house; go to Mary's on one day and Elizabeth's the next day; suggest that you could all play together.

2. Borrow from a friend; call a neighbor; go home at lunch.

3. Ask if they could hold the book for you; borrow from a good friend; ask if the book will be at the library later.

4. Ask Tony to help you clean your room (a true friend would do that!); ask Tony to wait; ask your mother if you could clean your room and do one extra chore later if she lets you play now.

Follow-up: Discuss the concept of brainstorming with your students: first, generate lots and lots of ideas, even ones that may seem silly; then begin to eliminate the ones that don't seem good. Explain that when there is no clear-cut answer, a lot of good thinking will help narrow down your choices to several possibilities.

Name _____ **Date** _____

4·4   # Thinking Harder

Sometimes problems can be solved by thinking them over for awhile. What are at least three possible solutions for each of the following problems? Think before you answer.

1. Both Mia and Elizabeth invited you to their houses. You like both of them, but you can't be in two places at one time. What could you do?

a. _____

b. _____

c. _____

2. It's the day of the big volleyball game at lunch. Oh, no! You left your gym shoes at home and your mother has already gone off to work. What will you do?

a. _____

b. _____

c. _____

3. There is a book sale in the library. You really want to buy the book about papier-mâché projects, but it costs a dollar more than you have with you. It's the last day of the sale. What might you do?

a. _____

b. _____

c. _____

4. Your mother wants you to clean your room before company comes over. It's a mess (as usual). But your friend Tony wants you to play ball with him before it gets dark. You only have about an hour, and you really want to play with Tony. What will you do?

a. _____

b. _____

c. _____

Copyright © 2009 by John Wiley & Sons, Inc.

When You Have Problems   **155**

4.5 I Am Having a Really Bad Day

Objective

The student will identify several acceptable procedures for coping with a perceived or legitimate crisis in the classroom.

Rationale

We all have them—days that start out bad and only get worse. For some students, this can be a chain of events that leads to emotional shutdown, aggression, or annoying behavior that disturbs everyone in the classroom. If students can learn ways to handle their bad days, this skill can empower them to take steps toward helping themselves.

Thinking Questions

1. Have you ever had a really bad day? What happened to you? (*overslept, forgot homework, had a cold*)

2. Why do you think that when a day starts out bad, it seems as though the whole day goes bad? (*you are thinking negative thoughts from the beginning, you're already behind in your schedule*)

3. What does it mean to "start the day over"? (*try to imagine a new beginning point, put the bad things behind you*)

4. What are some ways that you can help forget about the things that are pulling you off track? (*focus on your work, talk to someone, find a quiet place where you can settle yourself down for a few minutes*)

5. Sometimes you might feel as though you are having a crisis, and you just can't go on. What are some examples? (*you just can't think about what you're supposed to be doing, keep crying, someone keeps bothering you in class*)

6. What are some ways in our classroom that you can help yourself calm down and get through your bad day? (*time-out, draw or write, talk to the counselor*)

Activity

Directions: Read about the children on the worksheet who are having bad days. What are they doing to deal with their problems?

Answer examples: 1. Tell the teacher you need a quiet time-out.   2. Change activities to something you like to work on.   3. Talk to a friend.   4. Talk to the counselor.   5. Think about the things you can do well.   6. Learn how to calm yourself down.

Follow-up: Discuss ways that are acceptable methods of dealing with a crisis, a really bad day, or a stressful situation. Have students draw posters of students engaging in these behaviors, and display them around the room.

Copyright © 2009 by John Wiley & Sons, Inc.

Name _____ Date _____

4.5   I Am Having a Really Bad Day

What are these children doing to help them deal with a really bad day? Write down what you think.

1. Ryan is bothered by the noisy children around him and is starting to get angry. He doesn't want to lose his temper, but he is getting more and more upset. He asked his teacher if he could go to a quiet place to calm down for a few minutes.

   _____

   _____

2. Sheri was absent for a few days and doesn't understand how to do the math problems on the worksheet. The teacher asked her to wait for awhile until she could help her. Sheri is trying and trying to figure out the math, but she just feels stupid. She decided to set it aside and work on her spelling assignment that is fun for her.

   _____

   _____

3. Jorge's mother overslept, and he missed the bus, so he was late to school. He came to school worried, but his friend Yoshifusa told him that he would help him with the morning assignments that he missed.

   _____

   _____

4. Belinda's mother is in the hospital, and Belinda just can't concentrate on school activities because she is worried about her mother. She asked if she could talk to the school counselor about her feelings.

   _____

   _____

5. Ashley isn't a very fast runner, and she doesn't like playing tag at recess. Her friend Kate told her that it doesn't matter if she can run fast because Ashley is one of the best readers. Ashley thanked her friend for reminding her of what she can do well.

   _____

   _____

6. A.J. looked at the test in front of him, and his mind went blank. He started to panic, but then he remembered to breathe in and out slowly a few times, focus on just the first question, and remind himself that he will probably think of the answer because he studied all of this last night.

   _____

   _____

When You Have Problems   **157**

4.6 I Don't Understand What to Do

Objective

The student will identify ways to handle a situation in which he or she does not understand the task and needs clarification.

Rationale

Although we as teachers try to be as clear as possible, sometimes students just do not get what to do. The task may be a bit too challenging, maybe our explanations were not clear enough, or perhaps the student didn't feel well enough that day to put forth some extra effort. Whatever the reason, the student legitimately does not understand the task. This lesson focuses on helping the student figure out what to do when he or she is faced with this problem.

Thinking Questions

1. What is something that is really hard for you to learn? (*a computer game, math with regrouping, finding the main idea, giving an oral book report*)

2. What are some reasons that you might not understand what to do? (*it's too hard, the teacher talked too fast, absent, not interested*)

3. If you didn't know how to do something, whom could you ask? (*the teacher, the teacher's assistant, a friend*)

4. If you didn't understand written directions, what could you do? (*read them again slowly and carefully*)

5. If you wanted to learn how to play a game but weren't able to ask someone how to play, what could you do? (*watch for awhile and see if you can figure it out*)

6. Why do you think a teacher might tell you to look again or try again rather than just tell you the answer to something? (*the teacher wants you to use your brain, thinks that you are really able to do it if you try*)

Activity

Directions: These children don't understand how to do something that is important. What is the problem in each example? How could the child figure out what to do?

Answer examples: 1. *Problem:* The teacher is talking too fast. *Solution:* Ask the teacher to repeat more slowly.   2. *Problem:* Everyone else seems to understand but me! I must be stupid. *Solution:* Raise hand and ask for help.   3. *Problem:* Absent for a week and missed instruction. *Solution:* Stay after school for help.   4. *Problem:* Didn't hear the directions. *Solution:* Raise hand and politely ask the teacher to repeat them, or check with a neighbor.   5. *Problem:* Don't understand what to do on the calendar. *Solution:* Observe the other children.

Follow-up: Share with students an example of a time when you didn't understand what to do (for me, for example, it was a computer training in-service in which I couldn't get something to work and everyone around me was talking about how easy it was). Talk about how it made you feel, and assure them that you understand their frustration. Include how you solved your problem.

Name _____   Date _____

4.6   I Don't Understand What to Do

These students are having problems because they do not understand what to do. What is the problem in each example? What is a solution?

1. Problem: _____

   Solution: _____

2. Problem: _____

   Solution: _____

Copyright © 2009 by John Wiley & Sons, Inc.

4.6   I Don't Understand What to Do (continued)

3. Problem: _____

    Solution: _____

4. Problem: _____

    Solution: _____

5. Problem: _____

    Solution: _____

Copyright © 2009 by John Wiley & Sons. Inc.

4.7 No Crying, No Whining

Objective

The student will state his or her problem in a controlled manner without crying or whining.

Rationale

People are more likely to listen to a complaint or problem if it is presented in a polite manner. Crying and whining behaviors draw negative attention to the situation. If a student can demonstrate some self-control in discussing his or her situation, it makes for a more pleasant climate, even in a problem situation.

Thinking Questions

1. Let's say I was writing something and my pencil broke. What would be a likely way to solve this problem? *(ask if you can sharpen it, use another pencil)*

2. If I decided to cry about it, what would you think of me? *(you were getting upset over something small, you were a crybaby)*

3. If you have a problem, why do you think it might be better to handle it in a quiet, calm manner? *(people would like you better, you can get attention for doing something good)*

4. When someone cries or whines about something going wrong, what could happen? *(people wouldn't want to be around them, they wouldn't get their problem solved anyhow)*

5. When you feel like crying or whining, what could you do instead? *(stop and think, calm yourself down, go to your list of alternative behaviors)*

Activity

Directions: Look at the children on the worksheet who are having problems in the classroom. What do you think each child could do instead of crying or whining?

Answers: 1. get another pencil   2. get a tissue   3. quiet down and read the story   4. do something while waiting

Follow-up: Discuss situations in which children have focused on crying and whining instead of doing what they were supposed to be doing. Discuss the difference between crying when you are hurt versus crying when you are frustrated. Are there ever times when it is appropriate to cry? Are there ever times when whining is appropriate?

4·7   # No Crying, No Whining

Each child below is having some kind of problem. Write what you think each child could do instead of crying or whining.

1. "My pencil is missing! It was my FAVORITE pencil! I can't write with any other pencil!! I can't do my work without my pencil! I need my pencil!"

_____

_____

2. "My nose is running. I have a cold. (sniff, sniff). I can't do my work. I can't write. I don't feel good. How do you expect me to work if my nose is running?"

_____

_____

3. "I don't like this story. This story is boring. I want to read about cowboys. This story is ten pages long. It will take too long to read it."

_____

_____

4. "Where is my mom? She was supposed to pick me up at two o'clock and it's two minutes after two o'clock. I wonder if she forgot me? Where IS she? She's not here! (sob, sob) Where is my mom?"

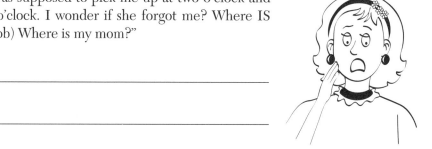

_____

_____

Copyright © 2009 by John Wiley & Sons, Inc.

4.8 I Don't Speak English!

Objective

Students will identify ways to assist other students who are not fluent in English.

Rationale

Many students in school do not speak English as their native language. Although there are teachers who are trained to help these students, often it is up to the classroom teacher to make sure that these students are given opportunities to fit in socially and to learn as much as possible. By having designated procedures in place, these students can follow steps to fit into the classroom as much as possible.

Thinking Questions

1. What would it be like for you if you were suddenly dropped into another country where you didn't speak or understand the language? *(very strange, frightening)*

2. How do you think you would learn the new language? *(listening to others, observing, taking lessons)*

3. Sometimes you might find that there are students in your class or school who do not speak English as their main language. Can you think of some other languages that might be spoken? *(Spanish, Japanese)*

4. What are some ways that you could help a student learn how to do things in the classroom? *(have a helper, give opportunities to observe others, specifically teach them)*

5. What are some ways that you could help such a student learn English? *(have them come over and watch TV with you, include them when you play, explain words to them)*

6. What are some ways that you could learn about their language and culture? *(ask them to bring in things from home, learn some of their words)*

Activity

Directions: How are these non-English speaking students being helped by classmates?

Answers: 1. showing them how to order lunch   2. teaching them words   3. including them at recess 4. learning some words in their language

Follow-up: If you have students who come from other countries, have them share some of their experiences with the class (if they feel comfortable doing so), teach the class a song or poem in another language, and talk about ways that the students are the same and different.

4.8   **I Don't Speak English!**

How are the students helping their friends who do not speak English?

1. "This is a hamburger, and this is a pizza. Which one do you want for lunch?"

    _____

    _____

2. "The teacher will be happy if you say 'please' and 'thank you.' Watch me. 'Thank you, Mrs. Martin!'"

    _____

    _____

3. "We are going to play baseball. Come with us!"

    _____

    _____

4. "How do you say 'My turn!' in your language?"

    _____

    _____

Copyright © 2009 by John Wiley & Sons, Inc.

4.9 Excuses, Excuses

Objective

The student will identify given excuses as legitimate or not acceptable, considering the circumstances.

Rationale

We often hear excuses for why homework wasn't turned in, why someone is late for class, or why it isn't necessary for someone to do the entire assignment. As teachers, we don't always know the entire circumstances surrounding the problem; however, we do know the students who are habitual in providing us with excuse after excuse. We should help students differentiate between giving a good reason for the problem happening and giving an excuse as a substitute for having a good reason. Help students realize that mistakes can happen to anyone, but if circumstances could be controlled and should have been controlled, an excuse is often not good enough to make up for not having something done.

Thinking Questions

1. What are some of the excuses you hear for not having something done? (*I lost it, I was too tired, I was busy*)

2. What would be considered a good excuse for not having your homework done? (*if you were in an accident, if the teacher forgot to pass out the homework*)

3. If someone gives excuses all the time, what might you begin to think about that person? (*doesn't really want to work, doesn't care, not responsible*)

4. When is an excuse good enough to get you out of something? When you couldn't control the situation or if you didn't want to change a situation? (*physical pain is usually a good excuse, poor planning is not*)

5. Are you responsible if your dog destroys a school book? (*you are responsible for the damage*)

6. If you are not careful about where you put things or what you do yourself, could accidents happen? (*yes*)

7. If accidents happen because you were careless, is that excuse acceptable? (*not if it is habitual—if you don't learn from the mistakes*)

8. Do you think most people would understand something going wrong for you if they knew the circumstances? (*hope so!*)

9. Why do some people get "excused" from school early or "excused" from doing extra work? (*depends on the circumstances: going to the dentist might be an emergency, that person's situation might be entirely different from yours*)

Activity

Directions: Students are to read the set of excuses and decide whether each excuse is acceptable to the point that there should be no consequences for missing or handing in late work. Encourage students to think hard about the situations. Is the student trying to get out of work or explaining a problem situation? If not enough information is given to make an informed decision, have students ask questions that they would need to know to make a judgment.

Answers:

1. Probably no (what was it doing sticking out of the car window?)
2. No (you are responsible for the dog's behavior, and you could have found another pencil)
3. No (you could control how late you were up)
4. Yes (going to the dentist is usually acceptable)
5. No (trying to blame Joe's mom is not good enough)
6. Probably yes (a promise was made to the brother and mother, so that would come first)

Follow-up: Impress on students the importance of planning ahead to avoid common household situations that turn into problems. Don't blame the dog, the wind, or the television. Direct the focus of whose responsibility it is to where it belongs.

4.9   # Excuses, Excuses

These students have many different excuses for not having something done or done right. Do you think each is a good excuse? Write YES or NO on the line next to each situation.

Copyright © 2009 by John Wiley & Sons. Inc.

_____ 1. I don't have my homework because it flew out of the car window last night when I was holding it in the wind.

_____ 2. My dog ate my pencil, so I couldn't finish my worksheet.

_____ 3. I was up too late last night watching a movie, and I overslept and couldn't finish my reading.

_____ 4. I'm late because I had to go to the dentist to get a filling in my tooth.

_____ 5. I'm late because I stopped to have breakfast at Joe's house, and his mom cooks slowly.

_____ 6. I can't come over after school to help you with your bike because I promised my little brother I'd take him to the store for my mom.

When You Have Problems   **167**

4.10 People Who Can Help

Objective

The student will identify several people who could help him or her with a problem.

Rationale

There are many human resources available to students if they are aware of them and willing to ask for help. This lesson asks students to think about some possible people who could be used as resources and ways that he or she might be helpful to the student in addressing a problem.

Thinking Questions

1. If you had a problem, what person or persons might you be most likely to talk to? (*answers will vary—friend, teacher, family member*)

2. Did everyone have the same answer? (*probably not*) Why? (*everyone has his or her own circle of resourceful people*)

3. How can family members or others help you with school problems? (*mother might talk to the principal, help you with homework; older sibling might help you out with a bully; a neighbor might help with driving or providing you with materials*)

4. How might school people help you with home problems? (*have some ideas for talking to your parents, a classmate might have had a similar problem*)

5. Do you think most people are willing to help other people? (*probably yes—ask students how they feel when someone asks them for help!*)

6. Did you ever have an experience when you felt bad and someone you least expected turned out to be a good listener or problem solver? Tell about it. (*answers will vary—the helpful person might turn out to be a teacher*)

Activity

Directions: Students are to list ways that the individuals on the worksheet might be able to help students with their problems. "Problems" is undefined and can be interpreted according to each student's own situation. The idea is to generally indicate how a person in that role (parent, sibling, neighbor) could be a resource in times of trouble.

Answer examples: the person might be a good listener, like working with kids, be especially understanding, or be protective of the student

Follow-up: Allow students to volunteer their responses if desired. If someone has an abusive father, it is unlikely that he or she would see that person as a resource since he is a problem. Perhaps the students could go to the father, however, if help was needed on building something, cooking something, or going somewhere. Allow students to personalize their responses if this is easier for them.

When You Have Problems

4.10   # People Who Can Help

If you have a problem, how could each of these people help you out?

1. A parent

   _____

   _____

2. Your older sister

   _____

   _____

3. The school counselor

   _____

   _____

4. A favorite teacher

   _____

   _____

5. The principal

   _____

   _____

6. Your best friend

   _____

   _____

7. A good neighbor

   _____

   _____

Copyright © 2009 by John Wiley & Sons, Inc.

4.11 Problem Solvers

Objective

The student will match students with problems to a likely solution or method of working out the problem.

Rationale

This is a review lesson, combining several types of problems and possible solutions. There are multiple ways to search for and reach resolution with problems. This lesson shows several techniques.

Thinking Questions

1. If you were having nightmares, would you work harder on your spelling words to take care of it? *(if your nightmares were about spelling tests, but they are probably not)*

2. If you were being bullied by a kid in another class, could you help solve the problem by asking your teacher politely for the glue? *(probably not—the solution doesn't fit the problem)*

3. What are sensible ways to solve these problems? *(think about the circumstances, what's causing the problem)*

4. What are some ways that we have talked about solving some problems? *(ask for help, take another look at the problem, think harder, avoid excuses, get help from a tutor, use an assignment notebook, do homework, use other people)*

5. If one solution doesn't take care of the problem, what should you do? *(keep trying to find another way to work on the problem, try another resource)*

Activity

Directions: Students are to match the characters on the left (who have a specific problem) with the solution on the right (that is specific as well).

Answers: 1. d   2. c   3. f   4. e   5. b   6. a   7. g

Follow-up: Have students discuss their responses. Ask for additional problem-solving ideas for each of the situations. Though only one matches on the worksheet, are there other solutions that could work for each situation? What?

When You Have Problems

4.11   # Problem Solvers

Match each student with a problem to the way that he or she worked on solving that problem. Write the letter next to each student.

Copyright © 2009 by John Wiley & Sons. Inc.

1. Jorge was getting bad grades on his spelling tests. ____

2. Marta couldn't read a lot of the words in her reading book. ____

3. Pete kept getting the wrong answers on his math. ____

4. Cindy kept forgetting to bring her art materials to school. ____

5. Artie was bothered by the boy who sat behind him in class. ____

6. Jeannine was worried that she was going to be late to school. ____

7. Fred got in trouble for yelling at the teacher when he couldn't find his pencil. ____

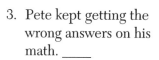

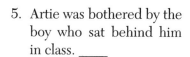

a. Her mother bought her an alarm clock so she could wake up on time.

b. He asked his teacher if he could move to another seat.

c. Her teacher found another student who was a good reader to help her with the words.

d. He took his spelling words home and studied them each night.

e. She wrote down things to remember in a little notebook.

f. He checked the numbers very carefully and looked over his work.

g. He worked on politely asking the teacher if she would help him find his pencil, please.

When You Have Problems

4.12 Keeping Track of Assignments

Objective

The student will demonstrate the ability to write down an assignment (given orally or taken from writing) on a piece of paper or in a notebook.

Rationale

As students become older, they usually work more with assignment sheets and coding homework assignments in notebooks. This is one way to help students remember their homework, become more organized, and begin using notebooks to keep track of specific tasks. As a teacher, however, you must be careful to teach your students how you want them to code the assignments in the notebook. (List the date? subject? pages? check when finished?)

Thinking Questions

1. If you had ten assignments to take home to do tonight, how might you remember to do them all? *(write them down, take all your books home, call a friend to help remember)*
2. How could you use an assignment notebook to help you remember what to do? *(write things down that you need to remember)*
3. What kind of information should be kept in the notebook? *(the subject, actual pages or materials needed, date that it's due)*
4. What could you put in your notebook to show that you finished the assignment? *(cross it out, put an asterisk or check mark)*
5. Why would a notebook be better than little scraps of paper? *(less likely to lose it, can check back on old assignments)*

Activity

Directions: A sample portion of an assignment notebook is drawn on the right of the worksheet, with the teacher giving the assignment on the left. Students are to write down what they could put in their assignment notebooks that would help them remember what to do.

Answer examples:

1. Spelling words—3 times
2. Reading—"Magic Violin"
3. Art—bring old clothes
4. Bring cookies for tomorrow
5. Take box home, put hat inside

Follow-up: Have students share their responses. Decide on a good system for writing down assignments. What shortcuts worked well?

4.12   **Keeping Track of Assignments**

What would you write down in your assignment notebook for each situation?

1. **Spelling:**

2. **Reading:** "Get the green book. Read the story, 'The Magic Violin'."

_____

_____

_____

3. **Art:** "Bring some old clothes to school tomorrow because we'll be doing some messy painting."

_____

_____

_____

4. **Don't Forget:** "James, will you bring in cookies for the party tomorrow?"

_____

_____

_____

5. **Don't Forget:** "Tomorrow bring in something that begins with the letter 'H'."

_____

_____

_____

Copyright © 2009 by John Wiley & Sons. Inc.

Classroom Tips for When You Have Problems

- Use magazine pictures of faces showing various emotions. What problem might each person be thinking about? Have students draw cartoons showing what the person could be thinking.

- Make posters emphasizing the techniques discussed for help with problem solving. Let students work in groups—one does the art, one can do the lettering, and so forth. Display the posters around the room or in the hallway.

- If you have students who are learning English as a new language, you may want to teach the other students some common phrases in their native language. Allow these students a chance to talk about their lives and their language, and share their culture with the class.

- Give peer tutoring a try. If you can find a few students in higher grades who can work with minimal supervision, have a half-hour set aside for the students to mix and work on fairly straightforward tasks, such as drilling on math flash cards, playing Go Fish with word cards, working together on writing and illustrating a story. *Problems to watch for:* students who try to take advantage of their tutors (have them sit out the next session as a consequence), not being clear on task directions for the tutors (write out specifically what the task is), or having too lengthy of a session (limit it to twenty to thirty minutes).

- There are many helpful people in a child's life. Have each student compile a small book containing pictures of friends, family members, and helpful adults at school, with several paragraphs written by the student telling about each person.

- Allow students to color, decorate, or otherwise personalize an assignment notebook in which they are to write their assignments every day. Come up with class codes for subjects, logos, mottos, and any other unique ways to individualize their homework and assignment sheets.

Part Two

Relating to Peers

One day while walking down the hallway at my school, I heard the wonderful sound of laughter behind me, so I turned around to investigate. I saw two little girls holding hands, skipping down the hall on their way to recess. I was pretty sure there was a good reason that skipping was not allowed in school (especially in the hallway in front of the principal's office), but I did not stop them. Instead, I asked them if they were best friends. They giggled and said yes. I asked how old they were, and one admitted to being six and the other to being six-and-a-half. I asked what they were going to do outside, and they giggled again. The one who was six said, "We're just going to be best friends." And off they skipped outside to recess. I remember thinking: what a wonderful gift it is to have a friend—and not only a friend, but a *best* friend.

My mind flipped through example after example of students who were excluded from groups; shunned because they smelled bad, laughed at because they wore the same clothes over and over, chosen last for teams because they were clumsy. I thought about a boy who hated recess because no one ever played with him. I remembered a girl who was the only one not invited to a birthday party. I was saddened by these examples of how hurtful children can be to each other.

But then I remembered something that had amazed me just months before. I had a boy named Leon, considered severely emotionally disturbed (SED), in one of my reading groups. He was short-tempered, argumentative, and disruptive in general to the other students. One day Leon came to my group with one of the other SED students, Jared. I asked why Jared had accompanied Leon. "We are partners," Jared explained. "When Leon starts to get mad, it's my job to tell him to calm down." Nodding, Leon added, "And when we partner-read, Jared will be my partner, 'cause I'm a good reader and he's not." What had happened was this: the special education teacher had paired them up to fill the gaps for each other. Two boys now had a responsibility to each other, which they took very seriously.

Students with even the most severe behavior challenges can find ways to work together with—and enjoy—their peers. The following material in Part Two will help you teach students to relate to one another:

- Parent letters
- Story: "Ralph and His Purple Face"
- Chapter Five: Learning and Working with Others
- Chapter Six: Making Friends
- Chapter Seven: Keeping Friends

PARENT LETTER #5

RE: Relating to Peers—Learning and Working with Others

Dear Parents,

Our next series of lessons involves getting along with other people, particularly classmates at school. School is sometimes the first place where children realize that they have to operate as part of a larger group. They can't walk around whenever they want to. They have to raise their hands to be acknowledged. And they usually have to sit at a desk. The school setting is an excellent place to learn lifelong skills that follow children into the workplace as adults: cooperation, ignoring disturbances, and developing leadership skills.

Some of the lessons in these chapters are about being a good leader, being a good follower, doing your share of the work, accepting the blame for mistakes, and not creating a classroom disturbance and yet ignoring those who do.

Although you may not have a household of twenty to thirty children all the same age, you may feel that sense of chaos and disharmony all the same! Here are some ideas to help reinforce these concepts at home:

- A family requires getting along with each other just as a classroom does. Assign chores on a rotating basis, based on ability and time and other factors that can make things equitable in your home. Work together as a family to make dinner, including cleanup, a pleasant time.

- Let children take turns experimenting in a leadership role in safe tasks at home. How will the yard work be done this weekend? Some children are natural organizers. Hand your child a pencil and paper and see what evolves.

- After completing a boring or unpleasant task together, reward the family by going out for ice cream (wearing the clean clothes that everyone helped wash, dry, sort, and put away).

- Don't try to be the judge in sibling arguments. Let them work it out, but keep your ears open! Ask children if they learned some coping skills at school during their social skills times!

Sincerely,

_____

Teacher

Copyright © 2009 by John Wiley & Sons. Inc.

PARENT LETTER #6

RE: Relating to Peers—Making Friends

Dear Parents,

Having a friend is probably one of the greatest gifts in life. Knowing that someone cares about you, saves a seat for you, and misses you when you are gone is truly precious. For most kids, it is pretty easy to throw them together in a mix of soccer teams, Scouts, or even recess. But for other kids, having a friend is a joy that is missing.

Going to a new school, being in a different class, being the oldest, being the youngest, not being "good" at something—these are all complications that can get in the way of making friends.

A disability on top of that, or past negative experiences, or a bully in the classroom make things worse. We want to give all children every opportunity to fit in socially.

Our lessons at school will work on techniques for making friends; they address being interested in others, being an interesting person yourself, helping others, saying nice things to others, being a good listener, and inviting others to join you.

Within your own family, you probably are part of several groups—perhaps church, community, hobbies, or sports. Use these activities to help your child work on the skills of making friends—for example:

- Have your child invite a new friend to join you at the movies or on a family outing.

- Take advantage of community sports teams, art lessons, camping, library activities, and so on. Your child will soon be part of a group.

- Encourage your child to have friends over to play, watch TV, or make a lemonade stand in the summer. Observe your child. Is he or she a follower? A leader? Cooperative?

- Ask your child questions about others in the class. Who is the best runner? Does anyone ride horses? Who won the spelling bee? Encourage your child to talk about and think about the others in his or her class. Give your child a reason to talk to other children.

Sincerely,

_____

Teacher

Copyright © 2009 by John Wiley & Sons, Inc.

PARENT LETTER #7

RE: Relating to Peers—Keeping Friends

Dear Parents,

Do you find that your child has a different best friend just about every week? Although making friends can be a challenge, keeping friends is a tough task as well. Friendships can and do change over time for many reasons, some of them very legitimate. As interests change and kids are shifted into different groups, the dynamics change as well. Nevertheless, working at maintaining a friendship even when things don't go your way shows something about commitment, understanding, and flexibility.

Our next set of lessons focuses on techniques for being a good friend.

The ideas include letting others pick what to do at times, sharing friends with others, not hanging around or begging too much, keeping promises, and sticking up for a friend who has a problem.

You will be cited often as a resource for your child to go to with a problem. You can help your child by being supportive of the ups and downs that occur with learning to be a good friend. You can help in these ways:

- Quietly observe how your child interacts with others. Is he or she too pushy? Always the one to decide what will be done? Gently suggest letting someone else pick an activity.

- Realize that friendships change. Your child will have more than one friend at a given time, and those friends will have other friends. By sharing friends, everyone gets to know more people. Hang on to that special best friend, but encourage other friends to come over and spend time with your child.

- Talk about the importance of keeping promises. Broken promises can lead to broken friendships.

- Discuss loyalty and comradeship with others. When one group of kids starts to bad-mouth someone else, help your child realize that if this is a friend, he or she should not be part of that hurtful activity. Your child should also understand that children who are getting involved in harmful activities should not expect your child to cover up for them, especially if other children are involved.

- Make your child aware that you are available to help out your child's friends, as well as your child. Listening goes a long way.

Sincerely,

_____

Teacher

Copyright © 2009 by John Wiley & Sons. Inc.

Story: Ralph and His Purple Face

Ralph was fun to tease. The kids in his class loved to tease him because he got very upset, and when he got upset, his face turned purple, and puffs of red smoke came shooting out of his ears.

Then they really had something to tease him about. Poor Ralph.

"Look at Ralph walk," cried Billy, laughing loudly. "He walks like he has ants in his pants."

The kids started to laugh at Ralph. He felt his face getting warm.

"Stop it!" cried Ralph. "These are very nice pants, and there are NO ants in them at all!"

But his face began to turn purple, and the red smoke was already starting to come out of his ears.

"Ha, ha!" laughed the kids. "Purple face, purple face!"

"That's enough," said Mr. Snaggle, the teacher, in a very stern voice. "It's time for math. Everyone sit down."

Everyone sat down, but Ralph knew they were still looking at him and laughing. Billy poked Ralph in the back while he was sliding into his seat. Ralph was getting madder and madder.

Copyright © 2009 by John Wiley & Sons, Inc.

"Take out your homework," Mr. Snaggle instructed the class. Then he looked at Ralph. "Ralph, what is the answer to the first problem?"

Ralph looked at his paper. "Thirteen. Oh, I mean thirty-one," said Ralph.

"Ha, ha!" laughed Pete. "Ralph doesn't even know his numbers."

"STOP it," said Ralph, turning purple.

"Stop it, stop it," sang Pete in a funny voice.

The red smoke started.

Later, on the playground, Ralph kicked the ball and ran to second base without stopping.

"Hey, purple face, you didn't touch first base," yelled Frank. "Cheater!"

"I am *not!*" Ralph yelled right back, beginning to turn purple. Frank grabbed Ralph's shirt. "Weirdo, weirdo!"

Ralph's ears looked like a red chimney. "Quit it!" he yelled at Frank and the other kids who were starting to laugh. "Stop teasing me!"

But the kids laughed even harder.

Mr. Snaggle called Ralph over to him. "Ralph," he began, "the kids tease you a lot, don't they?"

Ralph nodded. He didn't really want to talk about it.

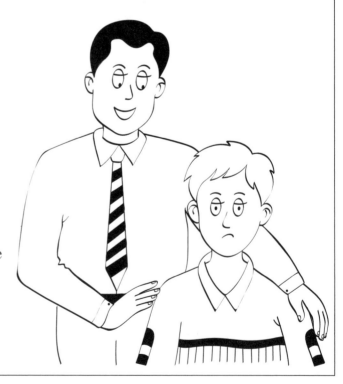

"Well, listen, Ralph. I have an idea. Next time they try to tease you or make you mad, just ignore them," he said.

Copyright © 2009 by John Wiley & Sons, Inc.

"Ignore them?" asked Ralph in disbelief. "But they really upset me, Mr. Snaggle! I can't help my purple face and red smoke!"

"I know it sounds hard," continued Mr. Snaggle, "but they'll give up if you pretend that you don't even hear them. Don't let them decide for you how you're going to act. *You* decide."

"It's hard," said Ralph quietly.

"They like to see your face turn purple," Mr. Snaggle continued. "And they think it's funny for red smoke to come out of your ears. Let's spoil their fun."

"Okay," said Ralph. "What should I do?"

"Well," said Mr. Snaggle, "try this: when they tease you, look away and don't say anything. Not one word. Just pretend they aren't there. If you think you're going to give in, look up at me. I'll wink, and that will mean I know you can do it. Hold out."

"I'll try, Mr. Snaggle," said Ralph, feeling a little better. "I'll have them wondering what's going on!"

His first chance came later that afternoon. Amy went by Ralph's desk and whispered under her breath, "Purple face, purple face." But Ralph just scratched his head and opened his spelling book to look at the words.

"Hey, where's the red smoke?" asked Fred. Ralph just turned his head and wrote his spelling words on a piece of paper.

Amy and Fred looked at each other in surprise. Nothing was happening!

Inside, Ralph smiled. He wasn't going to get mad!

The kids didn't know what was happening. They tried all Monday afternoon to get Ralph to turn purple, but it didn't work.

Copyright © 2009 by John Wiley & Sons, Inc.

They tried even harder on Tuesday. But Ralph didn't even turn light purple when they called him a bozo.

By Wednesday, the kids were getting tired of waiting for Ralph to turn purple. "He just doesn't get mad anymore," said Fred.

"Yeah," said Amy. "I don't know if we'll ever see that red smoke anymore."

By Thursday, the kids gave up trying anymore. They found out that it was more fun to play ball without fighting all the time anyhow.

On Friday, the kids found out something else about Ralph: he was an excellent speller.

Now instead of saying "purple face," the kids say, "Ralph, would you help me with my spelling, please?"

And Ralph just smiles and says, "Sure. I'd be glad to."

THE END

Copyright © 2009 by John Wiley & Sons. Inc.

Chapter 5

Learning and Working
with Others

5.1 Following the Leader

Objective

The student will identify characters who are following the requests or instructions of the group leader.

Rationale

When working in groups, some students may feel that they don't have to follow the instructions of anybody else except of an adult. When working in cooperative groups, however, each student may have the opportunity to be a student leader. They need to learn to function as both a leader and a follower within the group. This lesson focuses on the student as a follower.

Thinking Questions

1. What are some activities that you can do in a group? *(work on a poster for art, do a play, play a game, spelling Jeopardy)*

2. When you're working in a group, does it work well if there is no leader? *(only if everyone is cooperative)*

3. What if you were the leader of a group and your group was supposed to finish a huge mural for the wall? How would you help your group get the project finished? *(make some goals, assign different people tasks that they are good at, oversee the project)*

4. What if you ran into some people in your group who didn't want to work on the task? Why would that be hard for the leader? *(it would jeopardize the whole project for everyone, the leader would have to "get after" them, the project wouldn't be as much fun)*

5. How can a person be a good follower of the leader in a group? *(listen to the leader, don't argue, try to be cooperative)*

Activity

Directions: Students are to list the names of the characters on the worksheet who are being good followers. They are also to circle the student who is the leader of each group.

Answers: 1—Leader: Randy; followers: Josh, Ben.   2—Leader: Emily; followers: Nick, Luis.

Follow-up: Discuss the comments of the characters in the groups. Which were helpful? *(ones that related to the topic and the project)* Which followers were most helpful?

Name _____ Date _____

5.1   **Following the Leader**

These students are working on projects together, and each group has a student leader. Write the names of the students in each group who are good followers. Circle the group leader.

1.

Copyright © 2009 by John Wiley & Sons, Inc.

Good followers:

_____

2.

Good followers:

_____

Copyright © 2009 by John Wiley & Sons. Inc.

5.2 Being the Leader

Objective

The student will identify several characteristics of a good leader for a group.

Rationale

Being a good leader is not easy; nevertheless, assuming a leadership role in classroom activities is good for students. Skills such as pinpointing the task, including the opinions of others, assigning tasks, and keeping the group on task are all important for later leadership roles. This lesson asks students to evaluate the performance of characters in leadership roles.

Thinking Questions

1. Do you think it is easier to be a leader of a group or a follower? *(opinions will vary—the leader may have more responsibility, followers may not get to pick what they want to do)*

2. Do you think being the leader means you get to tell everyone else in the group what to do? *(no, it means "leading" or "guiding" the group)*

3. What if everyone has very different ideas about how to do something? What should the leader do then? *(listen to all of the ideas, have the group vote or come to a consensus)*

4. What should the leader know about the other people in his or her group? *(what their ideas are, what their skills are, how to ask questions about getting the task done)*

5. Why is it good to sometimes be a leader? *(learn to work with other people, be in charge, take responsibility for the product)*

6. If we had a list of characteristics of a good leader, what would we include? *(be clear, be fair, listen to everyone, don't be bossy)*

Activity

Directions: Students are to read the leader's comments in the situations on the worksheet and circle the student if they think he or she sounds like a good leader.

Answers: 1. no   2. yes   3. no   4. yes   5. yes   6. no

Follow-up: Discuss why certain characters sound like better leaders. What was the problem with the others? *(1—not a group effort; 3—bossy; 6—not a leader at all! Has no idea what to do!)*

5.2   **Being the Leader**

Each of the students is supposed to be the leader of the group. Which ones do you think are the best? Circle the students you would pick.

1. OK guys, we're supposed to work together on finishing the math problems. Bob, you do all of them and let me know when you're done.

2. Let's do a good job on our play. First, we'll read through it so we know all the words. Then we'll choose parts. Then we can practice. Does that sound good to everyone?

3. I'm the leader, so you HAVE to do what I say or I'll kick you out.

4. I think we should listen to everyone's ideas and talk about them. Then we can pick what to do.

5. Pete—you're the best artist. Do you want to do the drawing? Who has any ideas about what to put in the background?

6. I'm not sure what to do. Just do whatever you want.

Copyright © 2009 by John Wiley & Sons. Inc.

5.3 Ignoring When You Have To

Objective

The student will identify classroom events or disruptions that should be ignored.

Rationale

When students are supposed to be working on a task, noises, arguments, or generally distracting situations can be disruptive. In this lesson, students are to identify several disturbances that are better left ignored.

Thinking Questions

1. When you are working on something in the classroom, what are some things that might bother you or affect your concentration? *(people moving around, noises, distractions)*

2. Why would it bother you if someone was talking in a loud voice? *(you'd think about what the person was saying rather than what you were supposed to do)*

3. Would it bother you if someone interrupted you to talk about something else? *(it would probably disrupt the task)*

4. What might happen if you got involved in someone else's argument or conversation while you were supposed to be working on something else? *(it would probably disrupt the task)*

5. Why is it hard to ignore distractions? *(they seem interesting, you have to look up when you hear something loud for safety purposes, your work might be boring, it might involve a friend)*

6. What are some ways that you could ignore or tune out the distraction? *(look at your work, turn your back on the distraction, keep your mouth shut)*

Activity

Directions: The worksheet shows a classroom in which many disturbances are going on. The student is to put an X on the person or movement or thing that is distracting and should probably be ignored.

Answers: Principal/teacher interrupting; girl tapping pencil; boy yawning; teacher discussing problem with student; boy pulling girl's hair; two boys arguing; girl interrupting other girl who is working on a puzzle

Follow-up: Look around your classroom. What are the problem areas as far as having difficulty ignoring things? Can you have visitors later in the day? Do students know the routine for getting help? Do you discipline too loudly in front of other students? Can you help make it easier for students to ignore problems?

5.3   # Ignoring When You Have To

Put an X on each person or movement that you think should be ignored.

Copyright © 2009 by John Wiley & Sons, Inc.

5.4 Not Disturbing Others

Objective

The student will draw a picture showing a neutral situation or task performed in a disturbing or nondisturbing manner.

Rationale

Something as simple as walking across the room can be done in very different ways. Clumping loudly will still get the person to the other side—but so will walking silently. In a classroom situation, students should be able to perform simple tasks in a nondisturbing manner.

Thinking Questions

1. When people are supposed to be working or concentrating on something, what could be disturbing to them? *(people moving around, noises)*
2. Do you think people have some control over how they move, how loud they are, or how quickly they do something? *(yes)*
3. If you wanted to talk to someone across the room without disturbing others, how could you do it? *(get up and go over there, talk quietly, wait until a better time)*
4. If you are supposed to leave the room and don't want to disturb others, how might you accomplish that? *(go very quietly, don't walk between every single desk on your way)*
5. How could you help yourself remember to do things without disturbing others? *(think first, look around to see where people are and what they are doing—do they require quiet surroundings?)*

Activity

Directions: Students are given four typical classroom situations. They are to draw a picture of students carrying out that task in either a disturbing manner or a nondisturbing manner, depending on which one is not already drawn. Reassure students that their artwork is not the critical factor here—stick figures plus oral explanations are fine.

Answer examples:

1. Draw a student sharpening his pencils at the start of the school day.
2. Draw a student passing the paper by knocking it into the head of the person in front.
3. Draw someone closing the window slowly and quietly.
4. Draw someone yelling for the eraser.

Follow-up: Have students share their drawings and ideas with each other. Discuss how even seemingly small tasks can be made into a major problem just by doing it too loudly, at the wrong time, or without thinking through who might be bothered by the way it is done. Be sure to compliment students throughout the day who perform these simple tasks without disturbing others.

5.4   **Not Disturbing Others**

Draw a picture that shows how you could do the task on the left either by disturbing or not disturbing, depending on which square is blank.

	Disturbing	**Not Disturbing**
1. Sharpening your pencil		
2. Passing your paper forward		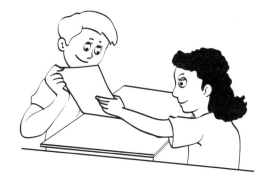

Copyright © 2009 by John Wiley & Sons. Inc.

Disturbing   **Not Disturbing**

3. Closing the window
   in the classroom

4. Asking a friend if
   you can borrow
   an eraser

Copyright © 2009 by John Wiley & Sons. Inc.

5.5 A Disabled Peer

Objective

The student will identify positive ways to interact with disabled peers in the classroom.

Rationale

More and more classrooms include students with identifiable disabilities—visual, auditory, or physical—and many of these students require adaptations in order to be successful in school. There are other students with emotional, behavioral, and various degrees of mental disabilities as well. In order to get along well in the classroom, students should have some idea of what is expected of students with disabilities, appropriate ways to interact, and ways to help out and be pleasant.

Thinking Questions

1. What would happen if someone came into the classroom who was missing an arm or a leg? *(we would be curious, want to know what happened, how he eats or walks)*

2. Do you think that this person would be able to do a lot of the same things that you do? What could he do? What would be hard for him to do? *(discuss)*

3. Sometimes children have disabilities that make things harder for them. Can you think of some that you may have heard about? *(autism, cerebral palsy, learning disabilities, attention deficit disorder)*

4. Everyone has trouble doing something. Some of these conditions might make it harder for a classmate to do everything you do, but do you think there are ways that you could help a classmate do well in the classroom? *(discuss; some students may have had experience with a disabled relative or friend)*

5. Do you think that people with disabilities want to be treated with respect? *(yes)* Why? *(so they don't feel different, stared at, made fun of)*

6. Some kids can learn the same things, but they learn in a different way. What do you think that means? *(might take them longer, might learn by seeing rather than hearing)*

7. Sometimes you might have a classmate who has a lot of difficulty staying on task, keeping his temper, or being quiet. What are some ways that you could help this student? *(tell him to stay focused, don't distract him, learn to ignore)*

Activity

Directions: On the worksheet are some examples of children with disabilities. Have the student circle the friend who is showing respect to the disabled child.

Answers: 1. A   2. B   3. A   4. A

Follow-up: Ask your school's special education teacher if he or she can talk to your class about educational disabilities and how these affect children. You might have students do some research on famous individuals who had a disability and overcame it. Be sensitive to students in your class who may have a disability. Some may be comfortable talking about this topic; others may want to blend in and not have it brought to attention.

5·5   **A Disabled Peer**

A student in each set below has a disability that makes it harder to learn in school. Circle the nondisabled student in each set who is showing respect to his or her disabled classmate.

1 A. "Hold on to my elbow. I'll walk to the lunchroom with you."

1 B. "I can do your work for you!"

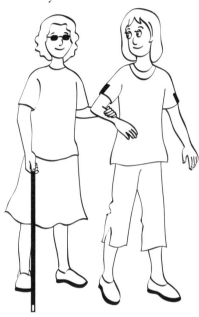

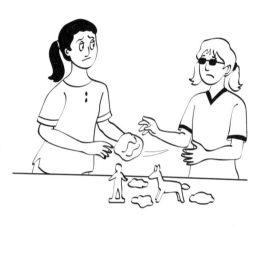

2 A. "Can I sit in your chair? I bet I can make it go really fast!"

2 B. "Would you like me to open the door for you?"

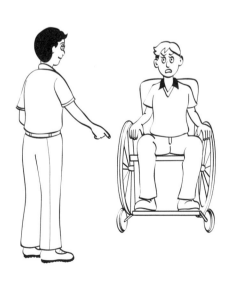

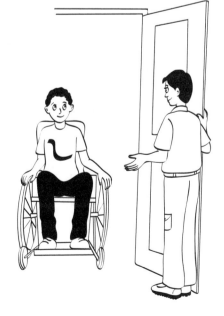

Copyright © 2009 by John Wiley & Sons, Inc.

3 A. "I won't tell you that word, but I will give you a clue."

3 B. "I'll just read the story to you."

Copyright © 2009 by John Wiley & Sons. Inc.

4 A. "You can play with us. Get a ball!"

4 B. "We don't want him on our team because then we won't win."

5.6 Bullies

Objective

The student will show how to deal with a bully at school.

Rationale

Bullying is an especially sad issue in that there are two sets of hurt people: the one who feels the need to push others around (emotionally and physically) and the victims of this aggression. It is a particularly tricky area to deal with, since the teacher may not see firsthand what is happening and the bully may take his or her issues outside school to finish up the intent to hurt someone. While we would like to believe we can help shape students into caring, nice people, unfortunately, there are kids who do not seem to care about others. One way to start is by providing an atmosphere of understanding and some safe zones for kids, with zero tolerance for malicious behavior.

Thinking Questions

1. What is a bully? (*your school may have a working definition or a policy in place—for example, someone who tries to hurt you, belittles others, might physically hurt another*)

2. What are some things that a bully might do at school to be mean to others? (*take their lunch money, call them names, trip them, try to get them in trouble*)

3. Why do you think there are some people like this? (*they want people to be afraid of them, they are selfish, they weren't brought up well, they like to tease people who aren't as smart [or fast or something else]*)

4. What are some things you could do at school if you saw someone being bullied? (*tell the teacher, tell the principal, tell your parents, try to talk to the bully*)

5. What if you were the one being bullied and were afraid to tell someone? What might happen? (*the bully wouldn't stop, the bully might come after you even more if you told on him*)

6. What are some things that we could do in this class, school, or neighborhood to stop bullying? (*give one warning and then a note goes home, have a policy of "play nicely or you can't play at all," provide a clear definition of what is and is not allowed*)

Activity

Directions: Here are some suggestions for what a child could do if someone was trying to bully him or her. Draw a picture to show how this suggestion could work at your school.

Answers: (will vary) 1. walk away from the bully   2. tell the bully to leave your friend alone   3. tell a parent   4. don't say anything   5. have your friends go with you   6. tell the bully that he or she is breaking the friendship rule

Follow-up: Depending on how prevalent this issue is at your school, you might want to discuss your school's bullying policy at a PTA meeting or send home a general newsletter about the policy. Be sensitive to the parents of a childhood bully; they may be embarrassed or may be in denial. This is truly one of the hardest situations to deal with as a teacher or parent.

5.6   **Bullies**

Select one of the following strategies and, in the space below, draw a picture to show how a child could use that strategy to deal with a bully.

1. Walk away
2. Stick up for a friend
3. Tell someone
4. Ignore
5. Stay with safe friends
6. Confront the bully

Copyright © 2009 by John Wiley & Sons. Inc.

5.7 Doing Your Share

Objective

The student will identify ways to split up a task fairly.

Rationale

When working on a group project, some members don't do their share. It is often difficult to divide up a project in such a way that all portions are equal. If everyone is cooperative, however, there is something that everyone can do to contribute to a well-done finished product. In this lesson, students are to think about how they can include everyone in some way in working on a project.

Thinking Questions

1. When working in a group, what happens if only one person does the work? *(it's not fair to that person because he or she had to work harder; the project is not a group effort, it reflects only one set of ideas)*

2. What if your group had an art project to do, and only one person liked to draw? How could the others contribute to the project? *(some could do the planning, the layout, gather materials, hold books, trace pictures)*

3. Do you think everyone could be involved in some way in a project? *(probably—using their own talents to contribute)*

4. Would it be fair if the people who could draw and liked to draw did all of the drawing and other people did something else? *(yes, as long as the product included everyone's thoughts and ideas and they contributed in some way)*

5. What are some other ways everyone could become a part of a project that a group is working on? *(get things, do research, hold papers, talk about the project in front of the class, use their own talents in some way)*

6. What if no one in a group liked to draw, but you were supposed to make a poster? How could the group make a well-done project? *(find another way to get pictures—use magazines, use the computer, use words, use another type of talent)*

Activity

Directions: Students are to split up task activities among members of a group in such a way that everyone is included.

Answer examples: 1. Read the directions/get the ingredients/stir in the ingredients/wash the dishes 2. Read the lines/work on costumes/make scenery/change the props 3. Get a partner and quiz each other/change roles and quiz each other/one person gives the quiz to everyone else 4. Rip up newspaper into strips/make the paste/put the strips on a balloon/paint the ball blue and green

Follow-up: Share responses. Perhaps students can divide into groups to discuss their answers and come up with the plans they like the best. Why are some plans unworkable? What were the best, or easiest, or fastest, or most fun ways to accomplish the tasks?

5·7   # Doing Your Share

There are four people in each group. Divide up each of the following tasks among the members of the group.

1. Bake a cake

_____

_____

_____

_____

_____

2. Put on a play from your reading book.

_____

_____

_____

_____

_____

Copyright © 2009 by John Wiley & Sons. Inc.

     Learning and Working with Others

3. Quiz each other on your spelling words; then everyone will take a test on the words together.

_____

_____

_____

_____

_____

4. Make a papier-mâché model of the Earth.

_____

_____

_____

_____

Copyright © 2009 by John Wiley & Sons, Inc.

5.8 Not Always "Me First!"

Objective

The student will identify characteristics of someone with a "me first" attitude.

Rationale

It's hard to work in a group with someone who always has to be first, who puts his or her needs above everyone else's. While students may not recognize themselves in these positions, it is important to agree that this type of attitude makes things difficult for everybody and generally doesn't gain much for the pushy person.

Thinking Questions

1. Have you ever been in a situation where somebody in the group felt that he or she had to be first? Tell about it. *(anecdotes should leave out specific names)*

2. How does it make you feel when someone insists that he or she has to be first, line up first, or do something else first, or he or she took something that should have belonged to everybody? *(angry, like you'd like to get back at them)*

3. What are some things you could do or say to someone like that without getting into a fight? *("Why don't you wait your turn?" "Could you hold on a minute? I'm almost done.")*

4. Is it sometimes better to just let a pushy person have his or her way, or should you always argue about it because it's not right? *(if you can let it go, let it go; some things aren't worth fighting about; nevertheless, the person needs to learn to give up that need to be first all the time)*

5. Are you ever one of the "me first" people? How? *(listen to anecdotes—talk about how important it was to be first)*

6. What are some things that are worth arguing about if you run into a "me first" person? *(your personal property, your safety, your school books and papers)*

7. How can students help each other get rid of the "me first" attitude? *(remind each other to share, allow others to go first intentionally at times, take turns being first at leading the line)*

Activity

Directions: The characters on the worksheet are all "me first" people. Students are to write down what they think the characters might be saying.

Answer examples: 1. "Get off the swing. It's my turn."   2. "I'm using the markers."   3. "I'm thirsty. I'm getting a drink first."

Follow-up: Discuss how the characters who were being pushed around could handle the situations without ending up in a fight or running to the teacher. Can the "me first" people be put in their place? How? Ideas: 1: The boy could negotiate ("I'll get off in five minutes. I just got on!"). 2—The girl could ask for the markers that aren't being used and remind the pushy girl that the markers belong to everyone. 3—The boy could say something like, "If you and your 'me-first' attitude can't wait, go right ahead. I can wait."

Name _____ Date _____

5.8   Not Always "Me, First!"

These students all have "Me First!" attitudes. What do you think each is saying? Write their words in the balloon.

Copyright © 2009 by John Wiley & Sons, Inc.

5.9 Cheating

Objective

The student will distinguish between cheating and not cheating behavior.

Rationale

When students are expected to do their own work but take shortcuts by copying the work of others, finding answers at the back of the book, or otherwise depriving themselves of the effort involved to learn something, they are basically cheating themselves. And the one who lets someone cheat off him or her is depriving the other person of the opportunity to learn something. Students need to understand the difference between group work and independent work.

Thinking Questions

1. What does it mean to cheat? *(steal the answers, not do your own work, take a shortcut)*
2. What is an example of cheating on math? A spelling test or reading worksheet? Playing a game? *(ask for examples)*
3. Why is it considered wrong to cheat? *(you are not doing your own work and in a sense stealing from the other person)*
4. Is it wrong or still cheating if you don't look at someone's answers but you let someone look at your answers? *(yes—you are depriving someone of honest learning opportunities)*
5. Why do you think people cheat? *(they don't think they can do the work, not smart enough, lazy, too tired)*
6. Is there ever a good enough reason to cheat? *(no)*

Activity

Directions: Students are to read a list of activities and decide whether it shows an incidence of cheating.

Answers: 1. no; group work is okay.   2. yes; straying eyes.   3. yes; having someone else do your work. 4. no; copying the directions is okay, just not the answers.   5. yes; copying the answers is wrong.   6. yes; letting a friend copy is cheating too.

Follow-up: Discuss each example of cheating. Discuss who is being cheated out of an opportunity to learn in each example. Explain that it is always better to do your own work. Discuss how each child in the example who is cheating could find a better way to get the work done or solve the problem.

Copyright © 2009 by John Wiley & Sons. Inc.

5.9   # Cheating

Is it cheating? Write YES or NO on the line after each item. Discuss your answers.

1. The teacher said you can work together in a group to get the map colored and

    labeled. _____

2. The class put up their "shields" while taking a test, but Ronald could peek around it to see the
    answers from his neighbor. He didn't copy, but he just wanted to see if his neighbor had the same

    answers. _____

3. Martha was sick for two days and didn't get her spelling words written. She didn't want to stay in

    for recess, so she asked her friend Jenny to write them for her. _____

4. Taylor was in the speech room while the teacher gave the science assignment, so Taylor copied from

    a friend's notebook the number of the pages that needed to be done. _____

5. Billy wasn't sure how to do his math, so he looked at the answers in the back of the book and wrote

    them down. _____

6. Sam spent the night at his friend's house. They realized that they hadn't written out their home-
    work. Sam did the math homework and his friend did the reading homework. Then they exchanged

    answers so they were both finished. _____

5.10 Listening to Other People's Ideas

Objective

The student will listen to another person and document or state his or her ideas.

Rationale

Sometimes in groups, only the speaker is listening to himself or herself. Others are thinking about what they are going to say and are not really listening. This lesson is an exercise in listening to others.

Thinking Questions

1. When you're in a group, are you the only one with good ideas? *(no, others contribute too)*
2. What's the best way to find out the ideas of other people in your group? *(ask them, then listen)*
3. How can you tell if someone is listening to you? *(he or she looks interested, is quiet, can repeat what you said back to the group)*
4. Tell me what I just said. *(something about how to tell if someone is listening to you)*
5. Why is repeating what someone says a good way to see if you were listening? *(you'll use the same words or ideas)*
6. Can you repeat an idea without using the same exact words? How? *(yes, paraphrasing is a higher-level skill than simply repeating; just use slightly different words that mean about the same thing)*

Activity

Directions: Students are to divide into small groups (unless your class is already quite small) and discuss topics selected from the worksheet. After listening to the others' comments on the topic, students are to jot a few notes about the other members' comments or ideas about each topic.

Answers: The responses, which will vary, don't have to be lengthy, but they should say something about each member's ideas.

Follow-up: Check with the members of the group as to the accuracy of the notes written about their comments. Was it hard to remember what each person said? Was it difficult to listen when you knew you were responsible for remembering?

Learning and Working with Others

5.10   # Listening to Other People's Ideas

Get into a small group. Listen to each other and, on the lines below, summarize each other's ideas about the following topics.

1. My favorite sport to play

_____

_____

_____

2. A great place to take a vacation

_____

_____

_____

3. A movie I would recommend to my friends

_____

_____

_____

4. What to do at your next birthday party

_____

_____

_____

5. Animals that make good pets

_____

_____

_____

Copyright © 2009 by John Wiley & Sons, Inc.

5.11 Someone Made a Mistake

Objective

The student will identify a character who made a mistake in given situations and identify how that person would probably feel.

Rationale

Everyone makes mistakes. How that mistake is handled, by both the person and the others, is a measure of social maturity. In this lesson, students are to think about how it would feel to make a mistake and come up with a socially appropriate response for others in the group.

Thinking Questions

1. Has anyone here ever made a mistake or done something embarrassing? *(yes—listen for anecdotes)*

2. When you made a mistake, how did you feel? *(embarrassed, sad, frightened)*

3. Did anyone stick up for you or try to make you feel better? *(teacher, friends, perhaps a stranger)*

4. How would you like someone to help you the next time you get caught in a mistake or embarrassing situation? *(depends on the situation—say something nice, help pick up things, don't call attention to the mistake)*

5. Is there a difference between mistakes and accidents? *(can't help an accident; a mistake might be able to be corrected through learning)*

6. Could an accident be a mistake in judgment, like running your bike into a tree or spilling something? *(probably—learning how to ride better or to control your arms when you're at the table can prevent accidents)*

7. No matter if it's a mistake or an accident, how should you treat someone who made a mistake? *(don't laugh at the person, try to help him or her)*

Activity

Directions: Students are to examine four situations and circle the person in each who has made a mistake.

Answers: 1. the girl   2. the girl reading   3. the girl playing tennis   4. the girl with the paper

Follow-up: Discuss how the circled person probably feels in each situation. How did the others in each situation respond to the person? 1—mean comment; 2—laughing; 3—belittling the girl; 4—calling attention to the problem. What would be a better response from the others in each situation? 1—help her clean the table; 2—say nothing; 3—encourage her to keep trying; 4—tell Sarah or just move the paper.

5.11

Someone Made a Mistake

Circle the person in each picture who made a mistake.

Copyright © 2009 by John Wiley & Sons. Inc.

5.12 Taking Turns

Objective

The student will identify ways that children can take turns to complete tasks or work on activities together.

Rationale

Some students are bossy—they want to be first and tell everyone else what to do. Others are passive—they do not take a turn when they should. Others still are impulsive—they complete something halfway and then expect someone else to finish. It is not only polite for those who are involved in a group project or activity to take turns, but it is a good learning experience to take a turn—for those who try too hard and those who do not try hard enough.

Thinking Questions

1. Let's pretend you are in line for free ice cream. What is going through your mind? (*"I can't wait." "Hurry up!" "I wish the line would move faster." "I hope there is enough for me."*)

2. Why is it hard to wait for something that you want? (*it's exciting!*) Why is it important to wait your turn? (*otherwise it would be a mess, with everyone rushing at the same time*)

3. What if your teacher asks a question for the class, and you know the answer but she doesn't call on you, even though your hand is up? How do you feel? (*disappointed not to get called on*)

4. Why does the teacher take turns calling on people? (*so everyone will have a chance*) If she doesn't call on you, does that mean she doesn't like you? (*no*)

5. What are some other school activities that you have to take turns on? (*computer, puzzles, classroom group games, sharing circle, show and tell*)

Activity

Directions: The children on the worksheet are supposed to be taking turns on the activity shown. Circle the child who is not taking a turn nicely, and write on the line what the child is doing

   Answers: 1. second; bossy, taking over   2. first: impulsive, not waiting for turn   3. second: not stopping 4. first: not giving the slower child a chance

   Follow-up: Discuss why each child wasn't taking a turn appropriately. Explain that even if you are better, faster, or more efficient at a task, it still is the fair thing for others who need more time or adaptations to have a turn.

5.12   **Taking Turns**

Some of these children are not taking turns on their activities. Circle the ones who are not taking turns nicely and write on the line what the child is doing.

Copyright © 2009 by John Wiley & Sons. Inc.

Learning and Working with Others   **211**

Classroom Tips for Learning and Working with Others

- Allow students to experience being a follower in a student-led group. Again, do not step in too quickly to try to solve problems; rather, let the student leader act as a leader. Compliment students who are cooperative followers for their contributions to the group. At the end, display the group's project, and ask the leader to list by name everyone who contributed.

- Allow students to take turns in a leadership role. It could be leading a small cooperative group, being the line leader down the hall, or even passing out papers. If members of the group try to bypass the leader to come to you with questions, give the authority back to the student.

- If you have a student who has a particularly difficult time ignoring someone or something, set up a special signal (a wink, scratching your nose) between yourself and the student to show that you noticed that he or she did a fine job of ignoring something. Just the knowledge that you are with him or her may give added power to overcome the tendency to say something about the disturbance.

- If possible, find a competing behavior for a student to work on when you sense that he or she is in a mood to disturb others, particularly if you know what's coming. If the student is about to blow up, send him on an errand. If an argument is brewing between two students, divide and conquer—time for new groups! For the student who has to have the class's attention by clowning around at the wastebasket, give her two minutes before lunch to tell her jokes and get a few laughs. Try humor. Tell the graffiti artist that you think she'd do a great job making a mural for the hallway—with her name signed on the bottom. Disturbers want attention. Try to find a positive outlet.

- Plan a special day in which you share an inspirational story or movie about a disabled child or adult. There are sports figures, celebrities, and people in your town who have disabilities and deal with them to be successful in their lives.

- After working on a group task, have students separately list their own contributions to the task and share these lists with others in their group. Do they agree on the assessment? Students may find by evaluating each other that their contribution was perceived as very worthwhile, even though they themselves may feel that they didn't do much. Always credit every member of the group, no matter how small the contribution was.

- Have a "You First" day or afternoon in which students actively give up their "right" to do something first. You may want to try secretly selecting two students in your class who will do this; at the end of the afternoon, see if other students can identify the ones who were chosen. Wouldn't it be great if everyone was so polite to each other that you couldn't easily guess the plants?

- Have a "hear and tell" session in which students get their moment in the spotlight—two or three minutes in which to talk about something. After speaking, other students summarize what the student talked about. Compliment the good listeners.

- Students may like to write their own endings to a story about someone making a mistake. Start the story orally in class, perhaps choosing a problem common to your students (forgetting something, playing poorly on a team) and let students make their own endings. Share stories, and praise the "good forgivers."

- Divide students into partners, A and B, and give them a short task (perhaps write something on a board, read a short story, make a list of spelling words, arrange cards in alphabetical order). Person A begins the task. After fifteen seconds, person B takes over. Switch people every fifteen seconds until the task is completed. Was it difficult or easy to divide the task? What was important to complete the task properly?

Chapter 6

Making Friends

6.1 Being Interested in Others

Objective

The student will identify several techniques for showing interest in others.

Rationale

The best way to make friends is to show sincere interest in other people. People love to have other people notice them and want to know more about them. Someone could find out things about another person by asking questions, noticing what he or she is doing or wearing, paying attention to skills or talents of others, and making eye contact. This lesson examines these and other techniques.

Thinking Questions

1. Why do you think it is important to have friends? (*more fun to do things together, can help each other*)

2. How could you show someone else that you would like to become friends? (*act friendly, show interest in them, share things*)

3. One good way to start is by being interested in someone else. What are some ideas for showing that you are interested? (*ask questions, hang around them, look interested*)

4. Why would this be better than just going up to someone and start talking about yourself? (*the other person might not be interested in hearing about you or what you are doing; the point is to find out about them*)

5. What's the difference between being interested in someone and being nosey? (*the other person will let you know when you've gone too far, being nosey implies you don't really care about the other person*)

Activity

Directions: Students are to read the brief description of three characters and write or tell at least two ways to show that person that they are interested in getting to know him or her.

Answer examples: 1. offer to play football, ask about his family   2. ask if you could watch her ride sometime, compliment her on her clothes   3. ask if you could join in a game, hang around Alex when there is a group

Follow-up: Share ideas for showing interest in these characters. Which are good ideas? Which have potential problems?

6.1   **Being Interested in Others**

Here are some people who might be fun to get to know. What are at least two things you could do or say to let the person know you are interested in getting to know him or her?

Copyright © 2009 by John Wiley & Sons, Inc.

1. Ramon plays football on the school team. He is from Mexico. His family just moved here this year.

   _____

   _____

   _____

   _____

2. Kris has a horse and loves to ride. She likes to wear different-looking clothes.

   _____

   _____

   _____

   _____

3. Alex always has good ideas for making up games. He makes everyone laugh and is nice to everyone.

   _____

   _____

   _____

   _____

6.2 Sharing About Yourself

Objective

The student will list ten things about himself or herself that would be considered unique or interesting.

Rationale

People are attracted to interesting people. Spending a little time being introspective, digging to bring out some unusual characteristics, is a worthwhile activity. No two people are alike, and things that make us different also make us interesting. Help your students center on their characteristics that are unique and appealing.

Thinking Questions

1. How are you different from everyone else in this room or group? (*name, family, physical appearance, talents*)

2. What are some differences that you are proud of? (*sports achievements, scholastic accomplishments*)

3. If you only had one minute to tell someone else about yourself, what would you be sure to include? (*most important thing—will vary!*)

4. Do you think that other people would find the "different" things about you interesting? Why? (*probably—because we tend to like things that are unusual, we notice those things*)

5. What about being "the same"? Do you think that would make you interesting to others as well? (*yes—because some groups of friends revolve around common interests*)

6. So if you were thinking about interesting things about yourself, would you include things that are the same, different, or both? (*a good blend of them all*)

Activity

Directions: Students are to list ten things about themselves that others would probably find interesting. Clues on the worksheet include sports interests, skills, trips, pets, family items, and music.

Answers: Answers will vary.

Follow-up: Have students share their lists with each other. What items appeared on most papers? What do students think is interesting about each other? Who thought of something unique to list?

6.2   **Sharing About Yourself**

List ten things about yourself that others might find interesting!

Copyright © 2009 by John Wiley & Sons, Inc.

1. _____
2. _____
3. _____
4. _____
5. _____
6. _____
7. _____
8. _____
9. _____
10. _____

6.3 Joining Clubs and Activities

Objective

The student will identify at least five clubs or activities that are available for him or her to join.

Rationale

Attending a group event or club is a natural way to make friends and meet people who have similar interests. Most schools have clubs or sports for students. Students who join in may be likely to develop some friendships based on common interests.

Thinking Questions

1. What are some activities that you could join if you wanted to get involved in some after-school programs? *(basketball, scouting, dance class, YMCA activities)*
2. What activities are you already involved in? *(bowling league, church groups, riding lessons, art club, spell bowl, other athletic or academic clubs)*
3. What are some things that you could do in the community with other people? *(roller skating, park activities, swimming)*
4. Can you think of some activities that don't cost a lot of money but you can still do with your friends? *(the dollar movies, after-school art club, painting and decorating signs for events)*
5. Why is joining a club or group a good way to make friends? *(you will be with people who like the same things, you will be working together on something so you will have things to talk about, people will get to know you)*

Activity

Directions: Students are to list at least five clubs or activities that are available at school, after school, in the community, or loosely organized by other friends.

Answers: Answers will vary.

Follow-up: Have students share their responses. Talk about how someone could start a new group if there was some interest in developing something at the school or in the community. Many small communities have started skate parks, community playgrounds, and art classes simply because someone expressed a need and gathered volunteers.

Name _____ Date _____

6.3   **Joining Clubs and Activities**

Write down at least five clubs or activities that you might be interested in joining or already have some interest in.

At School

_____

_____

_____

_____

After School

_____

_____

_____

_____

In the Community

_____

_____

_____

_____

Loosely Organized with Friends

_____

_____

_____

_____

Copyright © 2009 by John Wiley & Sons, Inc.

6.4 Inviting Others into Your Group

Objective

The student will cite examples of polite ways to invite someone to join a group.

Rationale

Sometimes groups are formed by choice; other times, by random. If a student has an opportunity to invite someone else to become part of a group, this is a socially mature thing to do. New students may feel hesitant or shy to break into a group. It may be threatening to allow an outsider to merge with an already established circle of friends. However, by enlarging the group to include others, the students are given an opportunity to share and explore new relationships—a growing experience.

Thinking Questions

1. How would you feel if you had just started at a new school where you didn't know anyone? *(lost, afraid, shy)*

2. What would be a good way to help a new person learn his or her way around if this happened at our school? *(assign someone to help the person learn where things are, tell everyone to be especially nice to the person)*

3. What if you wanted to invite someone to sit with your group at lunch but the others in your group didn't want that? What could you do? *(talk to the person later, sit with the new person yourself, try to convince the group to make room for one more)*

4. What good things might happen if you invited someone new to join your group? *(might make a new friend, the person might be fun and interesting, you'd feel good about it)*

5. What if the new person in your group turned out to be bossy or nasty to everyone? *(he or she probably wouldn't be asked back)*

6. Why might it be embarrassing to invite someone who wasn't popular or who was different into your group? *(the others might laugh at you or the person, might kick you out of the group)*

7. What do you think you would do in that situation? *(decide if you wanted to stick with the group or if you liked the new person and wanted to be friends on your own)*

Activity

Directions: Students are to decide which of the comments on the worksheet are good ways to invite someone to join a group. They are to put a check mark next to the good responses.

Answers: 1, 2, 4, 6, 7

Follow-up: Discuss what was rude or insensitive about numbers 3, 5, and 8. (These comments make the person sound as though he or she is last choice, very undesirable as company, and difficult to be nice to.) Even if the comments express how the group truly feels, how could the person be included in a polite manner? (examples: number 3—"You're on our team, Jeff"; number 5—"Let's wait for Amy"; number 8—"There's room over here".)

6.4   # Inviting Others into Your Group

Which of these are good ways to invite another person to join your group? Put a check mark next to your answers.

_____ 1. "Would you like to go swimming with us?"

_____ 2. "There's room on this seat of the bus. You could sit here with us."

_____ 3. "Well, there's no one else left, so I guess you'll have to be on our team."

_____ 4. "Why don't you come with us to the playground?"

_____ 5. "If we walk very slowly, we'll lose her."

_____ 6. "There's an arts and crafts session at the library. Let's all go."

_____ 7. "We're all going out for ice cream. Why don't you come?"

_____ 8. "I guess you'll have to join us for lunch. I was told to try to be nice to you."

Copyright © 2009 by John Wiley & Sons. Inc.

Making Friends

6.5 Breaking Into a New Group

Objective

The student will identify appropriate ways to become part of a group.

Rationale

It is hard to be new! It is especially difficult to work your way into an existing group of people when it seems as though everyone else knows and likes each other and you are the outsider. The new person needs to decide whether to be outgoing or sit back for a little while to understand the group dynamics before attempting to make a place for himself or herself.

Thinking Questions

1. Let's say you decided to join a basketball team that meets after school, but the teams have already been picked. What could you do? (*ask the coach to put you on a team, watch for awhile until there is a spot for you*)

2. Why wouldn't it be a good idea to say, "Hey, I'm really good! You should put me in right now!"? (*it's bragging; other people might already have their spots on the team*)

3. What if you joined a scouting troop and everyone else already had badges and you didn't have anything? How could you fit in? (*ask someone to help you; start earning badges, and don't worry about how many you have*)

4. Let's say you wanted to join a model car–building club and already had built some model cars. What would be a good way to let others know that you have some skills? (*ask if you could bring some cars in to show everyone; offer to share your paint*)

5. What if you wanted to join a gymnastics group but you had never done gymnastics before? (*try to find a group that is at your ability level; don't be afraid to ask for help; keep practicing so you will get better*)

Activity

Directions: Students are to read the descriptions of four children who are trying to break into a new group and select/circle the ones who are choosing good methods. Be prepared to discuss how each child is making an attempt to join the group.

Answers: 1. no—being very bossy   2. yes—waiting for an opportunity   3. yes—offering to share skills   4. no—not doing anything to join the group

Follow-up: Discuss what the children in numbers 2 and 3 are doing that makes it likely they will be accepted by the group. Discuss why the child in number 4 is not being obnoxious but also is not doing anything to get into the group. Make a class list of possible group activities and ways that a newcomer could successfully join that group.

6.5   Breaking Into a New Group

Which of these children are doing a good job of trying to break into a new group? Circle the ones who will probably be accepted.

1. Sharon wants to play soccer with the other girls at recess.

Copyright © 2009 by John Wiley & Sons. Inc.

6.5   Breaking Into a New Group (continued)

2.   Juan would like to work on a mural that the children are painting.

3.   Lizzie would like to roller skate with the other girls at the roller rink.

Making Friends

Copyright © 2009 by John Wiley & Sons. Inc.

4. Alex is watching the boys in his class play basketball, but he is too shy to ask if he can join them.

Copyright © 2009 by John Wiley & Sons. Inc.

6.6 Listening

Objective

The student will identify comments made by a character who appears to be listening to another character.

Rationale

Listening is an excellent way to make friends because most people like to be listened to. A way to show that you are listening is by making a comment that relates to what the person is talking about. In this lesson, the student is to listen (or read) and pick the character who is responding appropriately because he or she was listening to the person speaking.

Thinking Questions

1. Do you think more people like to talk or to listen? *(opinions may vary—possibly more will think there are more talkers than listeners because they themselves like to talk)*

2. Why would listening to someone talk be a good way to make friends with the person? *(you'd find out something about the person, his or her concerns, show that you are interested in this person)*

3. Why is it hard to listen? *(we want to do the talking, we feel that we have something more important to say)*

4. How could you show that you are listening to someone who is talking? *(look at them, be quiet)*

5. What could you say to someone after he or she is done talking that would show you were listening? *(ask a question about what he or she was talking about, ask for more details about the situation)*

6. Do you think you should pretend to be interested in someone and what he or she is saying even if you really aren't? *(perhaps by pretending at first, you might really get interested later, which may still be a polite way to make a friend; realize that not everything you say or do is interesting to everyone else)*

Activity

Directions: Students are to match the two participants in a conversation—the listener on the left with the one who is listening (and then commenting appropriately) on the right.

Answers: 1. b   2. d   3. e   4. a   5. c

Follow-up: How did the listeners show that they were listening? How were their comments polite and appropriate? Which ones asked for more information? How did each make the talker feel?

6.6   **Listening**

Match each student on the left who is talking to the student on the right who is listening.

Copyright © 2009 by John Wiley & Sons, Inc.

6.7 What Is Encouragement?

Objective

The student will identify a character giving an encouraging statement to another.

Rationale

Many students do not know how to encourage others. The idea of "me first" or being out for yourself often takes precedence over giving another person a little boost of confidence or stepping aside to let someone else have the spotlight. This lesson discusses what encouragement is and how to recognize an encouraging statement.

Thinking Questions

1. What does it mean to be "discouraged"? (*feel lost, hopeless, like you try but just can't get anywhere*)
2. When have you felt discouraged? (*ask for anecdotes about poor test performance or losing at a game*)
3. Did someone say anything nice to you when you felt discouraged that really cheered you up? What was it? (*perhaps a parent gave some support, a friend may have said "nice try" or something like that*)
4. What does "encouragement" mean? (*the opposite of discouragement—when you say something that makes the other person feel that there is hope*)
5. When you say something to give another person hope, how would the other person probably feel? (*perhaps a little better*)
6. How would that person feel about you, the encourager? (*would look at you as a friend*)
7. Even if what you said didn't make a difference or change anything, how would it still help the discouraged person? (*let him or her know you care*)

Activity

Directions: The student is to circle the student in the pair on the right who is giving encouragement to the discouraged student on the left.

> *Answers:* 1. second student   2. first student   3. first student   4. first student   5. second student

Follow-up: Discuss the specific comments of the encourager in each example. How did the comment give the discouraged person hope? How realistic (or valued) was the "hope" given? Does it really help to be encouraging, or is an encouraging word just a nice thing to say?

6.7   # What Is Encouragement?

Circle the student in each pair on the right who is saying something encouraging to the student on the left.

Copyright © 2009 by John Wiley & Sons. Inc.

6.8 Saying Nice Things

Objective

The student will state an example of a polite comment that could be made in given situations.

Rationale

Another good technique for letting someone know that you would like to be friends is simply that of making a nice comment. If students could accept the fact that a compliment, given in sincerity, is a perfectly fine way to approach someone else, perhaps they would try it more often. People like to hear nice things about themselves. Given the opportunity, we should do this consciously more often.

Thinking Questions

1. What is a compliment? (*something someone says that is nice, a comment that praises something you've done*)

2. When someone gives you a compliment, how does that make you feel? (*pretty good*)

3. Are there situations you can think of in which you could say something nice to someone else to make them feel better? (*ask for anecdotes*)

4. Would saying nice things about someone or to someone be a good way to make friends? (*yes*) Why? (*lets the other person know that you are friendly, positive, and interested in him or her*)

5. Why is it hard to say something nice about someone, especially after that person has said something rude or negative? (*then that person might think you're trying to be less of a friend to him or her, shows that you disagree*)

6. What would other people start to think about you if you said nice things about other people all the time? (*they'd respect you; maybe they would stop saying mean things about others because they know you would disagree with them*)

Activity

Directions: Given four situations, the student is to fill in the speech balloon to show what an appropriate nice comment might be.

Answer examples:

1. It's a very pretty color.
2. No, that might really hurt him. Leave Robert alone.
3. That kid is really good at softball.
4. Yes, I sure would—let me see your book.

Follow-up: Go through each situation, and try to view it through the eyes of the potential friend in each situation. How would the girl with the unusual dress respond? What about Robert? He seems to be unpopular. Even if you didn't want to be friends with him, how would saying something nice make you a better friend to the speaker? In number 3, the girl is talking right in front of the new boy. How would both children respond to a friendly comment? Discuss how your kind comments might be received by others who would overhear you.

6.8   # Saying Nice Things

What is a nice thing that you could say in each situation below? Write your answer in the balloon.

Copyright © 2009 by John Wiley & Sons. Inc.

6.9 Good Group Activities

Objective

The student will identify several group activities that would involve positive people and experiences in the school or community.

Rationale

Being a part of a group is a good way to meet others who have similar interests. It gives children something to talk about and provides them with something to do together. But not every group activity is one that will encourage friendship. Students should be on the lookout for activities that are going to result in good friendships.

Thinking Questions

1. We have already talked about clubs and activities that are available for kids to join. What are some? (*scouting, art club, after-school activities*)

2. Sometimes there are groups of people who do things just to be together rather than planned meetings all the time. Can you think of anything like that? (*going to a birthday party, roller skating, going to the movies with friends, horseback riding*)

3. When you go out with a group of friends, what are some things that you might need to be careful about? (*make sure they are not going to get you in trouble, come home on time, don't do something that will hurt someone else*)

4. It is important to make good choices for activities that you have been invited to. What are some consequences for getting involved with the wrong group of kids or finding out that you made a bad choice? (*get in trouble at home, become identified with a bad group*)

5. If you were going to plan a good activity for a bunch of your friends, what is something that you might do? (*go to the movies, play soccer, act out a play*)

Activity

Directions: Students should examine the six situations on the worksheet to determine which of the group activities would most likely be positive, good experiences. Students should be prepared to discuss their answers.

Answers: 1. yes; a birthday party is fun and involves everyone   2. yes; performing a play can be fun   3. no; smoking will get someone in trouble and is harmful to your health   4. no; writing notes about someone can be unkind   5. yes; a water park is great fun   6. no; parents are not at home

Follow-up: Discuss the answers to the worksheet. Discuss why even though an activity might sound like fun (numbers 3, 4, and 6), it has an element of risk that could end up being a bad choice. Have students come up with an alternative group behavior that the kids could do instead.

Making Friends

6.9   **Good Group Activities**

All of these children have been invited to participate in an activity with a group of other children. Circle the ones you think would be the best choices.

1. Attending a Birthday Party

2. Performing a Play

3. Smoking

Copyright © 2009 by John Wiley & Sons, Inc.

Making Friends   **235**

6.9 Good Group Activities (continued)

4. Writing Notes

5. Going to a Water Park

6. Having a Sleepover

Copyright © 2009 by John Wiley & Sons, Inc.

6.10 Having Someone Visit Your House

Objective

The student will identify ways to show friendship when a guest is visiting.

Rationale

It sounds fun to have someone come over to your house, but playing nicely is sometimes a challenge. Older siblings, younger siblings, unexpected other friends, broken toys, the weather—all can influence how the experience turns out. Having clear expectations for guests and showing good manners are just two of the ways to promote friendship, especially in your home.

Thinking Questions

1. When you have a friend come over, what are some things that you like to do? *(crafts, play football, build models)*

2. Have you ever had a friend over and then something goes wrong and you end up fighting? Tell about it. *(answers will vary)*

3. Do your parents have rules for you about when a friend visits? *(no fighting, no fits when it's time for the friend to go home, put everything away before the friend leaves)*

4. Has this ever happened to you: you wanted to play with a friend but you have an unexpected guest—a cousin from out of town whom you don't know very well but you have to do something with? What did you do? *(answers will vary)*

5. When you are a guest in someone else's house, what are some things that you should remember? *(thank the parents, be respectful of their furniture)*

Activity

Directions: Students are given a list of possible fun spoilers when a friend is visiting. Have them choose three, and illustrate a way that this situation could be turned into a good experience. (Students should draw on a separate piece of paper. Students who do not like to draw can be given the option to write a response.)

Answers: Answers will vary.

Follow-up: Have students share their answers and their drawings. You may want to have students form small groups and role-play each situation, first showing a likely unhappy response and then showing a possible positive outcome.

6.10   **Having Someone Visit Your House**

Here are some situations that might occur when you have a friend over to your house. Pick three, and draw a picture to show what you could do to make the situation better.

1. Surprise! You have to baby-sit your two-year-old brother while your mom goes to the dentist!

2. Your friend comes over after school but gets sick after eating ten bologna sandwiches.

3. You and your friend want to watch different shows on TV at the same time.

4. Your friend makes a huge mess of your room, but when it's time to go home, he doesn't offer to pick anything up.

5. While your friend is over, you get a phone call from another friend and want to talk to her, so you ignore your first friend.

6. You want to go outside and play basketball, but your friend wants to stay inside and play video games.

7. Your friend tells you that your room would look better if it was painted bright red, so he suggests getting some paint and redecorating.

8. Your friend comes over, but she invites several of her other friends to come over too, and now you are left out.

Copyright © 2009 by John Wiley & Sons, Inc.

     Making Friends

Classroom Tips for Making Friends

- Select one student at a time, and have other students come up with a list of five to ten questions that they could ask to find out more about the student. If the selected student is not too shy, have him or her sit in the center of a friendly circle and answer questions.

- Have students get into partner groupings and find out as many interesting things about each other as they can in two minutes. Share the findings with the rest of the class.

- Have each student make a poster or coat of arms displaying things about themselves that not everyone else might know. Using the list that was made in activity 6.2 for starters, students could set up a shoebox display of pictures, mementos from the past, and artwork that shows what they are like.

- Have students make a class list of favorite places to go and hang out with friends. Students can write or make advertisements telling why or how this is a good place to get together with friends.

- Organized social groups (church youth groups, scouting, swim teams) are good places to make friends based on common interests. Are newcomers welcome to the groups? Have students who are already members of such groups tell about their experiences. Why is it fun? Does it take more than an invitation to participate?

- Create a "Yellow Pages" type ad for use in the classroom with students drawing their own advertisements featuring help or assistance that they could give to others and are willing to share with others—for example, "See Latisha for Computer Help!" or "See Mark for a Portrait of Yourself." Students should realize that their services must be available to everyone and anyone in the class, not just a select few.

- Students can role-play examples of listening and not listening by writing and performing short skits. After each performance, have the participants explain what they were trying to show as examples of how you could tell if someone was really listening.

- When students work together in small, cooperative groups, they tend to be more supportive and encouraging with each other. Assign tasks that can be worked on, turned in, and evaluated together. Watch for kids who are encouraging each other, and make class comments such as, "I would like to be in THIS group. Boy, do they support each other and help each other out!"

- Pass out stickers in the classroom to students you hear saying something nice about someone else. Don't comment about why you are giving a sticker; let the kids watch and catch on.

- Have students look through a local newspaper to find as many group activities as they can for a given week: library readings, community parties, volunteer training, and so on. See how long a list your class can come up with.

Chapter 7

Keeping Friends

7.1 Learning from Your Friend

Objective

The student will identify examples of things that can be taught from a friend.

Rationale

Part of friendship is learning new skills or learning about ideas from others. (Think about all the things that are taught and learned incidentally by older and younger siblings.) By spending time with someone and observing what he or she does, a person can learn a lot. This is an informal education that can be quite helpful in making and keeping friends.

Thinking Questions

1. If you wanted to learn how to throw a football, who would you ask? (*brother or sister, parent, coach*)

2. Who is good at swimming? Dancing? Horseback riding? Gymnastics? How did you learn these skills? (*probably someone taught them*)

3. What are some things that friends of yours could teach you? What are they good at? (*sports, drawings, games*)

4. Can a friend teach you other things besides skills or games? What else could a friend help you with? (*homework, how to get along with siblings*)

5. Can a friend teach you anything about how to handle a problem that you may be having? How? (*the friend might have had a similar problem*)

6. Do you think that part of friendship is learning from your friend? How? (*your friend might know things that you don't, and if you can do it together, then you have something else that is fun to do together*)

Activity

Directions: Match the friend with what he or she can teach someone. Be prepared to discuss how the friend is being helpful.

Answers: 1. c: teach how to fish   2. d: explain how to do a math problem   3. a: give advice on how to handle a problem with a teacher   4. b: demonstrate how to do a group cheer

Follow-up: Discuss how each friend on the worksheet taught, demonstrated, or was a role model to someone else. Discuss how learning from a friend is different from learning from a teacher, parent, or other adult. Is it easier? In some ways is it harder? Everyone has something to learn and something to teach. What are some specific examples that students can think of in their own lives?

7.1 # Learning from Your Friend

Each of these friends has something to teach. Match the friend to what he or she is teaching.

1.

a. getting along with a teacher

b. being part of a group performance

c. the best way to do a skill

d. explaining a good way to help solve a math problem

2.

3.

4.

Copyright © 2009 by John Wiley & Sons, Inc.

7.2 Being a Fair Friend

Objective

The student will state that being a "fair friend" means sharing the friend with others and not putting restrictions on the other person.

Rationale

Some students view a friend as their own personal property. Therefore, that person cannot talk to anyone else, play with anyone else, and must always be available for whatever reason the student wishes—to help with work, to be there to play. Being fair with others means allowing the other person freedom to live his or her own life, understanding that friendship does not come with unrealistic ties.

Thinking Questions

1. How would you feel if you were allowed to have only one friend? *(restricted, hard to pick only one)*

2. What if you were not allowed to play with anyone else, talk to anyone else, and you always had to help this person out whenever he or she wanted you to? Would this be fun? *(not really—it would be very limiting)*

3. What are some ways people might finish this sentence: "You can be my friend if . . ."? *(you give me that toy, you let me come over, you help me with something)*

4. Why do you think it is important to have lots of friends? *(one might move away, get to know more people, some things are more fun in groups)*

5. What do you think being a "fair friend" means? *(letting your friend do things on his or her own, having other friends, not saying "if" to them)*

6. Can you give some examples of not being fair with others? *(telling them who they can or cannot hang around with, changing friendships quickly, not really being sincerely interested in the other person)*

Activity

Directions: The student is to match the student who is being "unfair" with the reason on the right.

Answers: 1. d 2. c 3. e 4. b 5. a

Follow-up: Discuss how each student who was taken advantage of by the unfair friend could have responded politely, but with fairness in mind. How could each situation be remedied with both sides working together or still having fun?

7.2   Being a Fair Friend

None of these students is being a fair friend. Match the students with the reason why they aren't being fair.

1.

     You can't play with Sarah. You can play with Beth, though.

_____

    a. It's not fair to always expect some-one to do things your way or at your house.

2.

     You can be my friend if you let me have that ball.

_____

    b. It's not fair to make your friend do your work or it's his fault.

    c. It's not fair to make your friend give you things or you won't be friends anymore.

3.

     I have to clean out the garage. You better help me.

_____

    d. It's not fair to tell a friend whom he or she can or can't play with.

4.

     Don't leave me! You are the only one who can help me with this paper! You have to help me or I'll get a bad grade!

    e. It's not fair to make your friend do chores that you don't like just because he's your friend.

_____

5.

     Why do I always have to go over to your house? Why don't you ever come over to my house to play?

_____

Copyright © 2009 by John Wiley & Sons, Inc.

7.3 Sharing Friends

Objective

The student will identify ways that a friend can be shared with another person or situation.

Rationale

When someone has a best friend, it is often hard to see that friend having a good time with someone else. However, friends are not property, and it is reasonable to expect a friend to have other friends or to participate in an activity with others. A good friend won't make a big deal of this, but will accept the fact that at some point, he or she will do something with someone else.

Thinking Questions

1. How many of you have a best friend? *(show of hands)*

2. Why is it fun to have a best friend? *(someone you can count on, someone you especially enjoy being with, someone who lives close to you)*

3. Have you ever had a really good friend get invited to something that you were not invited to? How did you feel? *(probably left out, jealous)*

4. Is it really fair to expect a best friend to be your only friend? *(no, situations change and there are lots of other people around who might be fun to get to know)*

5. Why do you think it is hard to share your friend with other people? *(might worry that the friend will like someone better than you, that you'll be forgotten)*

6. How could making a big deal about your friend going off with other people hurt your relationship? *(your friend might be mad at you for being upset about it, you might miss out on something if other people want to invite you to something too)*

7. If your friend does get to do something that you can't do or aren't invited to do, how could you handle it? *(be a good sport, tell your friend you hope he or she has a good time, find something else to do)*

Activity

Directions: Students are to view each situation on the worksheet from the perspective of the character with a star beside him or her. They are to write or draw a response that shows how the starred student could share the friend with others.

Answer examples: 1. Show all three girls riding bikes. 2. "You could help me another time. Have fun at the party." 3. The boy who wasn't picked could say, "I'll wait for you after class, Andy." 4. The girl on the left could say, "Can I watch you, Sandy? I'd like to learn to dive, too."

Follow-up: It's hard to be the person who is left out, but learning to be gracious and accepting is a real step toward social maturity. Discuss how each person who was starred might feel left out or rejected at first; then discuss the positive ways that he or she could respond to the situation.

7·3   **Sharing Friends**

How could the starred student ☆ share his or her friend with others? Write your answer, or draw a picture to show a way.

Copyright © 2009 by John Wiley & Sons, Inc.

1.

2.

3.

4.

7.4 Laughing Together

Objective

The student will identify ways that friends can share a laugh together.

Rationale

There is nothing like laughing together to bring friends closer. Whether friends are sharing a funny anecdote, watching a comedy movie, or laughing at each other, this is a powerful way to share a strong emotion that helps cement a friendship.

Thinking Questions

1. Think about one of your best friends. Is this person someone who makes you laugh? Why? *(has a good sense of humor, knows what makes you laugh)*
2. Do you and your friend have embarrassing moments or silly stories that you laugh at? What are some of them? *(answers will vary)*
3. What's the difference between laughing with someone and laughing at this person? *(one includes both people, the other is mean)*
4. What are some things that make you laugh? *(when someone does something funny, when you make a mistake, when you just feel happy)*
5. Why do you think laughing with someone helps you enjoy being with that person? *(they are easy to be with, it's fun, it takes your mind off problems)*
6. What are some of your favorite things to do with a friend that involve laughing? *(going to the movies, putting on a play, playing a joke on your dad)*

Activity

Directions: Here is a list of possible activities that would involve laughing. Put a check mark in front of the ones that you think would be good ways to share a laugh with a friend. Be prepared to discuss your answers.

Answers: 1. yes   2. no–laughing at someone else like this is mean   3. no—only one person (the one who made the mistake) is laughing here   4. yes   5. no—involves danger   6. yes   7. yes   8. no—overdoing the joke; should have stopped earlier

Follow-up: Discuss the responses. Have the class plan some activities that involve laughing and sharing funny experiences with each other. Laughter is good for the soul!

7.4 <h1>Laughing Together</h1>

Here are some ways that you and a friend might laugh together. Put a check mark in front of the ones that you think are good ways to share a laugh.

Copyright © 2009 by John Wiley & Sons, Inc.

❏ 1. Watching an old movie that shows people falling down and losing their pants

❏ 2. Seeing a classmate trip over a book on the floor and fall down

❏ 3. Laughing at your friend when he makes a silly mistake on his math paper

❏ 4. Pretending that you are from another planet and talking with a funny voice

❏ 5. Blindfolding each other and walking across a street

❏ 6. Face painting each other at the school fun fair

❏ 7. Running in a three-legged race (where one leg from each person is tied together)

❏ 8. Telling everyone you see that day that your friend has green hair because he didn't know he had paint on his hand and touched his head

7.5 Keeping Your Promises

Objective

The student will identify realistic promises that a friend could make and keep to another friend.

Rationale

Some students make elaborate, unrealistic promises to others as an attempt to keep someone as a friend. While this may seem appealing to the person who is wanted as a friend, it is likely to result in disappointment and arguments once the promise is broken. Friends do promise each other things, and it is important to keep those promises. It is also important not to try to win a friend with enormous promises that can't be kept.

Thinking Questions

1. What kinds of promises do friends make to each other? *(not to tell secrets, to help each other out, to share things)*

2. What if you wanted someone to like you so you promised to give this person an expensive present to be your friend? Is that a good way to make friends? *(probably not—what if you didn't come through?)*

3. How could you tell if the friend really liked you or just liked what you could do for or give him or her? *(a real friend would like you without all those things)*

4. How would it make you feel if your friend promised you something and then forgot about it or changed his or her mind? *(angry at the friend, sad, betrayed)*

5. Why is it important to keep your promises? *(someone is counting on you, you should keep your word)*

6. If it is important to keep promises, why should you be careful what kinds of promises you make? *(make sure you can keep them, make sure you're not just trying to impress someone)*

Activity

Directions: Students are to look over the list of promises and put a check mark by the ones that someone could probably keep.

Answers: check marks by 2, 5, 7, 9

Follow-up: Discuss why the promises that were not checked are unrealistic or not safe promises. Can you make a promise for someone else? *(3, 8, 10)* Why are absolutes risky promises? (**always** and **never** *promises*)

7·5   **Keeping Your Promises**

Copyright © 2009 by John Wiley & Sons. Inc.

Which of these are promises that you think someone could keep? Put a check mark by the promises that are good. Add your own promises to keep.

1. ❑ "I'll never eat lunch with anyone but you. Ever."

2. ❑ "I'll ask my dad if you can go with us to the beach."

3. ❑ "I'll have my big brother beat up Ricky for you."

4. ❑ "I will always wait for you after school so we can walk home together."

5. ❑ "I'll save a seat for you on the bus if I get there first."

6. ❑ "Let's steal some candy from the store. I won't tell anyone if you get caught."

7. ❑ "You're sick, so I'll return your library book for you."

8. ❑ "If you'll be my friend, I'll have my father buy that remote control car for you. It's only $150!"

9. ❑ "I won't tell Debbie that you got a bad grade on your test."

10. ❑ "I'll make our teacher give you an A on that poster."

11. _____

12. _____

13. _____

14. _____

7.6 Sometimes Friends Disagree

Objective

The student will identify reasons that friends might disagree and suggest possible ways to resolve differences.

Rationale

Friends have arguments. Sometimes they might argue over small things such as what color to paint a model car. Other times the arguments might turn personal or even escalate into something that will end a friendship (betrayal, too many put-downs). But in the course of a normal friendship, people will have occasional periods of disagreeing. This does not mean the friendship has to end, but it might require some readjusting or forgiving to go on. It's all part of life.

Thinking Questions

1. True or false: If you have a friend, you will *never* have a fight or argument. (*false: everyone has times when they disagree*)

2. What are some things that you and a friend might squabble over? (*where to go, what to do, whose turn it is for something*)

3. When you fight with a friend, how does it make you feel? (*angry, sad, want to cry*)

4. What are some ways that you and a friend have made up after an argument? (*talk about it, don't argue about it, spend some time away from each other then get back together*)

5. What are some things you could do when you and your friend don't agree on something? (*talk about it, ask another person, take turns doing things*)

Activity

Directions: Here are some conversations between friends who are having a disagreement. Write how they might handle their problem.

Answers: Answers will vary.

Follow-up: Discuss ways that are healthy to handle a disagreement (*talking about it, trying to be fair, getting advice*) and ways that are unhealthy (*getting angry, hitting, calling names*). Make a class chart with two sides, and have students illustrate incidents that show healthy and unhealthy ways to handle disagreements. Talk about "two sides to every story" and what that means. No one is right all the time.

7.6   Sometimes Friends Disagree

Here are some conversations between friends who are having a disagreement. Write how they might handle their problem.

Situation 1

Juan: I don't want to see another dog movie. We saw what you wanted to see last time. We always see what YOU want to see.

Michelle: There aren't any other movies that we can both see. Besides, you wanted to see that last movie too. We both liked it, so why does that count as MY turn?

_____

_____

_____

_____

_____

Copyright © 2009 by John Wiley & Sons. Inc.

Situation 2

Andrea: I don't want to go to Mary's party. I don't like Mary. Let's not go.

Leah: Mary is my next-door neighbor. Our families are friends. I think I should go to her party.

_____

_____

_____

_____

7.6 Sometimes Friends Disagree (continued)

Situation 3

Manish: Hey, I let you borrow my bike and now it's all dirty and has a dent in it. I think you should fix it!

Theo: Well, when you borrowed MY bike you didn't clean it up, and besides, the dent was in your bike before I borrowed it!

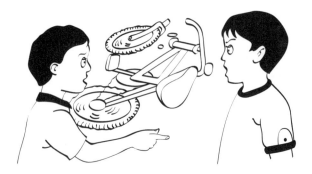

Situation 4

Yolanda: Let's go to the water park!

Ian: Let's go bowling!

Keeping Friends

Copyright © 2009 by John Wiley & Sons, Inc.

7.7 Sticking Up for Your Friend

Objective

The student will identify ways to show support for a friend in various situations.

Rationale

Friends stick up for each other, especially when the friend cannot defend himself or herself in a situation. Friends should not be friends only when it is easy. However, sticking up for a friend does not mean fighting. This lesson examines ways to show support for a friend.

Thinking Questions

1. What would you do if you heard people bad-mouthing your best friend? *(ignore, tell them to stop, threaten them)*

2. Why would it bother you if someone was saying bad things about a friend of yours? *(you like your friend and don't want him or her misrepresented, you don't want other people challenging your taste in friends)*

3. How could you stick up for your friend without getting into a big argument or fight? *(state what your opinion is and then walk away)*

4. What if your friend is in a situation where people are picking on him or her and your friend is too shy or scared to do anything about it? What could you do without fighting? *(tell an adult you trust, a teacher, a counselor; talk to the offenders; help your friend think of things to do)*

5. What if it didn't bother your friend one bit that other people were talking about him or her? Should you do something then? *(if the friend doesn't care, you might talk to the friend to make sure he or she really isn't bothered; otherwise it might be better to just leave the situation alone— let the offenders get tired and just quit)*

Activity

Directions: Students are to consider several situations involving a friend in trouble, and write down their answers as to what they would do in each situation.

Answer examples:

1. Say that you are watching them and tell the teacher if they take your friend's things.
2. Stay with Rob.
3. Tell Nina to be careful when she walks past the desk; she might hurt her arm by knocking your friend too much.
4. Tell Antonio that you will wait for him after school and help him get caught up.

Follow-up: Discuss students' responses. How many went straight to fighting and violence as their way of sticking up for the friend? Discuss the idea of sticking up for a friend by being a friend rather than having a confrontation with the other people.

7·7   **Sticking Up for Your Friend**

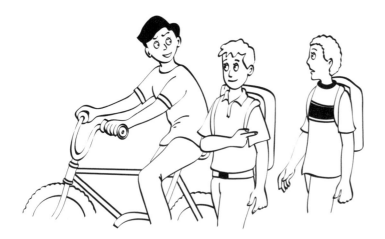 

Copyright © 2009 by John Wiley & Sons, Inc.

What would you do in each situation below? Write your answer on the lines.

1. Your friend is sick at home one day. Two kids want to go through your friend's desk and look for pencils and money. They ask you not to say anything to anybody.

   _____

   _____

2. You and your friend Rob are walking home from school together. Another friend, Gary, rides past you on his bike and asks if you want to ride to the lake with him. You want to, but, Rob and Gary don't like each other. You ask if Rob can go too, but Gary says no.

   _____

   _____

3. Nina keeps knocking into your friend whenever she passes by her desk. You know that Nina is doing it just to be mean. Your friend is too shy to tell the teacher or say anything to Nina.

   _____

   _____

4. Antonio had to stay in from recess for not doing his homework. Two girls go by the classroom and make fun of him. They are calling him names and saying that he is stupid. You know that Antonio was sick last night and that's why he didn't do his homework.

   _____

   _____

7.8 Helping Someone with a Problem

Objective

The student will identify possible strategies for helping a friend with a specified problem.

Rationale

Friends share their problems with other friends, and at times students may find themselves in a position to help out a friend with opinions or advice. This lesson involves the student in evaluating ideas for helping a friend with a problem.

Thinking Questions

1. Have you ever had a friend come to you with a problem? If so, what did you do? *(listen, give advice)*

2. Does your friend expect you to solve the problem or just give your ideas? *(probably just give ideas and helpful comments)*

3. When you want to help a friend solve his or her problems, do you think there is more than one possible way to work things out? Why? *(probably; there are usually several alternatives available)*

4. How did it make you feel to be able to help out a friend? *(good, powerful, happy)*

5. If you can't actually do something to help a friend with a problem, what are some other ways you could help? *(listen, tell your friend to talk to an adult, be there for your friend instead of leaving him or her alone)*

Activity

Directions: The student is to evaluate several different ideas for solving a friend's problem. There may be more than one possible good answer. The student is to write YES or NO indicating his or her thoughts about the answers.

Answers: 1. *yes:* second and fourth answers   2. *yes:* first and fourth answers   3. *yes:* third and fourth answers

Follow-up: Discuss why certain answers were discarded and why others were more reasonable alternatives. Come up with a generalized list of helping responses, such as *listening, being sympathetic,* and *offering to help practice a skill.*

7.8   # Helping Someone with a Problem

Your friend comes to you with a problem. What could you say? Write YES or NO on the line to show good answers.

1.

"You could move into my house. I have a nice sister." _____

"Can you talk to your parents about her?" _____

"Let's go through her stuff and hide everything." _____

"I'll help you talk to your sister and explain how you feel." _____

2.

"Why don't you practice with me after school?" _____

"Football is stupid. Just give it up." _____

"Move to another school district. Maybe you could make the team there." _____

"I'll help you work on passing the ball." _____

Copyright © 2009 by John Wiley & Sons, Inc.

7.8 Helping Someone with a Problem (continued)

3.

"I'll take some out of my mother's purse." _____

"Don't say anything about the window. They won't catch you." _____

"I could lend you some, but I have to put some in the bank." _____

"You better tell your parents. I'll go with you." _____

Copyright © 2009 by John Wiley & Sons, Inc.

7.9 Telling Someone If a Friend Needs Help

Objective

The student will identify an appropriate source if a friend indicates he or she is in need of serious help.

Rationale

If the situation is such that friends listening and being sympathetic is enough, that's great. Some situations may arise, however, that call for involvement of someone else who can do more to help with the problem. In this lesson, the student is asked to suggest others who can help.

Thinking Questions

1. If your friend broke his pencil, would you be able to help him? *(yes)* How? *(lend him one, buy one for him)*

2. If your friend broke his ankle, could you take care of the problem? Why or why not? *(probably not—that's a serious medical problem, but the student could call for help, stay with the friend while waiting for someone else to help)*

3. Why is it harder to handle the second incident than the first? *(much more serious to have a broken ankle than a broken pencil)*

4. When you know your friend has a problem that is more than you can handle, who are some people who could help? *(parent, teacher, doctor, counselor)*

5. If your friend is not willing or able to get help alone, what could you do to convince your friend to let you get help or how could you actually go for help? *(explain to your friend that the problem requires more expert help, promise to keep it confidential if that is a problem, talk to your own parents if that is appropriate)*

Activity

Directions: The student is to identify an appropriate source of help for each of the situations that his or her friend is experiencing on the worksheet.

Answer examples: 1. school counselor, teacher   2. older friend or sibling   3. teacher, principal   4. school counselor, principal, teacher   5. nurse, doctor, parent   6. bus driver

Follow-up: Go through each of the situations, and evaluate them in terms of the seriousness of each. Which involve emotional problems? Which are physical problems? Why are these problems more serious than those on worksheet 7.8?

7·9   # Telling Someone If a Friend Needs Help

Who is someone you could go to if your friend needed help?

Copyright © 2009 by John Wiley & Sons, Inc.

1. *I feel so sad. I hate school. I don't like my family. I just don't want to live anymore.*

2. *Allen wants me to try some drugs. I don't really want to, but I'm afraid he'll make fun of me if I don't.*

3.  *The other kids are making fun of me because I'm in a wheelchair. I don't even want to go to school anymore.*

4. *Someone at home is hitting me. I'm afraid. I don't know what to do.*

6. *Those big kids said they were going to punch me out after school in the back of the bus. I'm afraid.*

5.  *Oh no—I think I broke my arm! It really hurts!*

1. _____

2. _____

3. _____

4. _____

5. _____

6. _____

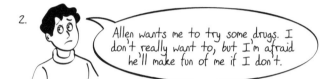

7.10 Friendships Change

Objective

The student will identify reasons that a friendship can lapse or change.

Rationale

There are some lifelong friendships, but the reality is that most friendships change over time. When people move away, develop different interests, or grow apart for many reasons, the friendship itself changes. This is not necessarily a bad thing, but it can cause some sadness, especially for children.

Thinking Questions

1. Who is the friend you have had the longest? *(answers will vary)*

2. Why do you think you have been friends for so long? *(live close to each other, love horses, like each other's families)*

3. Think about someone who used to be a friend of yours, but now you don't really do much with that person. What do you think happened? *(found new friends, didn't see each other very much)*

4. What are some ways that people stay in touch with each other even if they live far apart? *(write, call, visit, e-mail)*

5. Why do you think having new hobbies or interests might change a friendship? *(the other person isn't interested in what you do anymore)*

6. In what ways is having new friends a good thing? How can it be a sad thing? *(good: new people can teach you new things; sad: you might not do the same things you used to do because your friend isn't around)*

Activity

Directions: Here are some children who are not really best friends anymore. What happened to their friendship?

Answers: 1. moved away   2. different interests   3. disagreed about something important to them   4. no time to spend together   5. personality change

Follow-up: Friendship is a very important part of life. Whether friends are short term or lifelong, they all contribute something vitally important to us. Have your class celebrate a Friendship Holiday in which friendship is honored. Find poems, stories, quotes, and cards that address the value of friendship. Emphasize that being the best friend you can be to someone is a social skill that will help them out for their whole life—whether they have one friend forever or many different friends for different periods in their lives.

7.10   **Friendships Change**

Here are some children who are not really best friends anymore. Write what happened to their friendship.

1. **Cindy:** This is a picture of my friend Amy. We were best friends in first and second grade, but now she lives in Florida and I don't see her anymore.

   Amy: We wrote letters for a little while, but now I'm kind of busy because I'm in cheerleading and gymnastics.

_____

_____

_____

2. **Tim:** I used to see Jamal all the time when we played soccer together. But now I'm on a traveling baseball team.

   Jamal: I still like Tim, but I don't really run into him much anymore.

_____

_____

_____

3. **Isabella:** Patricia and I were friends until we couldn't work together on a big science project. I wanted to make a poster and she wanted to write a play.

   Patricia: I guess we each thought we had the best idea.

_____

_____

_____

Copyright © 2009 by John Wiley & Sons, Inc.

4. **Emily:** I get to take riding lessons every week! I love horses! But I don't have a lot of time to hang out with Luke anymore.

   Luke: Emily is always busy now. But I'm busy with soccer, so I guess I'm busy too.

    _____

    _____

    _____

5. **NeAsia:** Lauren and I were good friends until she started hanging around with Sophia and met all those other girls who think they are so popular.

   Lauren: NeAsia is so quiet; she just doesn't want to meet new people. I told her that she could be popular too if she wanted to hang out with us, but she doesn't want to.

    _____

    _____

    _____

Copyright © 2009 by John Wiley & Sons. Inc.

Classroom Tips for Keeping Friends

- During a sharing time or community circle, have each student pay a tribute to a friend who has taught him or her how to do something.

- During free time or recess, let students take turns choosing the activity with the understanding that no one complains about it; everyone participates. Let students learn to try something new.

- Write anonymous stories or essays about "My Best Friend." Have students try to guess who the essay is about if it is a classmate, and discuss the qualities that the author values in a friend.

- Have students make a class poster in which the skills or talents of various students are highlighted. Have students complete phrases such as: "When I want someone to talk to, a good person would be . . ." "If I want to play football, I would ask . . ." Explain that we often have different friends available for different activities. Not everyone likes to do everything with one friend; that's why it's fun to have lots of friends.

- Knock-Knock Day. Challenge students to find their best knock-knock jokes, get a partner, and take a minute or two before lunch (or recess or leaving for the day) to share their humor with the class.

- Make a paper chain with a sincere promise written on each link of the chain. Have students share their promises before linking them together and displaying the chain by draping it around the chalkboard or windows. Point out the symbolism of breaking the chain by breaking a promise.

- Use books (such as paperback series) with young characters, and find examples of friends sticking up for other friends. Students may want to work with partners on this task, each taking the side of one of the friends in the story.

- Assign each person in the class a "friend for the day" (or week). They are to look out for each other, help each other on school activities or other tasks, and perhaps even turn in assignments as a team. Rotate partners often.

- Make a class list of common school problems on one side (suggested by students) and workable solutions that students may have tried on the other side. Brainstorm together to come up with ideas to try.

- As a writing assignment, have students pretend to be "Dear Abby" advice givers for other students. Have an anonymous box where students can slip in letters or notes about their concerns. Pick appropriate letters and assign students to answer them sincerely. Share results.

- Invite your school counselor or principal or school nurse to talk to your class about child abuse, depression, dealing with disabilities, and other relevant topics that may pertain to your setting. Review sources of help and people who are trained to deal with these problems.

- Write a class play about friendship. The plot could be as simple as one friend betraying another in a school situation, with appropriate humor and characters thrown in to personalize it. One part of the class may perform for the other, and they could discuss thinking questions about the play and its outcome.

Part Three

Developing Positive Social Skills

Our community sponsors a program in which adult volunteers go in pairs to take children from low-income families shopping for the holidays. My assistant and I decided to participate and were given the name and address of a sweet-looking little girl whom I shall call Karlie. We didn't know her, though she was from our school. We were given a list of clothing sizes and a tip: *Hang on to her at all times.* For the next hour, we were in hot pursuit of a tiny second grader who threw tantrums; tossed random clothes into the cart; pulled items out of the cart; argued about colors, sizes, and styles; and insisted that she desperately needed sea monkeys.

I pulled the old "I'm calling Grandma on my cell phone to tell her we're coming home" trick, which settled her down briefly but left me feeling discouraged. At the checkout aisle, Karlie helped unload the items on the conveyor belt (including some gum and candy bars that she tried to sneak in) and flashed a beautiful smile to the cashier.

"Did you have fun, honey?" the woman asked Karlie.

Karlie turned on the charm and said, "Look! They let me get a pink umbrella! My grandma wouldn't let me have it the last time we were here!"

After delivering Karlie safely at home, my assistant and I collapsed, feeling as though we had survived a week's worth of indoor recess. The following day, I sought out Karlie's special education teacher to get more information on this puzzling child. It turned out that Karlie had been abandoned due in part to her attention deficit/hyperactivity disorder. She was in a treatment program in the morning and attended public school part time.

Although she was gifted academically, Karlie had few positive social skills, and she used them selectively. She was living with her elderly grandparents who were doing the best they could, but it was apparent that the situation was becoming worse. Here was a little girl with no friends, little respect for others, a highly impulsive nature, and a careless regard for how she appeared to others in public. Yet here also was a classic case of a child desperately in need of learning and exhibiting positive social skills.

The chapters in Part Three contain numerous activities that have proven to be extremely helpful with children like Karlie. Part Three contains these materials:

- Parent letters
- Story: "The Accident"
- Chapter Eight: Understanding Social Situations
- Chapter Nine: Positive Personality Attributes
- Chapter Ten: Getting Along with Others at Home
- Chapter Eleven: Everyday Etiquette

PARENT LETTER #8

RE: Developing Positive Social Skills—Understanding Social Situations

Dear Parents,

Have you ever visited another country? Everything is different: the language, the customs, clothing, transportation, and so on. It takes time to catch on to what is expected and what is appropriate. We do this by keeping our eyes open, paying attention to how people act, and watching what they do in response to each other. This is how we learn language as well. By using context, we can figure out what the words mean.

Now imagine having a tour guide. She might give you some pointers as to what to do or not to do in her country. She might teach you a few handy phrases to help you get around. She might also prepare you to make a good impression on your hosts by bringing an appropriate gift.

In a way, developing positive social skills is somewhat like this adventure. We want to help students know what is expected of them in social settings, teach them how to fit in, and equip them as much as possible with positive social skills so that they will have every advantage.

Some children have trouble understanding what is called for in many social situations. Whether it is at school, at home, going to a friend's house, or talking to people in a store, the experience may be confusing to the child who is not good at recognizing moods in people, knowing what to expect in a situation, or toning down his or her own voice to sound friendly.

These lessons give ideas for behaving appropriately around disabled individuals, respecting others' opinions, and paying attention to tone of voice, facial expressions, and the current setting before making demands on others.

You can help at home in these ways:

- Discuss your expectations for your child's behavior in social situations. Will Aunt Bertha try to kiss him? Should she ask to use the pool? Prepare your child for what's coming.

- Call attention to your own moods, facial expressions, and behavior as clues to how you are feeling. Ask your child to tell you what he sees. How do you feel? Why? Is this a good time for added stress?

- Make your values clear to your child. If he cheats at school, does this upset you? Is fighting permissible? What do you mean by "right" and "wrong"? Where will your child learn the values that will guide him or her through life? Decide!

Sincerely,

_____

Teacher

Copyright © 2009 by John Wiley & Sons, Inc.

PARENT LETTER #9

RE: Developing Positive Social Skills—Positive Personality Attributes

Dear Parents,

When you think of someone who is attractive, you probably think of someone who is friendly, interesting, and nice to be around. Whether the person is good-looking or athletic doesn't matter when you get right down to it. Nice people are nice people!

So how do people work on being nice?

The next set of lessons deals with developing positive qualities as a way to make friends and get along with others. These include developing interests, being a good sport, being tolerant of others, accepting the blame when appropriate, and being organized.

You can help reinforce as well as teach these ideas at home. Here are some suggestions:

- Encourage your child to seek out new experiences and find new interests. Check into sports programs, craft lessons, and volunteer opportunities.

- Model good sportsmanship. When something goes wrong, show your child how to handle the situation in a responsible manner. Show that there is no shame in being a good loser. It's easier to be a good winner; being a good loser takes work and a good attitude!

- If your child is a leader, use this ability to help organize the other children in the family. Ask this child to help you plan the family picnic, sort through the piles of clothing, and help make lists.

- When your child is at fault, help make it a little easier for him or her to accept the blame by treating the matter fairly and without extreme punishment, if appropriate. Thank your child for coming to you honestly—although you still expect amends to be made!

Sincerely,

_____

Teacher

Copyright © 2009 by John Wiley & Sons. Inc.

Developing Positive Social Skills

PARENT LETTER #10

RE: Developing Positive Social Skills—Getting Along with Others at Home

Copyright © 2009 by John Wiley & Sons, Inc.

Dear Parents,

This part is for you! Though we don't get to see our students in their homes very often, we know that what goes on at home can affect what happens at school and vice versa. If we are all stressing getting along with others in our day-to-day lives—whether it is at school or at home—we are teaching the same ideas: developing good relationships. Families are not as simple to define as in previous generations. A family might consist of two remarried parents, a grandparent in the home, step-siblings, and adopted siblings from other countries. Whoever it consists of, a family is an extremely important part of a child's life.

The lessons in this unit cover areas such as getting along with parents; fitting into a family of siblings as the oldest, youngest, or middle child; dealing with chores and homework; and having fun as a family. You can help in these ways:

- Explain your family rules clearly to your child. You might want to discuss the need for rules and the consequences if rules are not followed.

- Realize that your child is a unique individual, not simply "the youngest" or "my other son." Praise each child for his or her special accomplishments, and encourage interests.

- Be systematic and fair when it comes to chores.

- Everyone lives in the house, so everyone can contribute in some way to getting things done. Doing chores doesn't have to be viewed as punishment. It's just a responsibility that can make it easier for everyone if we all lend a hand.

- Remember that your children will probably not be in the house forever. Use the time you have with them to create a happy childhood, lots of good experiences, and the memory of a family who supports each other and loves each other. Look for ways to have fun together as a family.

Sincerely,

_____

Teacher

PARENT LETTER #11

RE: Developing Positive Social Skills—Everyday Etiquette

Dear Parents,

Have you ever been to a movie theater filled with children celebrating a birthday party? Or been to the grocery store and found yourself behind someone in the checkout lane who has a child who can't live without a candy bar and a magazine? Have you ever said (before you had children) that YOUR children would NEVER act like how someone else's children act? Well, now you know better! Kids are kids!

Our final set of lessons deals with teaching social skills used in everyday settings. We all hope that our children will grow up to be polite and respectful to others. Other skills, such as washing hands before eating, using good table manners, using appropriate language, and writing thank-you notes, are also included.

Perhaps the most important social skill covered in this series of lessons is the final one: discussion of the Golden Rule, to treat others as you wish to be treated. It says it all!

Help your child learn good manners at home:

- Specifically instruct your child how to introduce others and meet your friends when they come into the house. It doesn't have to be a formal thing, but make sure names are exchanged and there is good eye contact.

- Make hand washing, use of silverware, and passing plates around the table a part of your structured mealtimes. It's cute when a small child dives into the peas, but not so funny when someone who should know better attacks his or her food. Even if you don't have structured meals often, use the times that you do to work on these skills.

- Look for opportunities to teach your child about common courtesy when using public facilities such as a phone, transportation, or sitting in a crowded waiting room. Look for ways to show kindness to others.

- Take pride in the times when your child demonstrates courtesy to others. Compliment him or her on the thoughtfulness shown (even though it may surprise you!).

Good luck!

Sincerely,

_____

Teacher

Copyright © 2009 by John Wiley & Sons, Inc.

Developing Positive Social Skills

Story: The Accident

Cynthia and Linda were both students in Mrs. Clark's class, but that was about all they had in common. Linda was very tall; Cynthia was short. Linda liked to play baseball; Cynthia liked to draw. And they both had very different ways of telling people no.

When Linda didn't want something, she would take a deep breath and holler "NO!" at the top of her lungs. One day Michael asked if he could borrow her eraser. She yelled "NO!" so loudly that the force of her breath knocked the poor boy on the ground.

When she said, "no," she meant it! There was NO question about that.

Copyright © 2009 by John Wiley & Sons. Inc.

When Cynthia wanted to tell someone no, she always ended up saying, "Well, okay," which is not really "no" at all.

One day Nancy came up to her and asked if she could copy Cynthia's reading answers. Cynthia didn't want to give Nancy her paper, but she said, "Well, okay," and handed it over to her.

Mrs. Clark was watching them on the playground one day. Steven walked up to Linda, who had been playing on the swings for quite a long time, and asked politely if he could have a turn. Linda vigorously shook her head, took a deep breath, and yelled, "No! Now get out of here!"

So Steven went down to the next swing and asked Cynthia the same thing. Cynthia had just gotten on the swing and she didn't really want to get off, but she said, "Well, okay," and got off.

Copyright © 2009 by John Wiley & Sons, Inc.

Developing Positive Social Skills

Copyright © 2009 by John Wiley & Sons, Inc.

Mrs. Clark shook her head. She turned to Mrs. Smith and said, "I sure wish a little bit of Linda would rub off on Cynthia and a little bit of Cynthia would rub off on Linda. Then they'd both be able to say no without upsetting other people and themselves."

She walked over to Steven to tell him to give Cynthia her swing back. But Steven wasn't happy with that idea, so when Mrs. Clark's back was turned, he gave Cynthia's swing a really hard push! Actually it was a lot harder than he meant to push it, and the two girls were headed right for each other!

The girls started screaming! They knew they were going to collide. The last thing that Linda yelled was "NOOOOO!" and the last thing Cynthia yelled was, "WELL, OKAY!"

They hit. Hard! And both girls sat on the ground, rubbing the huge bumps that were already beginning to form on their heads.

"Are you all right?" asked Mrs. Clark, rushing up to them.

"Well, okay," said Linda.

"NO!" yelled Cynthia.

The girls looked at each other, startled!

"What did you say?" asked Mrs. Clark. "Did I hear right?"

Cynthia said, "NO!" and Linda said, "Well, okay."

The girls stared at each other with their mouths wide open. What had happened?

"Do you need to go home?" asked Mrs. Clark, looking a little worried.

"NO!" yelled Cynthia, sounding a lot like Linda. She covered her mouth with her hands. She meant to say "yes," but it came out wrong.

"Okay," said Mrs. Clark, holding up her hands. "I was just asking. Don't yell at me. What about you, Linda? Shall I call your mother?"

Linda shook her head because she knew her mother was planning to go out for the day, but the words came out, "Well, okay," and Mrs. Clark headed for the phone. She had sounded an awful lot like Cynthia.

As it turned out, Mrs. Clark called both parents, and both girls went home for the rest of the day with huge bumps and an ice pack.

It was not long before both girls figured out that all they could say were the last words that each had spoken before their swings had collided. Somehow in the accident, their voices had gotten mixed up and stuck on "no" or "well, okay."

"Do you want to take a nap?" asked Linda's mom when they got home.

Linda, of course, didn't want to take a nap—she wanted to go out in the back yard and play baseball, but the words came out, "Well, okay," and her mom pushed her into her bedroom.

"It's so nice to hear you using a quiet voice," she said. "I like that, Linda." Linda crawled into bed and found out that she really was pretty tired.

That night, Linda's mother fixed a big dinner. "Would you like to try some of this broccoli and spinach casserole?" she asked her daughter.

Copyright © 2009 by John Wiley & Sons. Inc.

Developing Positive Social Skills

The only thing Linda hated more than broccoli was spinach, but she was unable to say anything but, "Well, okay," and was faced with two heaping portions of the green stuff on her plate.

"I really like how you're trying new things, Linda," said her mom, smiling. "I always thought you didn't like these vegetables."

And it turned out that the stuff wasn't too bad.

After dinner, Linda's little brother, Jimmy, came up to her and asked, "Linda, would you help me with my homework? It's math." He stuck out his tongue.

Linda couldn't think of anything more boring than helping Jimmy with his homework, but she said, "Well, okay," and sat down next to him. Her little brother was so happy that he ran and got his favorite toy truck to give to her. Linda didn't care about the truck, but she felt good about helping Jimmy.

Copyright © 2009 by John Wiley & Sons. Inc.

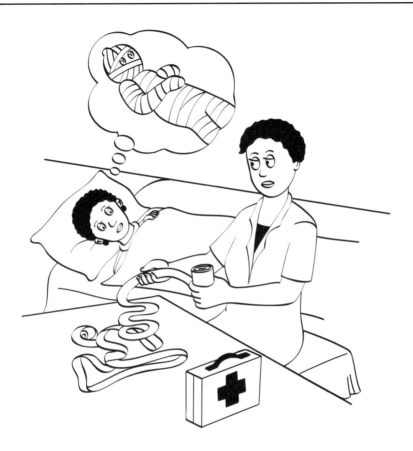

Meanwhile, Cynthia's mother was getting out rolls and rolls of bandages to wrap all over Cynthia's body, even though only her head hurt. "You poor dear," she said. "We're going to have to wrap you up and make sure you're okay, right sweetie?"

Cynthia groaned inside. She hated it when her mother covered her with bandages when only one little one was needed, but she was so used to saying, "Well, okay," that she opened her mouth and startled herself when she said, "NO!"

"What?" gasped her mother. "You don't want these bandages?"

"NO!" said Cynthia, almost falling off the couch with the force of her voice. "Well, okay," said Cynthia's mother, putting the first-aid kit away.

Cynthia couldn't believe it! The bandages were gone! This was great! Maybe this meant she wouldn't have to ride around in a wheelchair for a day either. Cynthia's mother sometimes went overboard when it came to taking care of Cynthia.

Later Alice, the girl next door, came over to play with Cynthia. Cynthia liked Alice most of the time, but she didn't like it when Alice took Cynthia's bicycle and rode it in the mud. But she always told Alice, "Well, okay," when Alice asked to borrow it.

Developing Positive Social Skills

Copyright © 2009 by John Wiley & Sons, Inc.

This time, however, when Alice asked about the bike, Cynthia kind of enjoyed saying, "NO."

"Really?" asked Alice. "Well, if you don't want to. I guess I'll just go home, then, and ride my own bike."

Cynthia didn't want to say "NO!" right then, so she closed her mouth tightly and cheered inside her head!

Later that night, Nancy came over to copy Cynthia's homework (she did this every night). Cynthia smiled as she saw Nancy walking up to the house. She was going to enjoy this.

"Hi there, Cynthia," called Nancy, waving her blank paper. "May I—"

The neighbors must have been pretty surprised when they saw a young girl blown across the front yard!

Copyright © 2009 by John Wiley & Sons, Inc.

At school the next day, the girls sat together in class. Cynthia wrote Linda a note that said: "Are you having as much fun with my voice as I am with yours?"

The note came back: "No! But I'm learning a lot!"

It turned out that both Cynthia and Linda had to work with the speech teacher for a few weeks before their voices completely returned to normal.

Linda worked on saying "no" in a quiet voice, but it still meant "no."

Cynthia worked on saying "no" when she really didn't want to do something, instead of letting people take advantage of her.

"I'm so proud of both of you," Mrs. Clark told them. "I think this has been a rather good experience for both of you, don't you agree?"

The girls looked at each other, smiled, and said together: "YES!"

THE END

Copyright © 2009 by John Wiley & Sons, Inc.

Chapter 8

Understanding Social Situations

8.1 Having Clear Expectations

Objective

Given a specific social situation, the student will correctly identify at least one plausible outcome or expectation.

Rationale

Many embarrassing social problems result from not clearly understanding the social situation itself. While this skill generally improves with practice and lots of social experiences, it is helpful to stop and think about what is involved in a specific social situation even before you are in the situation. For special students especially, thinking through the situation before it comes up is a real benefit to planning what will happen and how to prepare for what is expected of the student.

Thinking Questions

1. If you were invited to the circus, would you show up with skis and a tennis racquet? *(probably not)*
2. If you were supposed to give a speech, how would you feel if you walked into an empty room? *(confused, relieved!)*
3. How does it help you prepare for something by knowing what you are supposed to do ahead of time? *(you can rehearse, get things ready, buy something if you need to)*
4. How would you prepare if you knew you were going to the White House to have dinner with the president? *(might get new clothes, wash your hair)*
5. Why might it be embarrassing to show up at a party wearing the wrong clothes or coming at the wrong time or not bringing something you needed? *(makes you look silly or different from everyone else)*
6. Why might it be helpful to know as much as you can about something, such as a party or game or other event, before you go? *(so you can figure out what you'll need)*
7. Have you ever been disappointed because you expected something to happen at a social event and it didn't? Tell about it. *(perhaps a surprise party that wasn't or expecting someone to be there who didn't show up)*

Activity

Directions: The student is to read each of the four social situations and pick out the best answer that tells a logical expectation. Inform students that there is only one answer for each.

Answers: 1. c   2. a   3. b   4. c

Follow-up: Discuss why the unselected answers were not logical expectations. Why wouldn't the neighbors have a swimming suit ready for you? At what point are you expecting too much of someone else? Sometimes illogical things happen, and we are quite surprised; however, in most situations, there are certain things that we expect of others. Emphasize what is typical or normal in most situations, allowing for the fact that strange things do happen!

8.1   **Having Clear Expectations**

Read the following situations. What would you expect would happen in each? Check the best answer.

1. You received an invitation to a swimming party at a neighbor's house. You are supposed to arrive at four o'clock and stay for a cookout. Would you expect:

   _____ a. the neighbors to have your suit and towel for you?

   _____ b. to bring dinner for everyone there?

   _____ c. to bring your suit, dry clothes, and maybe some chips?

2. The principal walks into your classroom while the teacher is talking about growing plants. She stops to go over to talk to the principal. Would you expect:

   _____ a. to be quiet and wait for the teacher to finish talking to the principal?

   _____ b. the teacher to throw the plants on the floor?

   _____ c. the principal to look through the teacher's desk?

3. There is a new boy in your class. At recess time, he comes up to you and asks if he could join your group for kickball. Would you expect:

   _____ a. him to go around hitting everyone?

   _____ b. to let him play?

   _____ c. everyone to ignore him?

4. Your older sister lets you borrow her brand-new red sweater to wear to the football game. Would you expect:

   _____ a. to let your friend use it to clean up spilled soda?

   _____ b. your sister to let you keep it?

   _____ c. to be very careful not to get it dirty?

Copyright © 2009 by John Wiley & Sons, Inc.

8.2 Saying "No" Without Sounding Rude

Objective

The student will identify polite or acceptable ways to tell someone "no."

Rationale

Many times we are in situations where a refusal is perfectly acceptable. However, turning someone down or telling someone they can't have their way or what they want can sometimes be done in a hostile manner. Students should be aware that they can say "no" without conveying rudeness, anger, or hostility.

Thinking Questions

1. If someone came up to you and asked for all of your money, your best jeans, and your favorite toys at home, what would you tell him or her? (*"Forget it," "No way," "Are you crazy?"*)

2. How could you let that person know the answer is no in a very polite way? (*rephrase the above comments to things like "Sorry," "I can't do that"*)

3. What are some situations that you probably would say no to someone for? (*sharing something you're not supposed to, not being able to go somewhere with someone*)

4. If you said no to someone politely, would you have the same result? (*probably, although some people might require more persistence*)

5. How could telling someone no in a rude or mean manner make the situation worse? (*the other person might become angry, might be less likely to share something with you*)

Activity

Directions: The student is to circle the characters on the worksheet who are saying "no" politely and to put an X through the ones who are sounding rude. Stress that although the characters may not intend to be rude, the way the words come out make them sound impolite.

Answers: Circle: 2, 3, 6; X: 1, 4, 5

Follow-up: Have students rephrase the impolite-sounding refusals to make them more polite. The tone of voice used to refuse someone also conveys your intention. Have students practice using a pleasant or neutral voice quality when reading the characters' words.

Name _____ Date _____

8.2 Saying "No" Without Sounding Rude

These students are all saying "no" about something. Circle the ones who are being polite. Put an X through the ones who sound rude.

8.3 Don't Say "Yes" If You Mean "No"

Objective

The student will demonstrate telling someone "no" appropriately by drawing or explaining a solution to a specified problem.

Rationale

Some students have a somewhat different problem with the word *no*. They tend to be agreeable or commit to a situation even when they are unable to do what they just agreed to do. The skill of saying "no" instead of "yes" when it is called for is the focus of this lesson.

Thinking Questions

1. Have you ever agreed to do something for someone else even though you really didn't want to do it? Tell about it. *(have students relate anecdotes)*

2. Did it turn out to be a problem for you? If so, how? *(it might have taken more time, been a hard task, involved something the student didn't like)*

3. Are there times when you really should say no to someone? *(yes)* What? *(if the person asks you to do something wrong, if you know you could be in danger)*

4. Why do you think people agree to do things when they know it isn't the right time or could be dangerous? *(don't want others to laugh at them, be picked on, look foolish)*

5. What's the worst thing that might happen if you told someone no? *(the person would laugh at you, wouldn't be your friend)*

6. Is it better to put up with an embarrassing consequence than to find yourself in trouble or danger? *(yes!)*

Activity

Directions: Students are to draw a picture of a character saying "no" in each of the situations on the worksheet. The pictures can be explained in class or students can use speech balloons or other forms of writing to get their points across.

Answer examples:

1. "No, I just don't want to do that."
2. "No, that's not fair."
3. "I really can't tonight; it's my birthday, and I already have plans."
4. "I'm not feeling well; I think I should go home."

Follow-up: Have students share their ideas. Why were the situations on the worksheet potential problems? *(danger, cheating)* Is the greatest fear that the other person in the situation will not understand or accept the answer of "no"?

8.3   # Don't Say "Yes" If You Mean "No"

How could you say "no" in each of these situations? Draw a picture, and write how you would handle the problem.

1. An older kid wants you to smoke a cigarette or he'll call you a baby

2. Your best friend wants to copy your homework.

3. It's your birthday, and you are going bowling with your friends. Your neighbor asks you to baby-sit that evening.

4. You don't feel very well, but your teacher asks you to stay after school to work on the school newspaper.

Copyright © 2009 by John Wiley & Sons, Inc.

8.4 Not Hurting the Feelings of Others

Objective

The student will identify comments that potentially could hurt the feelings of someone else in that they are thoughtless or rude.

Rationale

It is very easy to make offhand comments about other people or their situations without realizing that you may hurt the other person's feelings, whether you intended to or not. Before speaking impulsively, students who are prone to do this should be conscious of how their words may affect the feelings of others.

Thinking Questions

1. Think for a moment about the things you are sensitive about regarding yourself. Without being specific, what are some areas that people might be touchy about? (*weight, looks, school difficulties, athletic inability*)

2. Can you think of any situations in which someone said something about another person's mistakes or weaknesses? (*ask for examples*)

3. How did the other person react? (*hurt feelings, anger*)

4. Do you think most people try to hurt other people's feelings? (*depends on the situation and person*)

5. How could you tell if what you said hurt another person's feelings? (*the person might look sad, cry, leave the group*)

6. How do people try to disguise their hurt feelings? (*act as if nothing happened, change the subject*)

7. Whether you hurt someone's feelings or not, there are comments that are just plain hurtful and mean. Can you think of examples? (*comments about someone's weak areas, habits, home situation*)

8. Does anything good ever come of being hurtful to others? (*not directly*)

Activity

Directions: The student is to read the list of comments and draw a sad face next to the ones that are hurtful. They do not need to draw anything on the positive or neutral comments.

Answers: Sad faces: 1, 2, 5, 6, 9, 10

Follow-up: Discuss students' reasoning for drawing the sad faces. Why were the comments hurtful? What weak area did the comment target? (*looks, inability, hygiene, finances*)

8.4   Not Hurting the Feelings of Others

Which of these comments might hurt someone's feelings? Draw a sad face next to the ones that are hurtful.

1. "You're really fat."

2. "Don't you know how to read that word? You must be really slow."

3. "Good try! You'll make a basket next time!"

4. "Would you please pass me my pencil?"

5. "Did you get that sweater out of the garbage?"

6. "Have you ever heard of using a toothbrush?"

7. "I like your tennis shoes."

8. "Ronald is the fastest runner in our class."

9. "We don't want Sarah to be in our group."

10. "Is that a big rip in the back of your shirt? Or is it just a stain?"

Copyright © 2009 by John Wiley & Sons. Inc.

8.5 What Is a Disability?

Objective

The student will identify physical or mental disabilities that he or she may be likely to encounter at school or in the community.

Rationale

Most of us feel uncomfortable at first in interactions with individuals who have an obvious disability. We may feel awkward as to what to do or say. The more students know about disabilities and are comfortable discussing situations involving disabled people, the more likely they will handle these situations appropriately.

Thinking Questions

1. What do you think of when you hear the word *disabled*? (*someone who is blind, in a wheelchair, crippled*)

2. There are lots of types of disabilities. Can you think of some that are physical? (*blindness, deafness, loss of limbs*)

3. Do people with those disabilities ever get better, or does the disability last their whole lives? (*may be improved somewhat, but the physical disability will always have to be dealt with*)

4. Can you think of any people who were physically disabled but were still able to do most everything they wanted to do? (*students may know of a local person, a famous athlete, Helen Keller*)

5. Just because someone has a disability, does that mean the person is sick or can't do anything fun? (*not necessarily—they find ways to adapt to their environment*)

6. Other kinds of disabilities might not be so obvious. Can you think of mental disabilities? (*Down syndrome, autism, learning disabilities*)

7. There are lots of students who may have to work even harder in school because of reading disabilities or learning disabilities. You can't tell by looking at someone, but these students, too, have to overcome special problems. Can you think of how this would make things in school tough for a student? (*harder to get through all of the assignments, might take longer to read, other kids might make fun of them*)

8. How do you feel when you see someone who is obviously disabled on the street or at a restaurant? (*awkward, curious*)

9. How do you think that person might feel? (*embarrassed that someone is staring, angry*)

10. If you didn't know whether a disabled person was bothered by his or her situation, how might you talk to that person at first? (*don't discuss the disability, listen before talking, don't stare*)

11. Do you think everyone who has a disability wants you to rush right in and help them, such as by opening a door? (*no*)

12. A disability might make things harder, but do you think it would have to slow someone down completely? *(no—there are many examples of people who have achieved much despite—or because of—a disability)*

13. How could you try to understand what a disabled person's life is like? *(read about it, talk to someone, observe, think through a day as a disabled person)*

Activity

Directions: The student is to read the list of disabilities and nuisances, and place a check mark next to those that are true disabilities.

 Answers: check mark: 2, 3, 6, 7, 8, 11

Follow-up: Go through each item on the list and discuss why it would or would not be considered a disability. *(having a hangnail is a temporary condition; being tall might make it harder to sit in a little car, but it would be possible to perform most everyday tasks)* Then consider the disabled items one by one with the thoughts of how a person with that disability could function well in everyday life, thereby not letting the disability make them seem disabled. *(being in a wheelchair limits mobility to some extent, but there are ramps, specialized cars, other motorized devices to make things accessible; deaf people can function well by signing, relying on vision, using special telephones that have written cues)*

8.5   # What Is a Disability?

All of the things on this list might make life a little harder for someone. Which of these could be considered disabilities, not just a nuisance that you have to deal with for a short time? Put a check mark next to the true disabilities.

❑ 1. Having a hangnail

❑ 2. Being in a wheelchair

❑ 3. Not being able to hear very well

❑ 4. Having red hair

❑ 5. Being tall

❑ 6. Being blind

❑ 7. Having only one arm

❑ 8. Not being able to read because the letters and words seem all jumbled up

❑ 9. Having a cold

❑ 10. Having a bloody nose

❑ 11. Having an artificial leg

❑ 12. Sneezing from hay fever

Copyright © 2009 by John Wiley & Sons. Inc.

8.6 People Who Are Different

Objective

The student will identify at least one characteristic of a person who is different from himself or herself and state at least one commonality.

Rationale

When we encounter a person who is different from ourselves, whether by race, interest, oddity, or any other feature, we may at first see the difference. With special children, this may manifest itself as staring, embarrassing questions, or intense curiosity. Differences can be interesting and understood. This lesson focuses on finding common areas that a student could explore with a person who is perceived as different from himself or herself.

Thinking Questions

1. Is everyone in this room exactly alike? *(no)*

2. In what ways are people different? *(race, physical characteristics, sex, emotions)*

3. Sometimes you may run into a person who is really different from yourself, like someone from another country. What kind of differences might there be between you and that person? *(language, culture, interests, clothing)*

4. Do you think there would be anything in common between you? What? *(might like to eat the same things, play games together, laugh at same things)*

5. Some people are different not only in the way they look but in how they act or what they believe. What are some different church groups? Political groups? Clubs that people can join? *(Baptist, Catholic; Republican, Democrat; Elks, Lions)*

6. Just because someone is different from you in some way, does that mean you have nothing that you could do or enjoy together? Explain. *(no—we all have differences, but we have common points as well)*

7. Do you think if you tried hard and thought hard, you could find something in common with almost everyone? *(probably)*

Activity Five

Directions: Five characters are pictured on the worksheet. Students are instructed to choose one who is different from themselves in some way and to list at least three activities or topics of conversation that they could possibly have in common.

Answer example: 1: Maria is from another country, but we could probably play cards together, jump rope, toss a ball, walk in the woods, or play with dolls.

Follow-up: Have students discuss why they selected the character they did. What aspect was very different from a characteristic you possess? What topics or interests seem to appeal to almost every child, no matter what country they are from or their social status?

8.6   **People Who Are Different**

Pick one of the five people from this worksheet who is different from you. List at least three things that you could do together or talk about.

1. Maria is from Bolivia. She does not speak any English. She has eight brothers and sisters.

_____

_____

_____

2. Dylan is in a wheelchair. He was born with a spine injury and will never be able to walk.

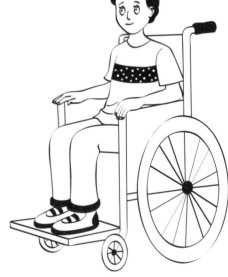

Copyright © 2009 by John Wiley & Sons. Inc.

8.6 People Who Are Different (continued)

3. Carolyn goes to a different house of worship from everyone else in your class. Her worship service is different from yours.

_____

_____

_____

4. Tommy is a Native American. His skin is dark, and his grandparents know how to do traditional dances.

_____

_____

_____

5. Carlos lives in a mansion. His parents have eight cars and an enormous swimming pool. He travels to other countries on vacations.

_____

_____

_____

Copyright © 2009 by John Wiley & Sons, Inc.

8.7 Tone of Voice

Objective

The student will correctly identify the intended meaning of a statement by applying tone-of-voice cues.

Rationale

Words are just words until the meaning behind them is conveyed and received by the listener. Students sometimes focus only on the words without listening to the tone that carries the word. The speaker may say something angrily, teasingly, laughingly, or with some other emotion that may change the entire meaning of the words. To correctly understand social situations, students must be able to use the speaker's voice to help interpret the situation.

Thinking Questions

1. Listen to this: "Shut . . . the . . . door." What do I want you to do? *(shut the door)*

2. How could you say those three words and make it sound as if I was really angry? *(SHUT THE DOOR!)*

3. How could you say the same three words and make it sound as though I thought it was the funniest thing I had ever heard? *(with laughter)*

4. How could you make it sound as though I thought you were going over to close the window? *(Shut the **door**.)*

5. How does the way you say something change what you actually say? *(you emphasize different parts of the sentence)*

6. How would paying attention to someone's voice as he or she is talking help you understand the situation? *(you'd get clues from his or her face, clues from what words were emphasized, clues from the loudness or sharpness of the voice)*

Activity

Directions: Students are to read what the characters are saying, using picture clues and context clues to determine the tone of voice the speaker probably is using. Then they are to put a check next to the answer that matches the speaker's true message.

Answers: 1. a   2. b   3. b

Follow-up: Have students take turns reading the character's comments in an appropriate tone of voice. Discuss how the words they emphasize change the meaning of the message, as well as how the other clues (dogs' tails wagging, teacher's expression) help figure out what the speaker means.

8.7   Tone of Voice

Read what each person below is saying. Put a check next to the answer that explains what the person means.

Copyright © 2009 by John Wiley & Sons. Inc.

1.

Good morning, Mark. I said GOOD MORNING, Mark. Aren't you talking to anyone today?

❑ a. The teacher wants Mark to pay attention to her.

❑ b. The teacher wants Mark to have a good morning.

❑ c. The teacher wants Mark to talk loudly.

2.

❑ a. The boy hates dogs and is not enjoying himself.

❑ b. The boy is teasing. He loves the dogs.

❑ c. The boy was hurt by one of the dogs.

I just can't stand dogs. I hate them all. They are real pains to have around.

3.

The bell rang already... Find your seat.

❑ a. The teacher thinks the boy does not know what the bell means.

❑ b. The teacher wants the boy to sit down right away.

❑ c. The teacher wants the boy to look for a chair.

Understanding Social Situations

8.8 Facial Expressions

Objective

The student will identify feelings or emotions from a facial expression on a character.

Rationale

The way a person looks can give clues as to what he or she is thinking or feeling. An open mouth, gritted teeth, furrowed brow, red cheeks, and so on are all bodily expressions of inner feelings. Giving the student practice in identifying possible emotions based solely on a facial expression is a good exercise for reading social situations.

Thinking Questions

1. How can you tell if someone is really, really mad at you, even if he or she doesn't say a word? (*red face, tight mouth, clenched fist*)

2. Without words, how could you tell if someone was really sad? (*might have tears in eyes, mouth in a frown*)

3. Can you tell a lot about how someone is feeling even if he or she isn't talking? (*yes—from bodily clues*)

4. What are some other ways a person's face expresses feelings? (*eyes might be tight if they are angry, nose flaring, mouth pouting*)

5. What are some other types of feelings that might be easy to detect by looking at someone's face? (*sadness, happiness, surprise*)

Activity

Directions: The student is to match the facial expression with the probable emotion. Remind students to look for facial cues, such as eyes and mouth.

   Answers: 1. c   2. d   3. a   4. e   5. b

   Follow-up: Have students take turns imitating some of the expressions on the worksheet. How does it feel? Does making the facial expression help you feel angry, surprised, or puzzled? Would making your face smile and look happy help you to feel happier?

Understanding Social Situations

Name _____ **Date** _____

8.8 Facial Expressions

Match the facial expression with what you think the person is feeling.

1.

    a. very angry

    b. puzzled, not sure

    c. surprised

    d. pouting, feeling sorry for self

    e. bored, not thinking about anything

2.

4.

3.

5.

Copyright © 2009 by John Wiley & Sons, Inc.

8.9 Other People's Opinions

Objective

The student will identify characters who are treating another person's opinion with respect.

Rationale

All through our lives we run into people who have different opinions from ours. Whether we agree with these opinions or not, it is respectful to acknowledge them and allow the other person to express what he or she thinks. In this lesson, students are to identify people who are listening respectfully to another's opinion.

Thinking Questions

1. Who do you think is the best basketball player [or rock singer or teacher]? (*students will express opinions*)
2. Why were there different answers to that question? (*different opinions*)
3. Is there only one correct answer, or could different people have different ideas or opinions about that question? (*different opinions*)
4. If someone disagrees with your opinion about something, does that mean he or she is wrong? (*no—just another opinion*)
5. Does it mean you are wrong? (*no, again it's just another opinion*)
6. If someone says something that is not at all how you feel about the matter, what good would it do to tell him or her that you don't agree? (*probably very little good, may lead to an argument*)
7. Is it okay for you to express to someone else how you feel, even if you know he or she will disagree? (*sure, depending on the situation and your motive—not trying to start a fight*)
8. If two people totally disagree on something, having very different opinions, can they still be friends? (*yes, but they'll have to accept differences in each other*)

Activity

Directions: The worksheet shows five situations in which students are involved in listening to another person's opinion. The student is to note whether the starred student on the worksheet is respectfully listening to the opinions or not by writing YES or NO on the lines.

Answers: 1. no   2. yes   3. no   4. yes   5. no

Follow-up: Discuss how you could change the "no" responses to make them respectful or kinder. Were the characters who gave opinions being obnoxious, or were they simply stating how they felt? What experiences could the characters have had with Mrs. Jones or with dogs to make them feel the way they said they felt? How would our experiences shape our opinions?

Other People's Opinions

Which of the starred students are listening to another person's opinion with respect? Write YES or NO next to each situation.

Copyright © 2009 by John Wiley & Sons, Inc.

1.  "I like this game. It's really fun." "This is a stupid game. You don't know how to have fun!"

_____

2. "I don't think it's fair for one person to always be the captain of the team."   "What do you think we should do that is fair?"

_____

3. "I like Mrs. Jones." "I do, too."  "You're both nuts."

_____

4.

_____

5.

_____

Copyright © 2009 by John Wiley & Sons. Inc.

Understanding Social Situations

8.10 Is This the Right Time?

Objective

The student will identify whether the situation given is an appropriate interruption or action.

Rationale

Often an action or question in itself is perfectly fine, but depending on the setting, it may or may not be the best time to ask or do something. Students should first consider whether their need is appropriate to be dealt with at any given time before going ahead with making a demand on someone.

Thinking Questions

1. If you were in the middle of a busy street, would that be a good time to stop and play checkers? *(no)* Why or why not? *(lots of commotion going around, dangerous)*

2. Is playing checkers dangerous? *(not by itself)*

3. What would make that situation dangerous? *(the setting—where it was being played)*

4. Is there anything wrong with asking questions, asking someone to get something for you, or telling someone about what you did last night? *(probably not)*

5. In what situations would those things be difficult or bothersome for someone else? *(if the other person was busy, talking to someone else)*

6. Before you interrupt someone, why would it be helpful to check to see if it was the right time to interrupt? *(the other person won't pay as close attention if he or she is busy, might make a situation dangerous if they have to stop to listen to you)*

Activity

Directions: The student is to read each situation on the worksheet and decide whether it is the right time to complete the task. They are to check YES or NO.

Answers: 1. no   2. no   3. yes   4. no   5. yes

Follow-up: Discuss the appropriateness of the actions in each example. For each situation, decide when or where the action is best completed. Is it the action itself or the timing that is the problem?

8.10   **Is This the Right Time?**

Read each situation below and decide whether it is the right time for the character to do something. Check YES or NO.

1. The fire bell just went off! The class is supposed to line up quietly at the door and get ready to go outside. Is this the right time for Marsha to ask her teacher if she can call her mother to bring her doll to school?

   YES _____   NO _____

2. It is quiet time, and everyone is reading a book. Is this a good time for Bobby to take out his squirt gun to show his friend?

   YES _____   NO _____

3. There is a guest speaker in the room, talking about how to take good pictures with a camera. Is this a good time to ask how to use a flash with your camera?

   YES _____   NO _____

4. A new student is sitting at your lunch table. Everyone at the lunch table is good friends and you do a lot of things together. Is this a good time to talk about how you are all going to go bike riding together?

   YES _____   NO _____

5. You are eating spaghetti at a friend's house. The sauce is watery and spilling all over. Is this a good time to put your napkin on your lap and be careful while you're eating?

   YES _____   NO _____

Copyright © 2009 by John Wiley & Sons. Inc.

8.11 Understanding the Teacher's Moods

Objective

The student will identify the most probable mood of the teacher depicted on the worksheet, given facial and verbal cues.

Rationale

Part of a good teacher-student relationship is mutual understanding of the current mood that each is operating under. Teachers are human beings and are subject to responding to situations differently. By recognizing the mood of a teacher, a student can better assess the appropriateness of his or her requests and needs at that time.

Thinking Questions

1. What kinds of moods does your teacher get in sometimes? *(happy, angry, impatient, funny)*
2. What kinds of things might bring on those different moods? *(a bad day: losing something; a good day: well-behaved students)*
3. When is the best time to talk to your teacher about problems with your work? *(when he or she isn't busy or stressed, during a designated time)*
4. If you had a problem that maybe wasn't urgent and your teacher was very tired, why wouldn't that be the best time to talk to him or her? *(may not be as concerned or pay as much attention or listen as well)*
5. How can you pick the best time to approach your teacher with school problems? Home problems? Just general conversation? Complaints? Arguing about something? *(figure out what kind of reception you are likely to get—does the teacher listen more sympathetically when it's quiet and controlled in the class?)*

Activity

Directions: The students are to use picture and verbal clues to determine which word best describes the teacher's mood or feeling. They are to circle the word on the worksheet.

Answers: 1. tired 2. upset 3. excited

Follow-up: Some of the word choices may be perceived as quite similar in meaning *(tired/angry, upset/sad, surprised/excited)*. Discuss the subtle differences in these words and why the selected answer is a little bit more specific.

8.11   Understanding the Teacher's Moods

Which word describes how each teacher below feels? Circle your answer.

1.

happy   tired   angry

2.

upset   sad   tired

3.

surprised   quiet   excited

Copyright © 2009 by John Wiley & Sons. Inc.

8.12 Understanding How Other People Feel

Objective

The student will depict an example of each of the following emotions: jealousy, sadness, fear, excitement, happiness, and fatigue.

Rationale

Not everyone is either happy or sad. There are lots of emotions or ways of feeling that affect how we operate on any given day in different circumstances. In this lesson, students can show how someone might experience a certain feeling by depicting a situation or event.

Thinking Questions

1. Have you ever been really, really happy? Tell about it. *(anecdotes about parties, gifts, events)*
2. Have you ever been extremely frightened or afraid? When? *(anecdotes)*
3. What are some situations in which someone might feel impatient or short-tempered? *(waiting for someone who is always late, being in a hurry to get to a game)*
4. Does everyone feel the same way about the same events? Why would some people react differently? *(some people may love parties, others be shy in a crowd; a roller coaster may terrify one person but cause great excitement in another)*
5. Do you think people can control their moods, or do you think what happens to people has a lot to do with how they feel? *(a debate topic)*

Activity

Directions: Students are to draw pictures of people involved in situations that might affect their moods. They are to draw pictures that depict given moods in others.

Answer examples: 1. three friends together: two playing together with a toy and one left out   2. a sick puppy   3. seeing a robber   4. a big present under the Christmas tree   5. swimming   6. shoveling snow

Follow-up: Share students' pictures and ideas with the rest of the class. Search for common threads as well as situations that depicted very different emotions from different students.

8.12   Understanding How Other People Feel

Draw a picture of a situation that might make someone feel one of the following moods:

1. Jealous

2. Sad

3. Frightened

4. Excited

5. Happy

6. Tired

Copyright © 2009 by John Wiley & Sons. Inc.

8.13   What Are My Choices?

Objective

The student will state at least three possible alternatives for a character in a given situation.

Rationale

There is rarely one correct answer or behavior in most situations. Since students may tend to look for only one right answer, this is an activity in extended thinking—going beyond the obvious to think of other possible choices for the character in the situation.

Thinking Questions

1. Let's say you're sitting at the kitchen table with a pizza in front of you. What are you going to do? *(eat it, wait, smell it)*
2. How many different responses did we come up with for question 1? *(several)*
3. In most situations in which you have to make a choice, do you think there are only one or two possible choices? *(no, there are usually lots of alternatives)*
4. When you're faced with a problem, is there only one thing you can do? *(no; you can think through several possible solutions before deciding on one)*
5. What if two friends wanted you to go to the movies with them and they selected different movies? What are four or five different choices that you have? *(go with one, go with the other, don't go at all, invite another friend to go with you, invite the two to go with you)*

Activity

Directions: Each of the characters is in a situation in which he or she must consider several choices. Students are to list three additional options for the characters.

Answer examples:

1. Mark can swim another time; Mark can ask if his other friend can swim too; Mark can swim first, then see his friend.
2. Taylor can borrow a book; Taylor can call home; Taylor can talk to the teacher later.
3. Sam can talk to his teacher; Sam can confront the boy; Sam can ask a friend to walk with him.

Follow-up: Discuss the choices that the class wrote for each situation. Which choices are most logical or likely to cause the least conflict? Have students circle their best answer for each situation or the answer that they would choose in that situation.

8.13   What Are My Choices?

These students are in situations in which they must make a choice. List at least three other choices that each has in this situation. One choice for each is already given.

1. | Mark is invited to a swimming party, but his friend is not. |

Mark can go to the party by himself.

Mark is invited to a swimming party, but his friend is not.

_____

_____

_____

2. | Taylor forgot to bring her book to school. Her teacher seems to be in a bad mood right now. |

Taylor can talk to her teacher politely and explain.

_____

_____

_____

3. | Sam is being teased by an older boy on the playground. |

Sam could ignore the boy.

_____

_____

_____

Copyright © 2009 by John Wiley & Sons, Inc.

8.14 What Is the Right Thing to Do?

Objective

Given several situations involving a right or wrong choice, the student will identify the right answer.

Rationale

It seems that it's getting harder and harder to find clear-cut right and wrong answers to problems. Everything is complicated by situational ethics; different standards of moral behavior at home, school, church, and other settings; as well as unclear values. In this lesson, the premise is that it is not right to hurt others, cheat, steal, or lie.

Thinking Questions

1. What is wrong with stealing? *(taking something that doesn't belong to you, it leaves the person who was stolen from with problems, not fair to have something for free when someone else had to pay for it)*

2. What about cheating? *(it's not fair to use someone else's thoughts or ideas and pass them off as your own, cheats you out of a fair evaluation of your work)*

3. What are some other behaviors that most people tell you are wrong? *(killing, lying, hitting)*

4. Why do you think those are always wrong? *(involve infringing on other's rights, not character-building activities, can get you in bigger trouble)*

5. When someone says, "Don't you know the difference between right and wrong?" what does he or she mean? *(some things are clearly right or wrong; some things are always considered the right thing to do)*

6. What kind of trouble could someone get into for lying, cheating, or hurting someone else? *(trouble at home, trouble with authorities, could lose a friend, could be responsible for damages)*

7. Why do you think some people choose to do the wrong thing even if they know better? *(thrills, fun, really angry at something, don't think about it)*

Activity

Directions: The student is to put a check mark next to the response that shows the right thing to do in each situation. The situations involve ethical choices—choosing not to lie, cheat, or hurt someone.

Answers: 1. second answer   2. first answer   3. first answer   4. second answer   5. first answer

Follow-up: Discuss why someone might choose the incorrect answer as his or her choice of behavior in each situation. What motive might be involved? *(revenge, fear, embarrassment)* What are the rewards of choosing to do the right thing? Why should anyone choose the right thing if he or she wouldn't get caught or noticed anyhow?

What Is the Right Thing to Do?

Put a check mark next to the right thing to do in each situation below.

1. A boy has been hit on the head on the playground and is knocked out.

   _____ Go after the kid who hit him and beat him up.

   _____ Run for a teacher or adult who can help.

2. Your test is very hard, and you are afraid you won't pass.

   _____ Do your best anyway and keep trying.

   _____ Copy the answers from your friend who sits by you.

3. Your best friend wants you to come over for a birthday party this weekend and you said you would.

   _____ Go to the party.

   _____ Go—unless another friend has a better idea for doing something fun that day.

4. A girl went into the teacher's desk while the teacher was out of the room. The teacher said some money was missing.

   _____ Give the teacher some of your money.

   _____ Tell the teacher what you saw.

5. You said you would bring a favorite drink to school, but you forgot. Now the kids are mad at you.

   _____ Tell them you are sorry and will bring it tomorrow.

   _____ Tell them that your house was robbed last night and the robbers stole the juice.

Copyright © 2009 by John Wiley & Sons, Inc.

8.15 Going for Help

Objective

The student will identify a person or method to alert someone when help is needed in a given situation.

Rationale

Some social situations involve recognizing danger and potentially dangerous conditions. In these situations, students should have some idea of who could help or what they should do to assist.

Thinking Questions

1. What would you do if there was a runaway car going through your neighborhood? *(get out of the way, call the police)*
2. Would you try to jump in the car and stop it yourself? *(no!)*
3. What if you encountered someone who had stopped breathing? What would you do? *(call emergency number, police; some might say they know how to do CPR)*
4. If you encounter a dangerous or emergency situation, who are some people who might be available to help? *(fire department, police, adults nearby)*
5. What are some emergencies that could happen in your neighborhood? *(car accident, fire, broken glass)*
6. What is the emergency procedure in our city for accidents, fires, or need for police? *(review your situation—call 911 or whatever system is in effect)*

Activity

Directions: There are five situations on the worksheet that are potentially dangerous or at least bothersome. Students are to draw a picture depicting how they could go for help or alert someone to the problem.

Answer examples:

1. Call the fire department.
2. Take the little girl to her parents.
3. Tell an adult at the party.
4. Tell a security guard at the mall.
5. Call home from a cell phone or a public phone/walk bikes together to a public place.

Follow-up: Discuss what could happen if someone tried to solve the problem alone. For example, what if Danny tried to put out the fire? Or Rita tried to capture the dog? Discuss why the best first step is to alert someone else to help.

8.15   **Going for Help**

Each character below needs to go for help for some reason. Draw a picture of the way the person could go for help or get help.

1. | Danny saw some smoke coming from an empty building on the way to school.

2. | Rita saw a little girl get bitten by a big black dog in her neighborhood.

3. | Alison is at a party. Her friend is crying because she swallowed something that doesn't taste right. It might be poisonous.

4. | Ricky is walking through the mall parking lot. He comes up to a little boy who is crying because he can't find his mother.

5. | Emma is riding her bike through the park. Her friend rides through some glass and gets a flat tire. They are a long way from home.

Copyright © 2009 by John Wiley & Sons, Inc.

8.16 This Is a Molehill, Not a Mountain

Objective

The student will distinguish between social situations that are important (dangerous, long-lasting, hurtful) and those that are neutral or "not a big deal."

Rationale

If a student is bumped accidentally while standing in line to get a drink, many outcomes are possible. The "bumper" might be attacked; the "bumpee" might fall on the ground requesting an ambulance; or the word "sorry" might be heard, and that's the end of the incident. In general, this would be considered "not a big deal." It was, after all, an accident. However, many students just can't let it go: they blow up a trifle into an argument, have to get somebody back, and the situation continues to escalate. Although it is hard to figure out if a bump was truly an accident or a well-planned sneaky movement, it is best to treat this as a molehill, not a mountain.

Thinking Questions

1. What does this mean: "Don't make a mountain out of a molehill"? *(if something is small and not of consequence, then don't make a big deal about it)*
2. What if someone accidentally bumped into your desk and your book fell off? How could you react? *(just pick up the book, call the person clumsy, knock their book down)*
3. What if you were the person who accidentally knocked the book off? How could you respond? *(pick up the book, apologize, make a joke about it)*
4. What are some examples of irritating things that might bother you that wouldn't bother someone else? *(someone making noises, making faces, tapping on the desk)*
5. How could that irritating thing become a "mountain"? *(you have to retaliate, tell the teacher, shout at the person to quit it)*
6. Why might it be a good idea to ignore the molehills? *(the person will just stop, it's not worth getting excited about)*

Activity

Directions: Here is a list of some things that might happen to you. Which of these are "molehills" (small irritations) and which are "mountains" (large, important events)?

Answers: 1. small   2. large   3. large   4. small   5. small   6. small

Follow-up: Discuss the answers and talk about how a molehill could be made into a mountain. Talk about how what might be a mountain to someone is really just a minor thing. Discuss how some people are very sensitive and what is a molehill to one person might be a mountain to another.

8.16   This Is a Molehill, Not a Mountain

Here is a list of some things that might happen to you. Which of these are "molehills" (small irritations) and which are "mountains" (large, important events)? Write your answer on the line.

1. You left your name off of your spelling paper, and the teacher returned it to you to put your name on it.

   _____

2. You didn't pass your grade-level exam, so now you have to go to summer school.

   _____

3. Your mother is not answering her cell phone, and you don't have a ride home from the basketball game at night.

   _____

4. You forgot to bring your science project to school, so your father has to bring it in later.

   _____

5. Your team lost by one point, but you will play again tomorrow.

   _____

6. You are excited about going down the waterslide, but someone has cut in front of you.

   _____

Copyright © 2009 by John Wiley & Sons, Inc.

8.17 Teasing Can Be Funny

Objective

The student will identify situations in which teasing another person is appropriate.

Rationale

Sometimes teasing can be a show of affection, of camaraderie, of being part of an inside joke. On these occasions, teasing is appropriate if both parties view it as such. Making up nicknames, referring to embarrassing moments, and laughing at yourself are examples of ways that teasing can be appropriate.

Thinking Questions

1. Who here has a nickname? What is it, and how did you get it? (*ask for examples*)
2. Can you think of some celebrities or sports people who have nicknames? (*The Rock, The Fridge*)
3. Why is it funny for someone who is a huge wrestler to be called "Tiny"? (*because it is so different from what he really is*)
4. Can you give an example of when someone might have teased you in a nice way? (*calling my teacher "Mom" by mistake and having my friend laugh with me; scoring a goal with eyes closed— "you should go pro!"; falling down—"your name must be 'Grace'"*)
5. Does it hurt your feelings when someone teases you like that? Why? (*no, because you know they really like you and aren't making fun of you*)
6. Have you ever made a mistake and then had other people laugh *with* you about it? Explain. (*ask for examples*)
7. When someone teases in a nice way, how does that make you feel? (*that the person really likes you, that your mistakes aren't that important*)

Activity

Directions: How is someone teasing in a nice way in each example on the worksheet?

Answers: 1. giving a nickname 2. laughing about a mistake 3. laughing about the way you look 4. doing a playful trick

Follow-up: Discuss why each of the examples is teasing but not intended to hurt feelings. Discuss the benefits of being teased in this way. You may want to have everyone in the class come up with a nickname that they would like to be called.

8.17   **Teasing Can Be Funny**

How is someone teasing in a nice way in each example below?

1.

2.

Understanding Social Situations

Copyright © 2009 by John Wiley & Sons, Inc.

Copyright © 2009 by John Wiley & Sons, Inc.

8.18 Teasing Can Be Mean

Objective

The student will identify situations in which teasing another person is inappropriate.

Rationale

Teasing has a dark side. When someone is teasing but not in jest, or when the taunt hits close to something sad or hurtful, it ceases to be funny. If someone is sensitive about a personal issue (hair color, weight, family life), this is not a permissible area to be funny or sarcastic. Students need to be able to understand the social situation. Is this an appropriate time, situation, or person for teasing? If the intent is hurtful or if the reaction is hurt or sadness, then it is inappropriate.

Thinking Questions

1. There are times when teasing is playful and fun, but also times when it can be mean and hurtful. Even if you think you're being funny, if the person you are teasing is hurt or offended by what you say, then you should not do it. Can you think of any examples when someone might be hurt by teasing? *(if that person is fat, thin, poor, grieving, part of a racial/ethnic group, new to the group)*

2. Let's say there's a really skinny boy with the nickname "Toothpick." Why do you think he might not like that nickname? *(he can't help the way he looks, he wants to be known for more than what he looks like)*

3. Let's say "Toothpick" doesn't mind being called that; in fact, he likes it. How would you know it's okay to call him that? *(he would give permission, say something like "everyone calls me that," some kind of affirmation)*

4. How would someone feel if he always came in last in a race and you called him "Speedy" or if someone couldn't spell very well and you called her "Brain"? How could that be hurtful? *(it emphasizes the things they can't do)*

5. How could it be hurtful if you played a trick on someone, such as telling him that someone famous was coming to see him or that everyone was getting free tickets to something important? *(he would get his hopes up and then feel stupid if he acted as though he believed you; again, it is making someone feel badly)*

Activity

Directions: How is someone teasing in a mean way in the examples on the worksheet?

Answers: 1. making fun of something physical   2. playing a prank that makes the person feel stupid   3. giving a mean nickname   4. implying that a person isn't in the "smart" group

Follow-up: Discuss how the teasing in the examples is hurtful to someone. Discuss the importance of knowing how a person reacts when you determine whether or not it is inappropriate teasing. For example, if the boy with freckles doesn't mind being teased, then it might be an opportunity to connect or develop a friendship with the boy. But always be sure to try to read the social situation correctly so that you aren't hurting someone inadvertently!

Copyright © 2009 by John Wiley & Sons, Inc.

8.18 Teasing Can Be Mean

How is someone teasing in a mean way in the examples below?

1.

2.

8.18 Teasing Can Be Mean (continued)

3.

4.

Understanding Social Situations

Copyright © 2009 by John Wiley & Sons, Inc.

8.19 Appropriate Behavior for a Particular Place

Objective

The student will describe appropriate behavior for given settings.

Rationale

It might be okay to yell on the playground but not during a social studies test. It's fine to sing during music class but not during a fire drill. It's great to be quiet in a house of worship but not when you are leading a pep rally. Part of understanding social situations is recognizing what types of behavior are appropriate for specific settings.

Thinking Questions

1. When is it okay to be really loud and yell? *(on the playground, at a football game, when you are doing cheers)*

2. What are some occasions during which you should be quiet? *(at a funeral, during a prayer, during a test, when the teacher is talking)*

3. When is it okay to laugh? *(when you are at the movies, when you are watching a funny show on TV, when a friend tells a funny joke)*

4. When might you get yelled at for laughing? *(when someone is giving a demonstration, when someone is trying to listen carefully, when you are being mean to someone)*

5. How do you know when you are supposed to be loud, or quiet, or laughing? *(it all depends on the situation)*

6. If you aren't sure how you are supposed to act or handle a situation, what do you think is the best thing to do? *(be quiet and observe others, proceed carefully)*

Activity

Directions: List an appropriate behavior for each setting; then list an inappropriate behavior for each setting.

Answers: Answers will vary.

Follow-up: Have students share their favorite response. Discuss why a particular behavior is or is not appropriate for each setting.

8.19   Appropriate Behavior for a Particular Place

List an appropriate behavior for each place. Then list an inappropriate behavior for each setting.

1. **A hallway during a fire drill**

    Appropriate _____

    Not Appropriate _____

2. **On the sidelines during a soccer game**

    Appropriate _____

    Not Appropriate _____

3. **During a math test in the classroom**

    Appropriate _____

    Not Appropriate _____

4. **Painting in art class**

    Appropriate _____

    Not Appropriate _____

5. **Having a police officer talk about bike safety**

    Appropriate _____

    Not Appropriate _____

Copyright © 2009 by John Wiley & Sons. Inc.

8.20 Hints That You Are Doing Okay

Objective

The student will list at least four hints that confirm his or her behavior is appropriate at a given time.

Rationale

It takes only a moment or a small gesture to affirm students in their appropriate behavior. Finally! They get it! Affirming students' behavior can be as simple as a wink, a head nod, a thumbs-up, a quiet "Yes!" or any of a number of other hints. Teaching students to recognize these hints and giving them opportunities to respond to them can be a means of communication that they are doing a good job with their behavior. It is always nice for students to receive positive feedback that they are on the right track.

Thinking Questions

1. When a player makes a touchdown in football, how does the crowd (for his team) react? *(clap, cheer)*

2. How do you think that makes the player feel? *(great!)*

3. When you do something that makes your teacher or parents proud, how do they react? *(pat on the back, say "good job," take you out for ice cream)*

4. How does it make you feel when you are told that you're doing something really well? *(happy, proud of self)*

5. What are some ways that a person can let another person know that she is doing a good job? Here are some clues: something with your eyes *(wink)*; something with your thumb *(thumbs-up)*; something with your head *(nod)*; something with your hands *(clap)*; something with your voice *("attaboy", "good job")*. Can you think of others? *(hand pumping, fist bumping, chest bumping)*

6. Do you and your parents or a special friend have a secret code that means "good job" that you use with each other? Do you have a special way of communicating something with each other? *(answers will vary)*

Activity

Directions: Let's see if you can come up with different ways that people could signal each other to say "good job."

Answers: Answers will vary.

Follow-up: Have your class develop its own special signal of affirmation for each other. It could be a hand signal, some kind of movement, something that is unique to your class. Whether you use it for a day, a week, or for the entire year, students can use it to get the message that they are part of a group of students who are doing something right.

8.20   **Hints That You Are Doing Okay**

Let's see if you can come up with different ways that people could signal each other to say "good job." The first three will get you started.

1. A round of applause: students clap by moving their hands in a big circle
2. Two thumbs up; put up one thumb, put up the other thumb, shake them together
3. Wink; make eye contact, give a quick wink

_____

_____

_____

_____

_____

_____

_____

_____

_____

_____

_____

_____

_____

_____

_____

Copyright © 2009 by John Wiley & Sons, Inc.

Classroom Tips for Understanding Social Situations

- Before you go to the gym, attend a school play in another classroom, or go to an assembly, discuss expectations. Make predictions as to what will happen. After the event, go through your list. Was the event predictable? Did planning ahead for it make things go more smoothly?

- Plan a surprise party for your assistant or someone else you know well who is connected with your classroom. Discuss how lack of expectations is the key to having a good surprise. Show how taking away the clues of predicting makes the event a surprise.

- When someone is unnecessarily rude in conversation, ask for an immediate rephrasing of the response. "Could you try that again?" or "I'm sure you didn't mean that the way it sounded; would you like to repeat that?" might be ways to alert the speaker to be more polite.

- Modified assertiveness training might be helpful for some of the meeker students who are continually taken advantage of by others. Working in small groups, perhaps with the assistance of the counselor as coach, have students practice standing up for themselves, saying "no" appropriately, and sticking up for each other.

- Have a Disability Awareness week in your class, emphasizing how people with disabilities can compensate and achieve great things. Read stories of athletes with disabilities who have been successful in sports, share articles about devices invented to help people with disabilities function better, and invite a guest speaker who might be willing to talk about his or her disability with the students.

- Invite speakers who are from other countries or who have ties to another country to come in and talk about their customs, language, schools, and games.

- Make a tape recording of speakers demonstrating various tones of voice. Speakers could be in the midst of an argument or cheering at a ball game, for example. Have students use the clues to figure out what the speaker's mood is and where the speaker is at the time. Use comedy if appropriate.

- Cut out magazine pictures showing facial expressions. Have students write appropriate (even comical) captions to go with the expressions.

- Set up mini-debates: students have thirty to sixty seconds to make a point about an issue, and then others with a different view make their points. The topics should be simple: The Best Pet, The Most Important Holiday, A Great Meal. It is more important that students make good points and are clear in their presentation than what their choices truly are. Have other students in the audience discuss which side was more convincing, and why.

- When you are in either an especially good or a down mood, explain to your students how you are feeling and why (if appropriate). Give them a chance to learn to respect your feelings by allowing them to see how you are feeling. Show them you appreciate their concern. Respect is reciprocal; ask them to alert you to their moods or a particularly bad day that they are having. Communicate.

- During reading, stop often to reflect how the character in the story is probably feeling at that moment. Students may enjoy keeping a diary for a few days as a favorite character. What would Little Red Riding Hood be thinking about after her first visit with the wolf? Would Goldilocks be worried about breaking the chairs? Create an awareness of feelings in others.

- Collect newspaper articles about local events that illustrate right and wrong. Perhaps there are some local heroes who helped someone out, as well as a few who got caught for hurting someone else or destroying property. What would a student court decide as a sentence for the destruction? What penalties were given?

- If appropriate, discuss the Code of Hammurabi (king of Babylon), an ancient system of legal codes. How would his system work today?

- Have students write creative stories with the general theme of "Emergency"! Although the story can be fictional, have students show how an emergency situation could be handled correctly in the story. They may have to do some research to be accurate (What's the treatment for rabies? How do firefighters put out a fire? What do you do if someone swallows cleaning fluid?)

- Help students recognize the difference between teasing as a pleasant experience versus teasing to show meanness by watching clips from television shows. Have students identify which type of teasing they are viewing and note the response of the person who is being teased.

- Select a "Hint of the Week" for students to pick and practice. Teach students to encourage each other by developing a signal that they can share with each other to affirm positive social skills.

Chapter 9

Positive Personality Attributes

9.1   Developing Interests and Hobbies

Objective

The student will identify at least five interests or hobbies of importance to himself or herself.

Rationale

Part of what we share with each other is things about ourselves that make us interesting or unique. Having a hobby or spending time pursuing our own interests are ways that we can develop our own personalities. This lesson encourages students to explore new interests as well as to identify current areas that are important to them.

Thinking Questions

1. What is a hobby? *(something that you spend time doing for enjoyment, a favorite activity)*
2. What are some examples of hobbies that people might have? *(golfing, collecting things, painting)*
3. What are some examples of things that people might collect? *(shells, rocks, stuffed animals, baseball cards)*
4. Why do you think it is important to have hobbies and interests? *(makes you an interesting person, might lead to new friends, can learn a lot about something you are particularly good at)*
5. How could you go about learning a new hobby or getting involved in something new that interests you? *(look for classes, do some reading, talk to people, visit a library or museum)*
6. Have you ever been in a situation where you thought you wouldn't be interested in doing something or trying something but after you did, you were hooked? Tell about it. *(ask for anecdotes)*
7. What good things could come about from trying new things? *(find out you're really good at something, meet new people)*

Activity

Directions: Students are to check at least five items from the list on the worksheet (including ideas of their own) that they are interested in.

Answers: Answers will vary.

Follow-up: Have students share their ideas and hobbies with the class. What discoveries did they make about each other and themselves? Who had an unusual interest or hobby? What experiences did they have with a certain hobby or activity?

9.1   # Developing Interests and Hobbies

Here is a list of some things that you might be interested in doing or learning more about. Add your own ideas to the list. Then check five that you are most interested in.

❑ playing softball

❑ playing basketball

❑ collecting coins

❑ training dogs

❑ painting

❑ reading books

❑ riding a bike

❑ putting on a play

❑ writing stories

❑ swimming

❑ cooking

❑ making things out of clay

❑ sewing

❑ doing cross-stitch

❑ riding horses

❑ archery

❑ bowling

❑ playing piano

❑ _____

❑ _____

Copyright © 2009 by John Wiley & Sons. Inc.

Positive Personality Attributes   **331**

9.2 Being Patient with Others

Objective

The student will identify characters on the worksheet who are exhibiting patience with someone else.

Rationale

A nice personality attribute in others is patience, whether it is with circumstances or with others. If students want to be well on the road to getting along with others, the virtue of patience is well worth developing.

Thinking Questions

1. How do you feel when you're in a big hurry and you have to wait for someone to find his or her shoes or make a phone call? *(impatient, angry)*

2. What are some times that you can remember when you were very impatient with someone? *(ask for anecdotes)*

3. Can you control how fast other people move or what other people are doing all the time? *(no)*

4. When you find yourself being impatient and you can't do anything about it, what are things you could do? *(do something else, talk to someone, tell the person that you are in a hurry and to be ready next time, try to calm down)*

5. If someone is making you impatient and feels badly about it, what could you say or do to let the person know that it's okay? *(tell them it's okay, help them do whatever is keeping them busy, act as if it doesn't bother you)*

6. How do you feel when you are the one who is making someone late or frustrated? *(frustrated also, afraid the other person will be angry)*

Activity

Directions: There are eight situations on the worksheet that depict students in situations involving another person. The student is to circle the characters on the worksheet who are showing patience with someone else.

Answers: Circle: Carla, Liz, Joanne, Brian

Follow-up: Discuss the circumstances in each of the situations on the worksheet. How did the impatient people come across to the students? How did the patient people handle the situations and turn the inconvenience into something positive?

Name _____ Date _____

9.2   Being Patient with Others

Which of these students is being patient or trying to be patient with someone else? Circle the names of those being patient.

Copyright © 2009 by John Wiley & Sons, Inc.

9.3 Being a Good Sport

Objective

The student will write an appropriate comment to show that the character is being a good sport in frustrating situations.

Rationale

It is hard to be a good sport in situations that are disappointing, difficult, or annoying. People who show good sportsmanship, however, are much nicer to compete with and probably end up having a better experience. In this lesson, students are given the opportunity to demonstrate good sportsmanship by writing comments that indicate acceptance of the disappointing outcome.

Thinking Questions

1. Have you ever played a game of basketball or football and lost the game by only one point? How did that make you feel? *(angry, sad, frustrated)*

2. What are ways to show that you are a good sport, even if you or your team loses a game? *(congratulate the other players, don't say bad things about the other team, don't blame the referees)*

3. What are some ways that people show poor sportsmanship? *(just the opposite of the above answers)*

4. What are some situations, besides playing sports or games, that might make someone feel like being a bad sport about something? *(not getting a grade you thought you deserved, losing a contest, being caught doing something you are embarrassed about)*

5. When you show good sportsmanship, how does that affect you and other people? *(you—makes you a better person, shows good judgment; others—sets a good example, contributes to good mood, shows you are a good competitor)*

Activity

Directions: Students write comments that reflect good sportsmanship in the situations on the worksheet.

Answer examples: 1. We'll win next time!   2. I'll send Alison a card anyway.   3. I'll thank my uncle for the gift.   4. I'll just pay the fine without complaining.   5. I guess you're the faster runner, Tim.

Follow-up: Discuss how good sportsmanship applies to all sorts of situations, not just sports. How does being a good sport in the situations help the person out, even if he or she must accept the disappointment?

9.3   **Being a Good Sport**

What could these people say in these situations to show that they are good sports?

1. Joe's basketball team lost by one point.

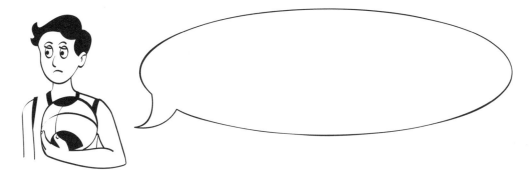

2. Mary is the only girl in her class who wasn't invited to Alison's birthday party.

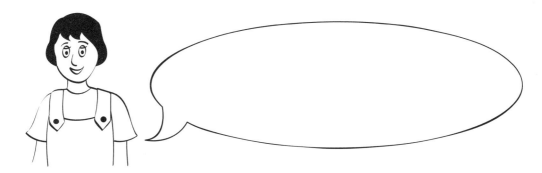

3. Jack wanted a game for Christmas from his uncle, but instead he got a shirt and a tie.

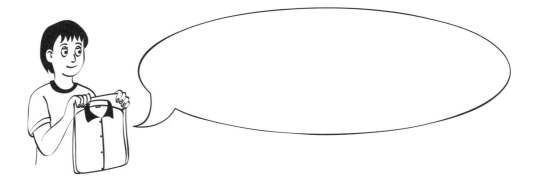

Copyright © 2009 by John Wiley & Sons, Inc.

Positive Personality Attributes

9.3 Being a Good Sport (continued)

4. Catherine forgot her library book and had to pay a fine. Her little brother had hidden it from her.

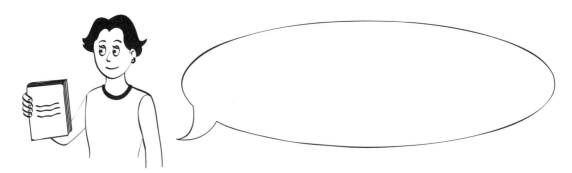

5. Both Tim and Lisa want to sit in the front of the sports car, but Tim got there first and won't move.

Copyright © 2009 by John Wiley & Sons. Inc.

Positive Personality Attributes

9.4 Don't Exaggerate

Objective

The student will explain why an exaggeration is inappropriate and reword a comment in a clearer way.

Rationale

Communication is important when expressing an idea, reporting an event, or describing a situation. When students exaggerate, it's difficult to figure out precisely what is going on and what is important. Students must realize what an exaggeration is and why it is not helpful when clear information is important.

Thinking Questions

1. Have you ever known anyone who had a tiny injury, such as a bump or little cut, and acted as if someone should call an ambulance? What did you think of that? *(silly, maybe funny, annoying)*

2. Have you ever heard of someone trying to get somebody else in trouble by stretching the truth just a little bit? Explain. *(saying that someone hit harder than they did, did more damage than actually was done)*

3. What does it mean to exaggerate? *(go beyond the truth, make up something that is bigger, worse, more sensational)*

4. Why would people exaggerate when they are talking about how good they are at something? *(they want to make it sound as though they are really athletic or smart; perhaps they want attention)*

5. How does it make you feel when someone stretches the truth a lot? *(you don't really believe the person anyway, wonder why the person can't tell the truth)*

6. If you saw an accident, why would you want someone to explain what happened clearly, and not by exaggerating? *(you want the facts, you want to know how bad something really is)*

Activity

Directions: The children on the worksheet are exaggerating quite a bit! Can you reword what they are saying to make it clear and true?

Answer: 1. "I cut my finger."   2. "The high school kids are pretty big."   3. "The principal told me to please pick up the trash."   4. "Three other people scored points."   5. "It took me about an hour to do my homework last night."

Follow-up: Discuss the difference between exaggerating to be untruthful and annoying versus embellishing to make a good story. Colorful language is wonderful, especially in writing. This might be a good opportunity to talk about fiction and nonfiction.

Name _____ **Date** _____

9.4   **Don't Exaggerate**

These children are exaggerating quite a bit! Reword what they are saying to make it clear and true.

1. "I have a horrible paper cut! I don't think I can write with that hand! Look! I'm bleeding all over!"

_____

_____

_____

2. "I had to walk past the high school kids, and they were all at least ten feet tall, and they looked really mean"

_____

_____

_____

3. "The principal screamed at me for about an hour because I dropped one little banana peel on the lunchroom floor."

_____

_____

_____

Copyright © 2009 by John Wiley & Sons, Inc.

9.4 Don't Exaggerate (continued)

4. "I was the only player who did anything for our team! It was like I was out there by myself!"

_____

_____

_____

5. "I slaved over that homework practically ALL NIGHT."

_____

_____

_____

Copyright © 2009 by John Wiley & Sons, Inc.

9.5 Thinking of Others

Objective

The student will identify situations that show consideration for someone else.

Rationale

A positive personality attribute is the ability to show consideration for others—to put the needs of others first, even if yours must wait. This lesson gives students examples of being considerate.

Thinking Questions

1. If you and a friend were out running in the heat and were both thirsty, how would you decide who got to drink from the water fountain first? (*first one there, might let the friend go first, might decide who was thirstier*)

2. What if another person heading for the water fountain was holding his throat and choking and coughing? Who would go first? (*probably the person in distress*)

3. Why is it nice to let someone else go first if he or she is in pain or in a hurry? (*the other person's needs are very important to them, might be a more critical situation*)

4. What does it mean if someone says you are very considerate? (*you consider—or think about—other people*)

5. What are some ways that you could think about other people's needs before your own at home? school? the community? (*pick up your room/be quiet when someone is working/don't litter*)

Activity

Directions: The students are to check each example that shows consideration of someone else's needs or situation.

Answers: Check marks: 1, 2, 4, 6, 8, 10

Follow-up: Discuss how consideration was shown in each of the examples. How was the other person put first in each case? In the examples of inconsiderate behavior, what could have been done to show thinking of someone else first?

9.5   Thinking of Others

Which of these behaviors show that you are thinking about someone else's needs? Put a check mark by each answer.

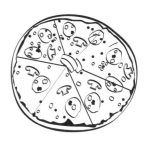

_____ 1. You let Pete go ahead of you in line for a drink because you know he is in a bigger hurry than you are.

_____ 2. It's your mother's birthday, and you made her a special card.

_____ 3. You want to go out for pizza for dinner, so you make sure everyone knows what you want to do.

_____ 4. Your cousin is staying for a week. You find out what she likes to do so it will be a fun time.

_____ 5. The bathroom is a mess! You make sure your mother knows so she can clean it up for you.

_____ 6. Your sister has a flat tire on her bike. You pump it up with air for her.

_____ 7. You have to get up earlier than anyone else in your family to catch the bus. You make a lot of noise so someone else will wake up and keep you company.

_____ 8. It's time to change the bedding in the guinea pig's cage. It's Joshua's turn, but you know he has not been feeling well, so you take care of it.

_____ 9. You are tired after playing tennis, so you put your tennis racquet on the kitchen table instead of in the hall closet.

_____ 10. You are really good at jumping rope all by yourself. Your friend wants to double-jump. You don't really want to, but you know she likes to jump with you.

Copyright © 2009 by John Wiley & Sons, Inc.

9.6 Being a Good Leader

Objective

The student will identify leadership qualities in a person as someone who steers a group in a positive or helpful direction.

Rationale

If we start with the premise that a leader is someone who directs the activities or thinking of the group, then we would expect a good leader to be someone who leads others in a positive direction. Someone might be particularly good at getting the group to follow some bad advice and get them in trouble, and although the leadership might be effective, the end result is not good. Emphasize that a good leader steers the group toward an end result that is positive and helpful to everyone.

Thinking Questions

1. Who are some people you can think of who are good leaders? *(principal, captain of sports teams, class leaders)*

2. Why is that person a good leader? *(helps others out, makes good decisions, listens to everyone in the group)*

3. How would you feel about someone who was a good leader and got everyone to follow him or her, but everyone ended up in trouble? *(angry, wouldn't want to follow them again)*

4. Is someone a good leader if he or she can get everyone to do what they want, but duck out or disappear when the group gets in trouble? *(no)* Why or why not? *(the leader should stick with the group, not abandon them; otherwise, the leader is just using them)*

5. What could we use as a definition of a good leader? *(someone who is good at leading and leads toward good or positive results)*

Activity

Directions: The student is to select the character from each pair who is demonstrating good leadership in each situation. Remind students of the definition of a good leader.

Answers: 1. second student   2. first student   3. first student   4. second student

Follow-up: Discuss the possible outcome of each situation if the first person's advice was followed, and then under the leadership of the second. How does this help decide who is the good leader?

Positive Personality Attributes

Name _____ Date _____

9.6

Being a Good Leader

Circle the student in each pair who is being a good leader.

Copyright © 2009 by John Wiley & Sons, Inc.

Positive Personality Attributes

9.7 Being a Good Follower

Objective

The student will take direction from another student-leader in a group activity.

Rationale

It is fun for students to pretend to be "the teacher," but frustrating when they quickly realize that the other children aren't paying attention to them for more than a few moments. As we do more and more with small groups, it is important for students to assume leadership abilities. Teaching peers is an excellent way for students to gain self-confidence and master the material they teach as well. Other students in the group, however, need to respect that leadership. Someday it may be their turn.

Thinking Questions

1. What are some activities that we do that only the teacher can lead? (*introducing a new math lesson, giving a spelling test, reading the announcements*)

2. What are some activities that students can lead? (*helping with the lunch count, weather report, show and tell, being line leader*)

3. When one of the students is the leader, how should the other students act? (*respectfully, do what the student-leader says*)

4. Why do you think it's hard to follow the instructions of a student rather than the teacher? (*a student might make mistakes, can't really keep you in from recess*)

5. Why do you think it might be important to learn to follow the leader's directions, even if it is a student and not the teacher? (*the teacher has given that student a job to do, it shows respect to others, I will want them to do what I say when it's my turn to be the leader*)

Activity

Directions: The children on the worksheet have a student showing them what to do. Which one in each pair is being a good follower?

Answers: 1. second one   2. first one   3. second one   4. first one

Follow-up: Have the class come up with a list of common class activities in which they can take turns being the leader. Work on developing student leadership skills by preparing the leader and giving the followers opportunities to be respectful and compliant.

Name _____ **Date** _____

9.7   **Being a Good Follower**

These children all have a student showing them what to do. Circle the one in each pair who is being a good follower.

Copyright © 2009 by John Wiley & Sons, Inc.

1.

2.

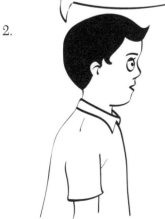

3.

4.

Copyright © 2009 by John Wiley & Sons, Inc.

9.8 Admiring and Complimenting Others

Objective

The student will provide examples of statements that show admiration for another person.

Rationale

There's nothing like getting a sincere compliment to help a friendship grow. This lesson gives students opportunities to think of appropriate compliments to give others in typical situations.

Thinking Questions

1. Has anyone ever admired you for something? Tell about it. *(ask for examples)*
2. Why does it feel good to have someone give you a compliment? *(emphasizes the good things about you, shows that someone noticed you)*
3. Do you think it is hard or easy to give compliments to others? *(sometimes hard if you don't know the other person well; others might be easy if they are good at doing many things)*
4. Is there anyone who wouldn't like to be admired or complimented sometimes? *(maybe someone who was very shy and didn't want attention)*
5. If someone does something that you admire, how could you let her know without embarrassing her or calling a lot of attention to her if she is shy? *(say it quietly, find the right time and place, be sincere)*

Activity

Directions: Students write an example of what they could say in the given situations to express admiration or a sincere compliment.

Answer examples: 1. "You did a nice job." 2. "You played really well last night." 3. "I like your drawings. Could I see some more?" 4. "You've got a great bike." 5. "You're a good speller, Dottie!" 6. "Good luck tonight, Miguel!"

Follow-up: Discuss how a good compliment avoids calling attention to anything bad. For example, instead of mentioning that Amanda only messed up once, don't mention the mistake at all. Share ideas for making sincere, appropriate compliments in these examples.

9.8   **Admiring and Complimenting Others**

What is a compliment you could give or something nice you could say to each of the following people? Write what you could say.

1. Amanda played a piano selection in front of the class. She messed up only once.

   _____

   _____

2. Ricardo caught a touchdown pass in the game last night. The team won the game!

   _____

   _____

3. Shelley is really shy. You know that she is a really good artist from the sketches all over her notebook.

   _____

   _____

4. Mike got a new mountain bike.

   _____

   _____

5. Dottie won the spelling bee for her class.

   _____

   _____

6. Miguel is the fastest runner in the whole school. He will be in the track meet after school.

   _____

   _____

Copyright © 2009 by John Wiley & Sons. Inc.

9.9 Apologizing and Accepting the Blame

Objective

The student will identify characters who are sincerely accepting the blame or apologizing for a given situation.

Rationale

Another quality that we admire about others is the ability to admit when they are wrong and accept the blame. Consider this in contrast to someone who believes that he or she is never wrong, never guilty of anything, always looking for someone else to pin the problem on. There is no disgrace in admitting to have done something wrong, especially when you are willing to make amends.

Thinking Questions

1. Have you ever been in a situation in which your parents or some other adult made you apologize to someone even though you felt you had done nothing wrong? Tell about it. *(ask for anecdotes)*

2. How did that make you feel? Were you really sorry? *(probably not)*

3. Why do you think people expect other people to apologize for making a mistake? *(it's polite, lets the other person know that you realize you made a mistake, shows that you were concerned about what happened)*

4. Even if someone says, "I'm sorry," can you tell if that person is sincerely sorry about what happened? *(look for facial expression, what the person does about the problem)*

5. Why is it important to accept the blame if you are in a situation in which you did something wrong? *(shows that you are mature, responsible enough to admit to doing something wrong, takes the blame off of someone else who might be blamed)*

Activity

Directions: Students are to decide whether they think the character who is apologizing is truly sorry and accepting the blame or not. They are to write YES or NO on the lines.

Answers: 1. no   2. yes   3. yes   4. no   5. no   6. no   7. yes   8. no

Follow-up: Discuss how each of the "no" students handled the situation. What excuses were given? Who was blamed for the problem? How did the "yes" students try to take care of the problem?

9.9   Apologizing and Accepting the Blame

Some of these students are apologizing or accepting the blame for something that they did. Write YES or NO if you think they are sincerely sorry.

Copyright © 2009 by John Wiley & Sons, Inc.

Positive Personality Attributes

9.10 Finishing the Job

Objective

The student will explain what is needed to finish a job.

Rationale

How many kids start something (a project, a story, cleaning out a desk) and then completely abandon it after only a few minutes? It seems as though finishing the job is a difficult task. This is true even in social settings. Can a student finish a conversation or follow through on a promise to do something for a friend? People who do not follow through on their tasks tend to let friends down.

Thinking Questions

1. How would you feel if you asked a friend to help you with a puppet show, and after helping you for about ten minutes, after you got everything out and made all your plans, the friend said he was bored and left? (*I'd feel mad, let down, angry about having to pick everything up*)

2. Have you ever had a friend over and after playing for awhile, your mom said that you had to clean up everything? And then your friend decided he needed to go home and you were stuck with cleaning up? Has that ever happened to you? (*undoubtedly*)

3. What if you were planning a party for someone and there were all kinds of plans made, but when it came time to actually get everything and do everything, everyone left but you! How would you feel? (*dumped on, like others were lazy*)

4. When you are given a job to do, should you do it until you get tired and then quit? (*no—should do the whole thing*)

5. What if you decide after you get started that you really don't want to do the job—that it isn't fun like you thought it would be? (*if others are depending on you, you should do the job*)

6. What does it mean to be dependable? (*people can count on you*)

7. What does it mean to finish the job? (*work until everything is completely finished*)

8. What if you think the job is finished, but someone else doesn't think so. For example, if your mom says to clean your bedroom and you throw your socks under the bed, did you finish the job? (*no*) Why not? (*the room isn't cleaned up*)

Activity

Directions: Here are some situations in which the children were given a job to do. They did not finish their job. What do they need to do to finish the job?

Answers: 1. put books in their desk, clear off the top of the desk   2. put names on their papers, staple together   3. finish giving the spelling test   4. take turns reading

Follow-up: Keep your eyes out for opportunities to address this skill of finishing the job. There are a lot of self-starters, but those who finish (and finish correctly) are not as plentiful. Be sure to reward good finishers.

9.10   **Finishing the Job**

These children did not finish their job. What does each child need to do to finish the job? Write your answers on the lines.

1.

_____

_____

2.

_____

_____

Copyright © 2009 by John Wiley & Sons, Inc.

          Positive Personality Attributes

3.

4.

Copyright © 2009 by John Wiley & Sons, Inc.

9.11 Thinking Ahead

Objective

The student will identify possible obstacles to completing an activity and take steps to prevent them.

Rationale

Having a clear idea of the outcome of an activity, or what the end is supposed to look like, can be helpful to students in order to plan what they need for the job. For example, if a student is coloring a picture that needs five different colors, it would be efficient to get all five colors at one time rather than make five trips to the crayon box. By thinking of the end first, students should be given the opportunity to work through the job in their mind, which should avert some delays or obstacles and prevent finishing the job. Socially this is also important: students who make promises, plans, or social obligations will be able to follow through by making sure they are able to do what they say they will do.

Thinking Questions

1. Guess what! We're going to have a great big special class party on December 25! Can you all come? *(no—everyone is on Christmas vacation)*

2. Is it a good idea to check the calendar before planning a big party? *(yes)* Why? *(because something you can't change might already be planned)*

3. What if I told you that we can paint the gym bright red but we only have blue paint? Do you see a problem? *(we will have to get some different colored paint)*

4. What if everyone in the class wanted to use a classroom computer to work on a project that had to be done at the end of the day but we have only three computers? How could you think ahead to make sure you got your work done? *(have a sign-up schedule, use the computers by table number, if you see an empty computer use it while it's free)*

5. Let's say that the whole class can play a game at the end of the day if everyone has all of their work done. How could you plan ahead for yourself? *(use time wisely)* How could you think ahead so that the class could get to play the game? *(keep an eye out for those who might need help getting their work done)*

6. Sometimes it is helpful to think about the end first and then make sure you can do everything in between to get the job done. Can you think of some school examples? Maybe things that need to be done by the end of the day? *(certain class assignments, bookbags packed, games put away, change the calendar, clean out the hamster's cage, spend time on the computer)*

7. How could you plan ahead during the day to make sure everything gets done? *(stop every once in a while and check, think about what might go wrong)*

Positive Personality Attributes

Activity

Directions: These students did not plan ahead! What has gone wrong, and what can each do to get back on track?

Answers:

1. ran out of time; stay in for recess and finish
2. wrote too big, wrote in pen, made a lot of mistakes; start over
3. not enough cookies for everyone; break some in half and share
4. the glue wasn't dry; might have to salvage what you can and start over

Follow-up: Start using the phrase "think ahead" when assigning an independent task. Have students identify possible obstacles that they may encounter before beginning. It may be tempting to stop a student when you see that he or she is going off track, but it may be a more valuable lesson for the student to realize he or she didn't think ahead.

9.11   **Thinking Ahead**

These students did not plan ahead! Tell what has gone wrong. Then write one thing that each can do to get back on track to finish the job.

1.

_____

_____

_____

2.

_____

_____

_____

Copyright © 2009 by John Wiley & Sons, Inc.

3.

I thought there were 20 kids in the class, but I forgot about the ones who come only in the afternoon. I only brought 20 cookies and there are 24 kids.

_____

_____

_____

4.

I glued all of my words on the paper, but the glue isn't drying and they all got stuck together.

_____

_____

_____

Copyright © 2009 by John Wiley & Sons, Inc.

9.12 Having a Sense of Humor

Objective

The student will identify which child in each pair is demonstrating a sense of humor in a social situation.

Rationale

Life is full of setbacks, disappointments, and challenges. How we react to these situations says a lot about our character. Responding with a sense of humor helps us regain some control over the situation, helps others feel comfortable, and helps to put a seemingly negative situation into perspective.

Thinking Questions

1. What does "having a sense of humor" mean? (*you try to laugh at something, laugh at yourself, look for something funny about a situation*)

2. What are some things that you should not make jokes about? (*serious things, such as a relative dying, someone getting in trouble, teasing that might be hurtful*)

3. Let's say that a friend tripped in the lunchroom and dropped his tray. How is he probably feeling? (*embarrassed*)

4. What is something that you could say that would show a sense of humor and help lighten the situation? (*"Some people will do anything for attention!" "I didn't like the lunch today either!"—and say this while you are helping the student pick up the spilled food!*)

5. Let's say that someone accidentally thought you were a boy (if you are a girl) and was very sorry and embarrassed about the mistake. How could you make that person feel okay by using a sense of humor? (*"Don't worry; everyone makes that mistake! I really have to get a new hair style!"*)

6. What could you do if someone bumped into your desk and accidentally knocked a puzzle off that you were working on? Maybe you are really angry, but how could showing a sense of humor calm you down too? (*realize that it's not all that important, it's just a puzzle; invite the person to help put it back together*)

Activity

Directions: Which child in each pair is showing a sense of humor in the situation?

Answers: 1. second   2. second   3. first   4. first

Follow-up: Discuss how a sense of humor helps regain control, helps others feel comfortable, and can put things into perspective.

9.12   # Having a Sense of Humor

Circle the child in each pair who is showing a sense of humor in the situation.

1. Eric didn't hear his group leader when he asked him a question, so Eric gave the wrong answer.

2. Someone accidentally stepped on Madison's painting in art class.

Copyright © 2009 by John Wiley & Sons, Inc.

Positive Personality Attributes

3. Ben wasn't looking where he was going and walked into a classmate.

4. Someone drank Orlando's chocolate milk by mistake.

Copyright © 2009 by John Wiley & Sons. Inc.

Classroom Tips for Positive Personality Attributes

- Have an "Interest Fair" in which students can set up a booth displaying their hobbies by using pictures, displaying trophies and ribbons, or books showing something about their hobby. Let students work at their booths for half of the class on one day; then switch and let them be visitors the second day.

- Students can practice being good sports by making it a policy for both teams to slap hands with the other team after a game is played. There is to be no grumbling or arguing over the game; only "nice job" or other words of praise.

- Assign students to think "you first" for a week, allowing someone else to go first or be the recipient of thoughtful behavior. By doing at least one good deed every day for a week, this may become a habit. Encourage students to talk about the rewards that they experienced at the end of the week.

- Research famous political individuals and decide whether they were good leaders. Upper elementary students might be assigned someone from a particular country who has been newsworthy in the past. Based on the outcome of the individual's leadership, would they be considered good leaders?

- Have a wall of compliments. Write examples on colored paper ("Nice job! I like how you did that!") and display them on one wall in your room or the hallway. When someone is at a loss for something complimentary to say, refer him or her to the wall or hall.

- Set a good example for your students by admitting when you make a mistake. It's hard for adults to apologize to a child or take the blame for something when it is deserved. This is the kind of example that really makes an impact on children.

- Have a class day in which everything gets cleaned up and organized. Demonstrate that time spent in organizing things is time well spent. Assign students a buddy to help them check things out to make sure everything's in place.

- As an experiment, give the students all of their written assignments at one time, first thing in the morning. Tell students that they are to come up with a written plan about how they will accomplish all of the tasks. Afterward, discuss how the plan worked. Is it easier for some to have the whole picture and chip away at tasks, or do some children do better by being given small doses of assignments with lots of teacher support? Discuss how the day went. Some very well-organized students may want to do it this way all the time.

- Call attention to students who are demonstrating a good sense of humor at the moment that they display this trait. Explain that even though such-and-such happened, the student showed a good attitude and was able to laugh or make a funny comment that was totally appropriate.

Chapter 10

Getting Along with Others at Home

10.1 Obeying Parents

Objective

The student will identify characters who are complying with a request from a parent.

Rationale

Obedience—or lack thereof—is at the heart of many social problems. A first step toward learning obedience is acknowledging the command or order; the next is deciding to comply. Parents make many requests of children every day, and the child's response may depend on his or her mood, appetite, choice of activities, time of day, or even learned negativism. One lesson will not teach a child to become obedient. This lesson addresses the student's ability to identify obedience on the worksheet in common examples.

Thinking Questions

1. What are some orders or requests that your parents give you at home? (*pick up clothes, don't yell, wipe your feet*)

2. What do your parents expect you to do when they ask you to do something? (*do it, obey*)

3. Why do you think your parents like it when you obey them? (*shows that you can follow directions, shows respect to them, makes their job easier*)

4. Have your parents ever asked you to do things you didn't want to do? (*probably*)

5. What happened when you didn't obey? (*got in trouble, some sort of punishment, was ignored*)

6. Why do your parents ask you to do things? (*want you to learn how to do something, learn how to work, do your share*)

7. Have your parents ever asked you to do something that would put you in danger or hurt you? (*the hoped-for answer is "no"*)

8. Why is it a good idea to obey your parents? (*they know more than you, shows respect, it is expected*)

Activity

Directions: The worksheet shows six examples of children who have been given requests by their parents. Based on the drawings and comments, the children are or are not obeying their parents. Students are to circle the ones who are and put an X through the ones who are not.

Answers: Circle: 1, 3, 5; X: 2, 4, 6

Follow-up: Discuss the potentially harmful or dangerous consequences that could occur by the child's disobedience in these circumstances (*sister could get in trouble if left alone at home; an unfastened seat belt could result in a severe injury in an accident*). In the less serious instances, why is it important to good family functioning for the children to comply with the request? (*helps everyone get along with each other, family members share jobs*)

Name _____ Date _____

10.1   **Obeying Parents**

Which of these children are obeying their parents? Circle the children who are; put an X on those who are not.

Copyright © 2009 by John Wiley & Sons, Inc.

10.2   Consequences of Disobedience

Objective

The student will identify a likely consequence for a given disobedience.

Rationale

It may be annoying when a child asks, "Why?" or constantly questions an order given by a parent; however, if the child is able to understand how the obedience is beneficial to him or her, it may help the child comply. Nevertheless, "because I said so" is sometimes the only answer that is necessary. In either case, it is important for the child to be able to think through the consequences of not being obedient.

Thinking Questions

1. Have your parents ever asked you to do something that you really didn't want to do? What? *(probably—a distasteful task, something that took a long time)*

2. What happens if you ask, "Why?" after a parent tells you to do something? *(might take time to explain, might tell child to do it without questioning)*

3. Do you always have to know why you are supposed to do something? *(no—in a fire you wouldn't stop to ask questions, you'd just follow instructions to get out)*

4. Why do you think some people don't like to have their orders questioned? *(might be questioned in a haughty way, defiant, might think you are looking for a way out)*

5. How do you think your parents feel when they find out you have been disobedient, especially to another adult? *(probably ashamed, angry, mad!)*

6. Most of the time when you have been disobedient, did it turn out that you regretted it? *(the answer hoped for is "yes")*

Activity

Directions: The children on the worksheet have been disobedient. Students are to draw a picture or write something to show a possible consequence of this disobedience.

Answer examples:

1. Rachel's parents will worry and call the police.
2. Mike will spend the night cleaning out the garage instead of camping.
3. Amy will be late for the bus, looking for her shoes.
4. Andrew will have cold hands and head.
5. The dog will eat the doughnuts.

Follow-up: Discuss the consequences suggested by the students. Were some of the consequences the result of the parent's imposing punishment? Or were the consequences a result of naturally occurring circumstances? Do students think that the only negative consequence to disobedience is getting in trouble with the parents?

10.2   # Consequences of Disobedience

These children have been disobedient to someone or to an order. Draw a picture or write what could happen because of this disobedience.

1. Rachel went to her friend's house after school instead of going straight home.

2. Mike wanted to go on a camping trip overnight, but he didn't clean out the garage like he was supposed to.

3. Amy didn't put her shoes away before going to bed. Her mother told her that the bus would be coming earlier the next day.

4. Andrew's dad told him to wear a hat and mittens to school, but Andrew didn't. Then the snowstorm hit!

5. Tara's grandmother asked her to put the doughnuts on the table where the dog wouldn't get them. Tara didn't.

Copyright © 2009 by John Wiley & Sons, Inc.

10.3 Rules for the House

Objective

The student will list or state at least five rules that apply in his or her house.

Rationale

There are rules at every house, though some are stated more clearly and powerfully than others. Is it acceptable to wear shoes in the living room? Are dirty clothes supposed to be brought to the laundry room? Who takes out the garbage? This lesson focuses on general household rules, as well as specific rules for different sections of the house.

Thinking Questions

1. What are some of the different rooms in a house? *(kitchen, closet, bedroom, bathroom)*

2. What are some rules for each of the different rooms in your house? *(bathroom: flush the toilet, wash your hands)*

3. Why are there different rules for the different rooms? *(each room serves a different purpose, different needs)*

4. Which rooms do you think are the easiest and hardest to take care of? Why? *(ask for opinions— some students may think cleaning is difficult, others may think organizing or sorting is harder)*

5. Do you think the rules for the kitchen are the same in every household? *(somewhat similar perhaps: clean up your own dishes, mop the floor, don't leave the drawers open)*

6. What are some rules for outside the house? *(wipe your feet when you come in, don't leave toys outside)*

7. How does having rules at home help everything get done in a better way? *(people can share the chores, people know what's expected of them, might get an allowance for helping, if no one breaks the rules everyone benefits by having a cleaner house)*

Activity

Directions: Students are to look at the floor plan of the house on the worksheet and write at least one good family rule for each room. This can be expanded to include yard rules, basements, or the garage, depending on the student and the house. The idea is to look for *family* rules, not specific chores for one person.

Answer examples: Front porch—wipe your feet; kitchen—wash hands before eating; bathroom—put a new roll of toilet paper on the holder when necessary.

Follow-up: Expand the rule making by including activities that usually take place in the room, as well as taking care of the room and its furnishings. For example, eating and talking might occur in the kitchen, so rules about having polite conversations during meals and no yelling at the table might be appropriate for the kitchen area.

10.3   **Rules for the House**

Write at least one good rule that you or your family might have for the rooms in the house. Add other buildings (garage, pool house) or places if your family has rules for other areas.

Copyright © 2009 by John Wiley & Sons. Inc.

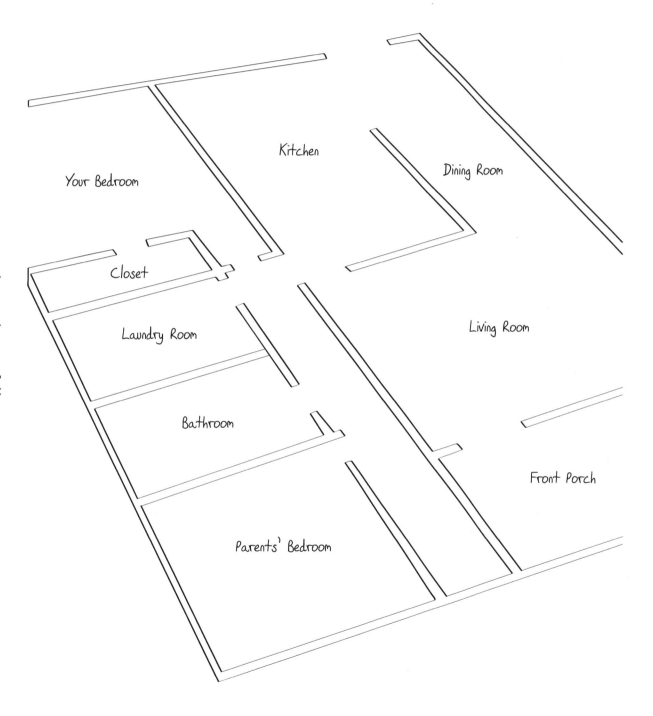

Kitchen

Dining Room

Your Bedroom

Closet

Living Room

Laundry Room

Bathroom

Front Porch

Parents' Bedroom

10.4 My Responsibilities

Objective

The student will identify at least three of his or her chores or responsibilities at home.

Rationale

Every family has plenty of jobs that need to be done. Even young children can be given simple but important responsibilities to do within the household. Some children might have the jobs of making their bed every morning, feeding the dog, or helping to set the table. Others might have to baby-sit for younger siblings or look after an aging grandparent. But each job is important, not only to contribute to helping the family but to help teach responsibility. There is usually always one student who will insist he or she does not have to do anything at home. I would inquire as to who brushes this child's teeth, who dresses this child, and who puts food in this child's mouth. Students quickly realize that "responsibilities" also means things that are necessary for them to do to function, not just typical chores or work activities.

Thinking Questions

1. What are some jobs that you are responsible for in your house? (*cleaning up your room, taking out the trash*)

2. Do you like your jobs? Why or why not? (*answers will vary*)

3. What would happen if you didn't do your job for a week? (*the work would pile up, things would be a mess*)

4. Some people get paid an allowance for doing chores or helping around the house. Do you think this is a good idea, or should people just do things to help out? (*answers will vary*)

5. Do you think it is a good idea that you have some jobs to do at home? (*the hoped-for answer is "yes"*)

6. How does doing your job help the family? (*gives parents time to do other things, teaches you new skills, makes the house look and smell better*)

Activity

Directions: Think about your responsibilities in your home as you go through each part of the day. Try to list at least one responsibility for each time slot.

Answers: Answers will vary.

Follow-up: Talk about the importance to the family of even the seemingly small responsibilities. How does each item affect the other members of the family? What are the consequences of not completing the task or responsibility?

10.4

My Responsibilities

Think about your responsibilities throughout the day. Write down at least one responsibility for each time slot.

First thing in the morning

Example: brush my teeth and put the toothbrush away

Breakfast time

Example: put dirty dishes in the sink

Before I go to school

_____

_____

When I get home from school

_____

_____

Dinnertime

_____

_____

Before I go to bed

_____

_____

Copyright © 2009 by John Wiley & Sons. Inc.

10.5 We All Have Jobs

Objective

The student will identify at least one responsibility for each family member.

Rationale

Ideally each family member will take on responsibilities and chores that help the family function well. Parents often do a lot of things for their children without being recognized or appreciated. Children, too, might be happy to know that their efforts are being noticed and praised. Even young children can do something to help out—perhaps picking up toys or taking a dirty dish to a sink. Cleaning a room is not necessarily a punishment, but something we all need to do once in awhile just to keep track of our shoes and library books.

Thinking Questions

1. What are some responsibilities that you have in your family? *(answers will vary)*
2. Do you do everything in your family, or do other family members help out? *(the hoped-for answer is that everyone in the family does something)*
3. What are some responsibilities that your parents do because you are not old enough or able in some way to do them? *(drive to the store, order things online, take care of the car, use knives)*
4. What are some responsibilities that kids who are a little older than you can do? *(answers will vary)*
5. What are some responsibilities that younger kids can do? *(answers will vary)*
6. Why do you think it is important that everyone in a family has something that they do to help the family? *(share the load, free up time for fun things, learn to be helpful)*
7. If you and your parents switched responsibilities for a day, what would you be doing? Would it be fun or hard? What would your parents say about your jobs? *(answers will vary)*

Activity

Directions: Have students list the members of their immediate family. List at least one responsibility that each person is responsible for.

Answers: Answers will vary.

Follow-up: Families have different ways of organizing themselves and different needs. Talk about how a large family might be different from a very small family. How would having a grandparent living in the home change things? How would having a new baby change things? Discuss the ways that each family member does something helpful.

10.5   # We All Have Jobs

List the members of your family or people in your house. What is one responsibility or job of each person?

Copyright © 2009 by John Wiley & Sons. Inc.

Person   ***Job***

_____   _____

_____   _____

_____   _____

_____   _____

_____   _____

10.6 People Are Busy

Objective

The student will explain the importance of being considerate in social situations involving tight schedules.

Rationale

Adults may be juggling one or two jobs. In addition to their schoolwork, teenagers have sports, school activities, and other social events that take up a lot of time. Younger children have homework, all kinds of lessons, and a lot of activities that they are involved in. It is hard to coordinate all of these schedules because people are busy. To help a family function smoothly during these busy times, it is important to be considerate of other family members by being on time and being flexible when you don't always get your way.

Thinking Questions

1. How many of you have busy parents? What do they do? *(work, go bowling, take care of the house)*

2. How many of you have busy brothers and sisters? What do they do? *(piano lessons, T-ball)*

3. How many of you are busy? What do you do? *(homework, play with friends, take care of the dogs)*

4. With everyone being so busy, do you think there might be times when there is a conflict? What does that mean? *(two things happen at once, too many appointments at the same time)*

5. With a busy life, what are some problems that might happen as far as making it to every game, every party, every activity? *(there might be times when you can't go, might be late)*

6. What are some ways you could get to a game, lesson activity, or appointment if your parents had to work and couldn't get you there? *(ask a neighbor, ask a parent of someone else on your team)*

7. What might happen if your mom or dad was late to pick you up? *(have to wait around, be bored)*

8. What could you do while you are waiting? *(start your homework, talk to friends)*

9. Do your parents ever have to tell you "no" because there is just too much going on? How does that make you feel? *(upset that you can't do things, left out)*

10. Even if you can't get your way, how could you politely discuss this with your parents? *(explain that it is important to you, ask if you can make other arrangements, accept it if it isn't going to happen for you)*

Activity

Directions: Each of these children is in a situation where something is a problem because people are busy. Write what that child could do or say.

Answer examples: 1. I will see my friend another day.   2. I need to go to the dentist so I don't get cavities.   3. I will stay right here and not move so Dad knows where I am.   4. I will make a Halloween card for Grandma.

Follow-up: Have students role-play these situations, showing first how the problem could become a complicated or unhappy event and then showing how the problem could be handled by being considerate.

Name _____ Date _____

10.6   **People Are Busy**

Each of these children wants something to happen, but there is a problem because people are busy. Write what each child could do or say.

Copyright © 2009 by John Wiley & Sons, Inc.

Copyright © 2009 by John Wiley & Sons, Inc.

Getting Along with Others at Home

10.7 Sharing with Siblings

Objective

The student will identify the item or place that is being shared with a sibling in given examples.

Rationale

Most siblings have to share things: toys, parents' time, a bedroom, or even other siblings. Part of getting along at home, especially if the student has brothers and sisters, is finding his or her place among the family by getting along with the other people who reside there. Sharing with others is not often easy, but it is part of being a family.

Thinking Questions

1. What are some things that you might have to share with brothers and sisters at home? *(a bedroom, clothing, toys)*

2. How do you share your parents with brothers and sisters? *(you might talk to them at different times, have them spend time with you at different activities)*

3. Who decides how things get split up among your brothers and sisters? *(parents, perhaps the kids themselves)*

4. Why is it necessary to share things with others at home? *(don't need two or three of everything, too expensive to duplicate, convenient to use same items)*

5. What are some things you could learn by having to share with others at home? *(need to pace yourself, accept rations, learn patience, learn to leave things in good condition)*

Activity

Directions: Students are to read the conversations between siblings and try to figure out what item is being discussed and shared. There are several possible answers to the situations. Have students think of alternative answers for later discussion.

Answer examples: 1. sweater, jacket   2. baseball, mitt   3. bedroom, back of the car   4. a game, toys 5. comic book, book of riddles

Follow-up: Have students share their responses. What clues were given on the worksheet? Why could different answers fit the description?

10.7

Sharing with Siblings

Read each conversation between the brothers and sisters. What is being shared in each situation? Write your answer on the line. There may be several possible answers for each item.

Copyright © 2009 by John Wiley & Sons, Inc.

Getting Along with Others at Home

10.8 Being the Oldest

Objective

The student will identify common characteristics of children who are the oldest of siblings.

Rationale

There are differing responsibilities for children in a family with several siblings. Birth order affects how that child is treated within the family, as well as how the child relates to others. This lesson discusses characteristics or situations common to the oldest child in a family.

Thinking Questions

1. Is anyone here the oldest child in a family? What is it like? *(ask for general comments)*

2. Do you enjoy being the oldest? Why or why not? *(some may like the responsibility and leadership, others may feel that the younger kids get more attention)*

3. What responsibilities might the oldest child have that others in the family wouldn't have? Why? *(watching the younger children, doing more around the house; older children may be more responsible, know how to do things that the younger ones don't)*

4. What might be some drawbacks to being the oldest? *(might not want the responsibility, resent being a leader, no role model to follow among other children in the family)*

5. How is being an only child like being an oldest child? *(there is only one to do chores and take responsibility, this child is the first one in both cases)*

6. Why might it be harder to be the parent of an oldest child? *(the parent is going through parenting for the first time, may make "mistakes" or be unsure how to handle things)*

Activity

Directions: Ten statements are listed on the worksheet. Students are to put a check mark by those that could describe a person who is the oldest in the family. Caution children that these are general statements; their own situations may be quite different, and there will be time to discuss their own experiences.

Answers: Probably 1, 2, 3, 5, 6, 7, 9, 10. Answers will vary depending on each child's experiences.

Follow-up: Discuss students' responses and personal experiences with being the oldest. Each situation may be different in terms of what it truly is like to be the oldest, but look for common threads. Is it different if the oldest is a boy or girl? Are younger siblings treated differently? How and why? Would the older children trade places with someone else in the family who is younger?

10.8   # Being the Oldest

Which of these statements could describe someone who is the oldest in the family? Put a check mark next to each one.

❑ 1. You might have younger children in the family.

❑ 2. You are expected to act grown up and set a good example.

❑ 3. You might have to baby-sit for others in the family.

❑ 4. You are the youngest of the children.

❑ 5. Your parents count on you to be responsible.

❑ 6. You are the first one to get new clothes.

❑ 7. You get to do things that younger children in your family don't get to do.

❑ 8. You have to go to bed before everybody else.

❑ 9. You might be bigger and stronger than the other kids in your family.

❑ 10. You know more about school than the others in your family.

Copyright © 2009 by John Wiley & Sons. Inc.

10.9 Being the Youngest

Objective

The student will identify at least two characteristics common to the youngest child in a family of several siblings.

Rationale

The youngest child in a group of siblings may be the "baby"; he or she may be ignored because there are many others; possibly this child is extremely special because he or she represents the last child who will be born in the family. Being the youngest has perceived advantages and disadvantages, which are discussed in this lesson.

Thinking Questions

1. What is it like having older brothers and/or sisters? *(ask for opinions, examples)*
2. What might be nice about being the youngest in the family? *(may be treated better, spoiled, don't have to do as much work)*
3. Are there things that the youngest might not be allowed to do? What and why? *(handle knives, stay out alone longer, ride a two-wheeled bike in the street—element of danger, lack of skill)*
4. What if you had older brothers or sisters who constantly got into trouble at school? How could that be a problem for the youngest? *(teacher may expect that child to have problems at school too, that this child will have bad examples to follow, indicates family problems)*
5. What if your older siblings were smart and good at everything? Do you think people would expect that of the younger child too? Why? *(probably—we tend to group family traits a lot because they come from the same parents and environment)*

Activity

Directions: The student is to fill in a simple chart by listing ideas about what would be advantageous to being the youngest in the family and then what would be a disadvantage. Clues are given for ideas to start with. Inform the children that you are seeking general responses, though you want them to draw from their own experiences if applicable.

Answer examples: Good things—last to have to go to school, have older brothers and sisters to help you with problems, parents might spend more time with you. Things that are not as good—have to go to bed early, last one to get the clothes (if handed down), perceived as "too little" to do things

Follow-up: Encourage discussion of what it is like to be the youngest in the family. How does it compare to being the oldest? What is it like having older siblings with good or bad reputations? Do they feel that parents treat them differently from the other children in the family? Is it harder or easier to get along with others if you are the youngest? The same?

10.9   **Being the Youngest**

What are some good things about being the youngest? What might be some drawbacks to being the youngest? Fill in your ideas in the "Good" and "Not as Good" columns. Think about bedtime, having pets, going to school, and doing chores, for example.

Good			Not as Good

Copyright © 2009 by John Wiley & Sons. Inc.

10.10 Being in the Middle

Objective

The student will identify at least one unique characteristic of each child on the worksheet.

Rationale

Middle children are not the oldest or the youngest but may have characteristics of both. Especially if there are many children in the family, these children have to be good at handling relationships from both chronological sides. Sometimes they are the "big brother"; other times they must defer to a sibling who is older than they are. Each child is an individual with special characteristics. Middle children in particular may need to recognize their own uniqueness from the others in the group.

Thinking Questions

1. What is it like to be a middle child? Can anyone give some experiences? *(some may enjoy it, others may feel lost or not noticed)*

2. How would being a middle child be similar to being the oldest? youngest? *(oldest: would have others younger than you in the family; youngest: still have older siblings around)*

3. How would being a middle child be different from being the oldest? The youngest? *(oldest: maybe wouldn't have quite as much responsibility as the oldest in the family; youngest: both are treated as younger members of the family, not allowed to do as much)*

4. If there were lots of kids in a family, do you think each one would be special in some way to the parents? *(yes)* How or why? *(because each has different abilities, interests, personality traits)*

5. How would having to get along with lots of children in the family help that person get along in life—at school, when they're grown-up, and around other people? *(getting along means just that— being able to get along with others. That's something that people need to learn to do throughout life. Having siblings means sharing, negotiating, getting attention, and experiencing things together.)*

Activity

Directions: Students are to select one unique quality about the characters who are pictured on the worksheet and write it on the line.

Answers: 1. plays piano   2. has brown hair   3. sings rock and roll   4. drew cartoons that were printed   5. loves animals

Follow-up: Discuss the responses to the worksheet. Besides the distinction for each student on the page, what similarities were given between the character and the other siblings? Do most siblings share some kind of ability? Are physical traits noticeable in families, such as the same hair color, skin color, and height?

10.10   **Being in the Middle**

Being in the middle means you might be compared to other kids in the family, but you are still an individual! What is different or unique about these children? Write your answer on the lines.

1.

> Everyone in my family plays basketball but me. I'm good at playing the piano.

_____

_____

_____

2.

> My brother has red hair and my sister has red hair. But I have brown hair.

_____

_____

_____

3.

> Everyone in my family likes to sing. My two sisters sing in the school choir, but I sing rock and roll with my friends.

_____

_____

_____

4.

> My brother can draw anything. My sister is a real artist. I like to draw, too. I drew some cartoons that got printed in the paper. No one else did that!

_____

_____

_____

5.

> My sister likes animals. My other sister likes animals sort of, but not as much as I do. I love horses and other animals! I collect them and draw them and think about them all the time. I want to work in a zoo!

_____

_____

_____

Copyright © 2009 by John Wiley & Sons. Inc.

Getting Along with Others at Home

10.11 My Parents Are Divorced

Objective

The student will identify ways that situations involving two households can be resolved positively.

Rationale

Students whose parents have divorced or separated have two households to deal with. There may be conflicting rules or procedures, other children in the household, stepparents, and sometimes parents who are not civil to each other. Each case is different, but students who can at least realize some possible difficulties and anticipate some solutions may get along with others at home as much as possible.

Thinking Questions

1. Some of you may come from a family in which there has been a divorce. What are some things that you have to think about or live with when there are two families that you are a part of? *(having new brothers and sisters, living in two houses, not getting to see one parent very often)*

2. Having two households can be difficult in some ways. What might be some hard things about that? *(changing houses on the weekends, having a parent who lives far away, having parents who have different rules)*

3. What are some things that would affect a child if he or she suddenly acquired stepbrothers or stepsisters? *(they might be the same age, might have to share a bedroom, might not like the personality of the kids)*

4. There are other reasons that a family might be split as well. What are they? *(one parent has died, a parent might be in the military and be away on duty, one parent is hospitalized, one parent might be incarcerated)*

5. What are some things that might be difficult for a single parent? *(spending time with the kids, making enough money to support the family, being lonely)*

6. If you are in a divorced or single-parent situation, what are some things that you could do to help the family run smoothly? *(don't complain about sharing, know when to ask your parent questions, don't make your parent feel guilty, try to get along with others)*

7. What are some good things about having a stepparent or stepsiblings? *(the stepparent might be really nice, happy situation at home, more kids to play with)*

Activity

Directions: Here are some situations that might be hard for children who have only one parent or divorced parents. How could each child help get along at home?

Answers: 1. offer to do chores   2. send pictures and letters   3. make two pictures—one for each parent   4. don't play one parent against the other, follow the rules   5. make room for new siblings

Follow-up: It is not the child's fault that his or her parents are divorced or separated. It is not the child's fault that a parent is not in his or her life because of life events. Reassure children in this situation that they still have many adults who care for them.

10.11   **My Parents Are Divorced**

How could each of the following children help get along at his or her home?
Write your answer on the lines.

1. Mom is very tired from working all day. When she gets home, she is
    too tired to clean up the house. Todd gets home from school an hour
    before his mother gets home.
    What Todd can do:

    _____

    _____

2. Julio's father lives many hours away from the family, and Juan gets to see him for only two weeks in
    the summer. Julio misses his father.
    What Julio can do:

    _____

    _____

3. It is Parents' Day at school, and Tina is supposed to draw a picture of herself for her parents. But
    her parents are divorced, and she doesn't know which parent to give the picture to. She doesn't
    want either one to feel left out.
    What Tina can do:

    _____

    _____

4. When Ray is at his mother's house, he is allowed to watch whatever he wants on TV. When he is at
    his father's house, he can watch TV for only an hour a day. Ray is angry that he can't watch what he
    wants at his father's house.
    What Ray can do:

    _____

    _____

5. Lizell's mother just got remarried, and now there are two new children who will be living in the
    house. There are only two bedrooms in the house.
    What Lizell can do:

    _____

    _____

    _____

Copyright © 2009 by John Wiley & Sons. Inc.

10.12 Talking with Parents

Objective

The student will identify characters who are attempting to talk to their parents in a rational, pleasant manner.

Rationale

Talking to parents at home may be more of a challenge for some students than we realize. Some students simply do not know how to get their parents' attention in an appropriate way. Instead, they beg, whine, demand, or yell. Parents are not likely to listen happily to such forms of communication. Other students may not feel that they can approach their parents when they need help or just want to talk. Encouraging students to try to talk to parents and do it in a pleasant manner is one step toward opening up lines of communication at home.

Thinking Questions

1. If you had a problem or were really worried about something, would it be easy to talk to your parents? (*ask for comments*)

2. Some people find it difficult to talk to their parents. Why do you think that might be the case? (*feel parents aren't interested, don't know how to approach the topic, don't want to reveal their thoughts to an adult*)

3. Do you think most parents are interested in what's happening with their children? (*the hoped-for answer is "yes"*)

4. Have you ever heard anyone say, "My parents just don't understand"? What does that mean? (*might mean that the parents aren't trying to understand the child or that the child hasn't done a good job of communicating with the parents*)

5. Do you think the age difference between parents and children has anything to do with a different viewpoint? (*in some cases, yes—the music, fads, clothing might be different*)

6. How would having different experiences affect the way someone feels about something? (*if someone wasn't interested in something or had no knowledge about it, that person couldn't really understand how someone else might feel*)

7. Do you think it's important for parents and their children to talk to each other? Why or why not? (*the hoped-for answer is "yes"—to express different viewpoints, understand each other, keep up with what's going on in each other's lives*)

8. What are some ways that kids and parents can communicate or talk to each other about important things? (*sit down and talk, spend time listening, think about the other's point of view*)

9. What are some ways that you could get your parents' attention if you wanted to talk to them? (*ask for time alone, write a little note, go to their office*)

10. What are some ways that you could understand how your parents feel about something? (*ask them, observe them, try to think from their point of view*)

11. If you feel that your parents aren't listening to you, what else could you do? *(try again, talk to someone else if the problem is serious, try at a different time)*

12. If you and your parents don't understand each other or agree on things, what are some things your family might do together to work out the problems? *(set aside time to talk with just the family, cool off and talk later, see a family counselor)*

Activity

Directions: Students are to circle the children on the worksheet who are truly talking to their parents, as opposed to arguing, whining, or begging.

Answers: 2, 4, 5

Follow-up: Have students determine why the children in numbers 1 and 3 were not concerned about talking to their parents, but rather getting their own way, actively and passively. How did the children in the other examples convey their concerns to the parent without being sidetracked by immature behaviors? Is the character in number 4 arguing with his mother or trying to convince her to see his point of view? Even though the mother in number 5 was busy, she wanted to listen to the poem. If the daughter had asked at a different time, would the mother's response have been different? Encourage students to talk to their parents, keeping in mind the setting as well as the approach.

Name _____ Date _____

10.12

Talking with Parents

The situations below show children and their parents. Circle the children who are trying to talk to their parents, not just trying to shut them out or argue.

Copyright © 2009 by John Wiley & Sons, Inc.

10.13 I Don't Need a Baby-sitter

Objective

The student will list at least three reasons that a baby-sitter might be a good idea.

Rationale

With parents working and having other obligations, children may be left alone or in the hands of a sitter. Children who are in upper elementary grades may feel that they are too old to have a sitter and resent having someone look after them, especially if the sitter is only a few years older than they are. Nevertheless, there are times when having an adult or older person around is a good idea for safety, school help, resolving problems, and generally taking responsibility.

Thinking Questions

1. How many of you have a sitter when your parents are gone? *(answers will vary)*
2. How does a sitter help your parents? *(provides safety when they are gone)*
3. At what age do you think kids don't need a sitter anymore? *(answers will vary)*
4. How could having a sitter around be helpful for safety? *(in case there is a fire, being able to drive, knowing how to swim)*
5. Even if you are old enough to be responsible for things, do you think a sitter could be helpful to watch out for younger children in your family? How? *(preparing meals, changing diapers, making sure that they are supervised)*
6. What are some things that a sitter should know how to do? *(call 911, make sure the kids are being watched, make kids behave)*
7. How can you show respect to someone who is supposed to be in charge of you while your parents are gone? *(do what they say, try not to fight with other kids, don't try to bend the rules)*

Activity

Directions: Put a check mark in front of the reasons that a baby-sitter might be helpful in a home.

Answers: Checks: 1, 3, 4, 5, 7, 8

Follow-up: Talk about the term *baby-sitter* and how it is funny to think about someone sitting on top of a baby. What are some other words that are used to refer to someone who helps watch over children? Why is it important to get along with this person, even if he or she is not a parent?

10.13   # I Don't Need a Baby-sitter

Which of these are good reasons to have a baby-sitter in a home, even if you are old enough to be responsible? Put a check mark next to each one.

❑ 1. If there was a fire, the baby-sitter could get the kids out of the house to safety.

❑ 2. The baby-sitter can do all of your homework for you while you watch TV.

❑ 3. The baby-sitter can handle your younger brother and sister who are fighting about what they want for a snack.

❑ 4. If you are having a problem with something on your homework, your baby-sitter might be able to help you with it.

❑ 5. If the weather is really bad and your mom and dad are delayed getting home from work, the baby-sitter will stay there until one of them gets home.

❑ 6. While the baby-sitter is talking on the phone, you can sneak out of the house and go over to see your friend.

❑ 7. You had a bad day at school, and your baby-sitter will listen to you talk about it.

❑ 8. The phone rings and you do not understand what the person wants, so your baby-sitter talks to the person on the phone and works it out.

Copyright © 2009 by John Wiley & Sons, Inc.

Getting Along with Others at Home   **391**

10.14 Family Fun

Objective

The student will identify several activities that a family could do together for fun or leisure.

Rationale

The times that a family can do things together may seem rare, considering everyone's different activities and schedules. Nevertheless, it is important for families to spend time together. There are many family activities that can be done on any budget, any time. Students will realize that their family is a social grouping that can be a lot of fun.

Thinking Questions

1. What are some ways that a family can have fun together? *(going on a picnic, taking a vacation, riding bikes)*

2. Has anyone ever taken a family vacation? Where was the destination? *(ask for examples)*

3. What are some things that a family can do together in the house or their own community? *(play cards, play basketball, go swimming, go to the zoo, ride bikes)*

4. Even though you might fight with siblings occasionally, what are things that you can do with brothers and sisters that are fun? *(board games, basketball in the back yard, riding bikes, building models, jumping rope)*

5. How is being part of a family different from being part of a group of friends? *(you will always be related by blood, always have the same background; with friends you're about the same age, but may change friendships with time and as you move)*

Activity

Directions: The left side of the worksheet lists parts of a conversation from a family engaging in a fun activity. The student is to decide what the activity is and write the letter of the answer on the line.

Answers: 1. d   2. c   3. b   4. e   5. a

Follow-up: After discussing the answers on the worksheet, have students think of and list other activities that a family can do together for fun. What conversational clues would give it away?

10.14   **Family Fun**

Match the way the family is having fun together with the clues in the conversations on the left.

1. "Yay!! You got them all down! It's a strike!"

a.

2. "Please pass the potato chips. Watch out for the ants!"

b.

3. "Don't splash me!"

c.

4. "Do you have any fives? Quit looking over here!"

d.

5. "Ha ha ha! I love this. Oh, here's a commercial. Let's get something to drink."

e.

Copyright © 2009 by John Wiley & Sons, Inc.

Getting Along with Others at Home   **393**

Classroom Tips for Getting Along with Others at Home

- Have students compile a list of requests that their parents have given to them in a one-hour (or one-afternoon or one-day) period of time. Discuss the requests. Are they mostly for chores for the children? Are the requests unreasonable? Should they be obeyed?

- Send home an informal survey to parents requesting lists of family rules. Are the rules similar among families? Would students like to trade family rules for a week?

- Assign a creative writing task with the title "The Day I Didn't Obey." Look for lots of interesting consequences!

- During community circle or sharing time, have students take turns talking about their jobs and responsibilities at home. How are these tasks the same as school tasks? How are they different?

- Compile a job description booklet of chores that students may do around the house. What is involved in cleaning out the closet? Ask students to be very specific. It is often lack of being specific that complicates a simple job.

- Designate a holiday for honoring siblings, and make cards in class for students to give to those at home. You may also wish to have students prepare small gifts such as a small plant or a cupcake. The next day, discuss the siblings' reactions. Were they surprised?

- With parents' help, have students make a photo-autobiography. Here is the chance for students to shine by concentrating on themselves. If desired, have students put their projects on a table and let students browse through each other's.

- If a child's family is going through a divorce, the child may need someone to talk to or listen to him. Every situation is different, but this may be a time in which the school setting is the most structured, familiar, and stable for the child. Bringing up this topic at community circle may be helpful if kept in general terms. Always be respectful of the family's privacy.

- As a homework assignment, have students sit down with a parent and talk for at least fifteen minutes every night. (You may have to adjust this to fit specific needs.) To get things started, give each student a question or topic to discuss each night. Require parents to sign a sheet to indicate that they had their nightly conversation. Both students and parents might enjoy this homework activity and keep it up beyond the week or two assigned.

- If you have a class camera (or are willing to donate yours for the project), send it home with each child in your class, one day at a time, and ask them to have a family picture taken. They may want to stage it, with the family doing something fun together. As an alternative, you could ask for vacation pictures or drawings showing how a family has fun together.

Chapter 11

Everyday Etiquette

11.1 Meeting Other People

Objective

The student will identify characters who are meeting other people by looking at the person, smiling, and saying hello or other greeting.

Rationale

Though most introductions are contrived and probably somewhat awkward for most students, it is a polite ritual to say "hello," put on a smile, and look the other person in the eye. In this lesson, students will concentrate on identifying those behaviors from characters on the worksheet.

Thinking Questions

1. When do you think you might meet new people? *(new kids at school, at a friend's party, church youth group)*

2. When you meet someone new, why is it important to look the person in the eye? *(show that you are interested in them, get a good look at them so you'll recognize them later)*

3. Do you think eye contact is important every time you talk to someone or just the first time you meet someone? *(in general, whenever you are talking to someone; shows interest and attention)*

4. What are some other things that you can do to show the person that you are polite and interested in them? *(smile, say hello, shake hands)*

5. Would you want to get to know someone better if he or she acted disinterested in you or snotty? *(probably not)*

6. Why do you think it's important to look friendly and interested in those you meet? *(so they will get a good impression of you, might open up a new friendship)*

Activity

Directions: The student is to identify which of the three elements for meeting someone is missing in the situations on the worksheet. Make sure students understand the three parts (looking at the person, smiling, giving a greeting) and that they are to write only the number of the missing element.

Answers: 1. 2   2. 1   3. 3   4. 2   5. 3

Follow-up: Have students role-play the situations on the worksheet, making sure that they are able to greet someone correctly (incorporating all three elements) after they have performed leaving one out. You can also have students make up their own skits, sometimes leaving something out so the others in the class can identify it.

11.1   # Meeting Other People

These people are meeting other people for the first time, but each is forgetting to do something important. Write the number of what was forgotten:

1 = look at the person   **2 = smile**   **3 = say hello or hi**

Copyright © 2009 by John Wiley & Sons. Inc.

11.2 Being a Guest in Someone's Home

Objective

The student will identify behaviors as appropriate and inappropriate and suggest alternative behaviors for those that are inappropriate.

Rationale

When a child visits your home, it does not take long to make an informal assessment as to that child's upbringing. We as parents are impressed when we meet a child who is polite, conversational, and helps clean up the room before going home. And certainly we hope that our children are making a good impression when they visit friends' homes. Being a guest sometimes comes with yet another set of rules as to what is appropriate.

Thinking Questions

1. Sometimes it is fun to have friends over to your house. What would you do at your house if you had a friend over? *(ride bikes, play video games, play outside)*

2. When you go over to someone else's house, do you act as though you are at home, or are there different rules? *(depends on the friend—maybe there are fewer rules)*

3. What does it mean when someone says that you are not a guest, you are family? *(it means that they are very close to you and that you will be treated just like one of their own children)*

4. What does it mean to be a guest when you go to someone else's house? *(you don't normally eat or sleep there, you will be there only a short time)*

5. Do you think guests get special treatment? *(probably; they are there because they were invited)*

6. When have you been a guest in someone's house? *(birthday parties, visiting relatives, when your parents were gone for a weekend)*

7. What are some ways that you could show that you have good manners when you are a guest in someone's house? *(be extra careful to pick up your stuff, offer to take the dishes to the sink, don't start fights with the other kids)*

8. When you show good manners to someone's parents or other adult, what does that say about you? *(polite, good upbringing!)*

Activity

Directions: These children are guests in someone's home. Which ones are not showing good manners? How could they improve their behavior?

Answers: 1. No; try the food anyway.   2. Yes; adults like to be talked to.   3. No; turn the TV down. 4. No; help clean up the toys.   5. Yes; offering to help is appreciated.   6. No; respect rules for taking off shoes in the house.

Follow-up: Have students share their particular house rules. Which rules are similar, and which are different? Have students pick one behavior that they would like to work on when they are a guest in someone's home. Afterward, they report back on how they did and if they received a compliment.

Copyright © 2009 by John Wiley & Sons. Inc.

Name _____ Date _____

11.2 Being a Guest in Someone's Home

These children are guests in someone's home. Circle YES if the child is showing good manners and NO if the child is showing poor manners. How could those not showing good manners improve their behavior? Write your ideas on the lines.

1. "I hate broccoli! It tastes yucky. It makes me want to throw up."

    YES   **NO**

    _____

    _____

    _____

2. "Hi, Mrs. Young. Thanks for letting me come over."

    YES   **NO**

    _____

    _____

    _____

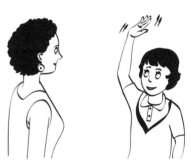

3. "I love this part! Turn it up really loud, and we can dance!! Your grandpa can't hear anyhow!"

    YES   **NO**

    _____

    _____

    _____

11.2 Being a Guest in Someone's Home (continued)

4. "We sure made a mess! Well, I gotta go! You clean it up; it's your house."

YES   **NO**

_____

_____

_____

5. "Here are my dishes. Do you want me to put them in the sink?"

YES   **NO**

_____

_____

_____

6. "It sure was muddy outside!"

YES   **NO**

_____

_____

_____

Copyright © 2009 by John Wiley & Sons, Inc.

11.3 Impolite Noises

Objective

The student will identify proper procedures for handling impolite noises in public, such as minimizing the noise, not calling attention to the problem, or saying "excuse me."

Rationale

Some noises can't be eliminated entirely, such as coughing or sneezing. However, they can be minimized and certainly should not be used to get attention. Other noises are impolite, such as slurping liquids or burping loudly. Students will first have to decide whether the noise can be helped, and if not, then how to handle the noise in public.

Thinking Questions

1. Have you ever had the hiccups when everyone around you was really quiet? Tell about it. *(you'll probably hear some good anecdotes!)*
2. What did the people around you do when you hiccupped? *(turned and giggled, stared, laughed)*
3. Some noises can't be helped, such as sneezing or coughing. But can the loudness be controlled? *(somewhat; you can stifle a sneeze and use a handkerchief or tissue)*
4. How could you lessen the noise if you had a sniffle from a cold? *(use a tissue instead of inhaling)*
5. Why do you think people consider burping to be impolite? *(some people overdo it, it calls attention to yourself)*
6. If someone around you makes an impolite noise to get attention or is trying to be silly, what could you do? *(ignore it)*
7. If someone makes an impolite noise and really couldn't help it, what should he or she do? *(say "excuse me" and don't make a big deal about it)*

Activity

Directions: The students are to match the picture portraying an impolite noise with the description.

Answers: 1. d   2. a   3. f   4. e   5. c   6. b

Follow-up: Sometimes you just have to scratch! Discuss why the noises pictured may be considered impolite in public. Stress that it is not the noise itself that is the problem (unless it is loud or annoying on purpose), but the context. Again, go over how each noise could be eliminated, reduced, or pardoned.

11.3   **Impolite Noises**

Match the picture of someone making an irritating noise with its description.

1.

2. HIC.

a. having the hiccups

3.

b. scratching

c. whistling

4.

d. blowing your nose

e. slurping

5.

f. sneezing

6.

Copyright © 2009 by John Wiley & Sons, Inc.

Everyday Etiquette

11.4 Saying "Thank You"

Objective

The student will state at least four occasions on which "thank you" is appropriate.

Rationale

"Thank you" is a phrase that we don't hear enough. We can prompt our children or students to express gratitude ("What do you say to your aunt for those nice clothes you got on your birthday—even if you wanted a game?"), but our larger purpose is to foster an attitude of gratitude. We can express simple thanks for small things such as receiving help or an act of kindness, and we can more elaborately express gratitude for huge, important acts in our lives.

Thinking Questions

1. I would like you all to look at me. Thank you! Now I would like you to close your eyes. Thank you very much. Now open your eyes. Thanks again. What are you wondering right now? (*what's going on! Why you are saying "thank you" so much*)

2. Why did I say "thank you" three times? (*we did what you asked*)

3. Do I appreciate your following my directions? (*yes*) Why? (*you didn't have to ask over and over*)

4. How does it make someone feel when they hear the words "thank you"? (*good, appreciated*)

5. What are some things that make you say "thank you" during the day? (*to the bus driver, the lunch ladies, when someone opens a door*)

6. What are some things that you could say "thank you" for? (*someone passing you a pencil, picking up something you dropped, helping you with a problem*)

7. Have you ever received a gift or gotten something really special that made you want to scream "THANK YOU!"? What was it? (*got a puppy, found out you were going on vacation, received a prize*)

8. How many times a day do you think you thank someone for something? (*answers will vary*)

Activity

Directions: Look at each picture. Finish what you think each person is saying.

Answer examples: 1. *Thank you for* getting that for me.   2. *Thank you for* the great food!   3. *Thank you for* noticing!   4. *Thank you for* inviting me.

Follow-up: Have students role-play these and other situations in which they could say "thank you" to someone. Sometimes just the words "thank you" are enough, but sometimes adding the reason for the gratitude is appreciated too.

11.4   Saying "Thank You"

Look at each picture. Finish what you think each person is saying.

1.

2.

Everyday Etiquette

Copyright © 2009 by John Wiley & Sons, Inc.

3.

4.

Copyright © 2009 by John Wiley & Sons. Inc.

11.5 Personal Questions

Objective

The student will state whether questions asked of someone else are appropriate.

Rationale

Children are curious and sometimes ask questions of others that adults would not. Curiosity can become offensive, however, when the questions are too personal and are not anyone else's business. Young students truly may not know that not all information is fair game for them. This lesson explains that some questions are not appropriate to ask others, depending on how well you know the other person and what the intention is in asking.

Thinking Questions

1. How would you feel if someone wanted to know when your birthday was and came right up and asked you? *(fine, happy for the attention)*

2. How would you feel if someone asked you about why your dad got in trouble at work and is it true that he was losing his job? *(not so good, angry, embarrassed)*

3. What is a personal question? *(something about you)*

4. Why do you think some people would not want to be asked very personal questions? *(might be embarrassing, don't want people to know their business)*

5. What are some areas that people might be sensitive about or wouldn't want to be asked questions about? *(their age, how much money they make, why they got in trouble, embarrassing home life)*

6. Is there a difference between asking questions because you are interested and asking questions because you are nosey? *(yes—the motivation is quite different)*

7. If a question makes someone else feel uncomfortable, how could you back off or talk about something else? *(ask different questions, don't ask any questions at all)*

8. If someone asked you a very personal question that you did not want to answer, what could you say to the person? *("sorry, that's not your business"; "I'm not supposed to talk about that"; "I don't know the answer")*

Activity

Directions: The characters on the worksheet are asking questions. Students are to circle the people who are asking nice, considerate questions. They are to put an X on the questions that are too personal.

Answers: Circle: 1, 3, 4, 7; X: 2, 5, 6, 8

Follow-up: Discuss the responses. Why were the X'd questions inappropriate to ask someone? Why would they be embarrassing to the character if he or she answered? What are good ways to answer someone who asked you these questions?

11.5   Personal Questions

Circle the students who are asking nice questions that show they are interested. Put an X on the questions you think are too personal.

Copyright © 2009 by John Wiley & Sons. Inc.

1.   Do you like school?

2.   Did you get an F on that?

3.   How many people are in your family?

4.   Do you live near here?

5.   How much money does your dad make?

6.   Why do you smell funny?

7.   Do you have any pets?

8.   Is it true that your family is getting kicked out of your house?

11.6   Mimicking or Imitating Others

Objective

The student will identify characters who are imitating others out of flattery or admiration rather than ridicule.

Rationale

There's a big difference between imitating someone you admire greatly and imitating someone with the intention of making fun of him or her. In this lesson, students are given the opportunity to distinguish between the two.

Thinking Questions

1. If you were pretending to be an animal, which animal might be easy to imitate? Why? (*elephant—swinging arm like trunk; lion—roaring; these animals have very distinctive characteristics*)

2. What are some things that people imitate or make fun of about other people? (*movements, voice, things that they say*)

3. Why is it funny to imitate the voice or movements of other people? (*you can exaggerate what they do that is unusual*)

4. How could imitating or mimicking others get you into trouble? (*the person might find out, could lead to hurt feelings, anger*)

5. Is it nice to imitate people who are doing something positive? What are some examples of positive imitating? (*wearing your hair or clothes like someone else, saying the same things they say, playing sports like someone who is good at it*)

6. What are some things that you would like to imitate about someone else? (*a good athlete's behavior, the way someone famous looks, a good attitude displayed by someone*)

Activity

Directions: Students are to circle the names of the characters on the worksheet who are imitating others in a nice way.

Answers: Maria, Anna, Ed and Fred

Follow-up: Discuss what is impolite or silly about the other characters' behaviors on the worksheet. Would those characters imitate the person if that person was aware of them? Is it ever okay to imitate someone else if it was done just for fun and the other person didn't mind?

11.6   # Mimicking or Imitating Others

Circle the names of the characters who are imitating others in a nice way.

Copyright © 2009 by John Wiley & Sons, Inc.

11.7 Behavior in Public Places

Objective

The student will identify the problem with the behavior displayed by characters in public places.

Rationale

There's a big difference between being in public and being in the privacy of your own home. When in public, you are sharing time and space with other people and must be considerate of everyone's needs. Students need to realize that they must be aware of their surroundings and their audience in public.

Thinking Questions

1. What does it mean if a place or event is "open to the public"? *(anyone can go there or attend the event)*
2. What are some public places in our community? *(zoo, park, library, restaurants, post office)*
3. What do you have to share with others in a public place? *(the view, tables, time, being waited on)*
4. Whose needs and interests do you have to consider when you are in a public place? *(everyone else who is there)*
5. Why can't you do whatever you want in a public place? *(it doesn't belong to you, it's not private property, someone might be offended or hurt)*
6. How does sharing public things benefit you? *(a community can afford to have a zoo or a nice library, the cost of the building is shared, you don't have to do the actual upkeep)*
7. Why is it important to remember that you are sharing public facilities with a lot of other people? How would it help you be on your best behavior? *(don't want to spoil things for someone else, be careful with things so others can use them, remember to share if people are waiting)*

Activity

Directions: After looking at the picture on the left, students are to write on the lines at the right the problem that they have discovered with the behavior.

Answers:

1. Graffiti is expensive to erase, often not nice.
2. Someone is walking on the grass (might be newly planted).
3. A boy is being pushy in line rather than waiting for his turn to buy tickets.
4. A girl is yelling loudly at a game, disturbing others.
5. The boy is making shadow pictures on the movie screen, distorting the picture.

Follow-up: Discuss alternative behaviors that the characters could engage in and still achieve their goal. How does their inconsiderate behavior affect or hurt anyone else?

11.7   **Behavior in Public Places**

What's wrong with the behavior of the characters in each situation below? Write your answer on the lines.

1.

     _____

     _____

2.

     _____

     _____

3.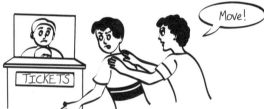

     _____

     _____

4.

     _____

     _____

5.

     _____

     _____

Copyright © 2009 by John Wiley & Sons, Inc.

11.8 Lining Up

Objective

The student will be able to form, stand, and wait in a line without provoking or being provoked by others.

Rationale

During a typical day, students have to stand in line. They have to line up for lunch, to go in or out of a classroom, to get on the bus to go home, for drinks from the water fountain, for fire drills, and lots more. You would think with all of the practice they have in standing in line that it would become second nature. However, when any two children are in close proximity and required to be quiet, be still, and not touch anyone else, it can become quite a challenge.

Thinking Questions

1. How many times a day do you have to line up? What do you line up for? *(list some examples)*

2. Why is it important to stay in a line? *(so you know everyone is there, so you don't wander all over the hallway and bump into people, makes it easier to count)*

3. What is the procedure for standing in line? *(boys on one side, girls on the other; keep one foot away from the person in front of you; no talking, hands at your side)*

4. Why do you think those procedures are important? *(because some people wiggle too much and touch others, if you're talking you can't hear directions)*

5. Why is it especially important to line up during a fire drill? *(if people are noisy and run all over no one will get to the door, have to be quiet)*

6. What is disturbing about having someone stand too close to you in line? *(don't want them to touch you, breathe on you, knock into you; might make you try to hurry when you aren't ready)*

7. Sometimes there is a line for girls and a line for boys. What are some other ways that you might line up? *(in the order that you finish your work, in the order that the buses come, alphabetical order)*

8. The whole idea about lining up is that everyone gets where they are going in an organized, safe way. What are some ways that our group could line up to make sure everyone does this safely and quickly? *(discuss class ideas)*

Activity

Directions: The line rules are: hands to self, quiet, and wait patiently. Which students are having trouble following these rules?

Answers: 2, touching; 4, making noises; 7, wiggling; 8, touching

Follow-up: Have students practice lining up in various ways. You may have a separate line for boys and girls, or alternating boy/girl. You may have students wearing red line up first. You may have students have a line buddy who will be next to them when they line up. Having a line leader and a line ender can also be helpful on a rotating basis. Varying your instructions can teach students to focus on what you say, since it will be different each time. For safety drills, however, make sure students follow the class protocol instantaneously.

11.8   **Lining Up**

The line rules are: hands to self, quiet, and wait patiently. Which students are having trouble following these rules?

Copyright © 2009 by John Wiley & Sons, Inc.

11.9 Table Manners

Objective

The student will draw pictures to illustrate several common table manners.

Rationale

Every family has different table manners. Families range from very informal eating habits (such as grabbing whatever you can find whenever you happen to get home) to more formal on special occasions (Hanukkah with relatives). It is important for children to know what behaviors are expected from them in different situations. Some families pause to have a blessing before eating. Others begin with the parents serving themselves first, followed by the children or vice versa. Twelve common behaviors are listed for consideration, although not all will be relevant to every family. Nevertheless, a student who could handle this degree of formality at a meal would be in pretty good shape to face anything!

Thinking Questions

1. What are some examples of good table manners? *(sit still, pass the food, wait to be excused, don't lick the knife)*

2. Why is it important to have good table manners? *(so you don't mess up the food, so everyone passes food in the same direction, show that you are considerate of others)*

3. What might be in front of you when you sit down at the table? *(plate or two, silverware, napkins, glass, bowls of food)*

4. What are the different items for? *(go through the purpose of each item listed in question 3)*

5. Why is it polite to wait until everyone else has been served before you start eating? *(shows that you aren't going to rush to beat everyone else, someone might need to have something passed and you'll have your hands free)*

6. What should you do if you don't like what is being served? *(say "no, thank you" politely, take a small amount, pass the bowl to the next person)*

7. Why shouldn't you argue or fight about things at the table? *(eating is a time to relax and let your food digest, arguing can make others upset, it's not polite to involve others at the table with your problems)*

8. After you are done eating, what could you do to help the cook? *(take your dishes to the kitchen, throw paper napkins away)*

Activity

Directions: The student has a choice of drawing pictures to illustrate four of the twelve table manners listed on the worksheet. They are to write the number of their drawing at the top.

Answers: Answers will vary.

Follow-up: Have students cover the number at the top, and let other students try to guess which manner they drew. Collect examples of all twelve from the class and display them so that they are in order, showing a complete dinner.

11.9   # Table Manners

Draw a picture to illustrate four of the following good manners.

1. Come when called.	5. Pass food before eating.	9. Be pleasant.
2. Sit quietly in your chair.	6. Ask politely for things you need.	10. Wait to take seconds until everyone has had firsts.
3. Wait to say grace.	7. Use your silverware correctly.	11. Ask to be excused.
4. Put your napkin in your lap.	8. Eat slowly and with your mouth closed.	12. Thank the cook.

Number _____

Number _____

Number _____

Number _____

Copyright © 2009 by John Wiley & Sons, Inc.

11.10 Eating Out

Objective

The student will circle the characters who are showing polite behavior in a restaurant.

Rationale

Waitresses and waiters are not slaves, waiting at the customer's beck and call. When people go out to eat, sometimes expectations change, and they are not as considerate to the servers or the customers who will follow them. Showing polite behavior in a public restaurant is something that children can learn at a young age. Even ordering politely for oneself is a helpful social skill, involving making decisions, speaking clearly, and looking someone in the eye.

Thinking Questions

1. What are some places where you might go to eat out? *(local restaurants)*

2. Why do people sometimes go out to eat? *(may enjoy certain ethnic foods, special occasion, no food at home)*

3. What is a fast-food restaurant? *(a place where you can get your meal in a hurry, have a drive-through)*

4. How is a sit-down restaurant different from a fast-food place? *(the waitperson takes your order, service is slower, may have more choice of items)*

5. How is eating at a sit-down restaurant different from eating at your own or someone else's house? *(don't have to wash the dishes, food is served by a waitperson, everyone can order something different)*

6. What table manners would be the same at a restaurant as at home? *(wait until everyone has been served, put your napkin on your lap, sit quietly)*

7. Since a restaurant is a public place, what do customers share? *(the waiter or waitress, the table— other customers after you, the restrooms, the waiting area before you are seated at a table)*

Activity

Directions: Students are to circle the characters on the worksheet who are displaying appropriate behavior in the restaurant depicted on the page.

Answers: Circle 2, 5, 8, 10

Follow-up: Discuss how the rude characters could change their speech or actions to be more appropriate for the restaurant. What other inappropriate behaviors could have been drawn on this worksheet, and why would they be impolite?

11.10   **Eating Out**

Circle the characters below who are showing polite behavior in a restaurant.

Copyright © 2009 by John Wiley & Sons, Inc.

11.11 Uninvited Guests

Objective

The student will give reasons why uninvited guests can become a problem.

Rationale

Children sometimes take advantage of situations in which they want to share a good thing with their friends, family members, and other people who may not be expected. Showing up at a party with a dog or cat may present problems as well. In most casual situations, the host doesn't mind if someone accompanies a child or understands the need to be a little flexible. But in some cases, it is important to remember that you can't just bring all your friends to something that only you were invited to. And, it's important to know the difference.

Thinking Questions

1. Let's say you were having a birthday party and your parents said you could invite five friends to go roller skating. One of your friends who came brought his three brothers with him. How would that affect the party? (*parents have to pay extra for the uninvited kids, not everyone would fit in the car, there might not be enough party favors or food*)

2. What if you were allergic to cat hair and a friend came over to spend the night and brought his furry cat with him? (*it would be a night of sneezing*)

3. How would you feel if you planned for your best friend to come over to play some video games, but he or she brought another friend whom you didn't know and the two of them played the games? (*kind of left out, have to change plans*)

4. What are some ways that you could handle those situations? (*make sure that if an exact count is needed, your friends realize extra people can't come; explain that you are allergic to cat hair; be nice to the friend anyhow*)

5. Would it be a problem if your mother said that you could have as many kids over as you wanted? (*no—you have parent permission*)

6. Would it be a problem having a lot of people over if you had a very small house? A sick grandmother? Another meeting going on? What do you need to think about before you invite a group over? (*what the conditions are at home, whether your parents give permission, if it is the right time and place*)

7. If you had a cousin staying with you for awhile and you received an invitation to a party, what could you do? (*ask if your cousin could come, make sure your cousin has something to do until you get back, be polite no matter what happens*)

Activity

Directions: Here are some uninvited guests. Why is it a problem in this situation?

Answers: 1. not enough room   2. parent doesn't want pets in the house   3. expensive to add another child   4. one child doesn't get along with the others   5. too many swimmers in the pool; not safe

Follow-up: For each situation, discuss why an unexpected guest might inconvenience someone. What could be done to prevent the situation? What could be done to handle the situation if it already happened? Finally, discuss the reality that there are people in the world who do not mind inconvenience at all; in fact, their philosophy is "the more the merrier." The important thing is that the child is aware that there are people who are not flexible and need structure, planning, and no surprises to function well.

11.11   **Uninvited Guests**

Here are some uninvited guests. Why are they a problem in each situation?

1. "Hi, Uncle Bob! Thanks for picking me up from practice. Here are my five friends who need a ride home too."

   _____

   _____

   _____

2. "I know my mom won't mind if I bring this snake home. It can live in my bedroom."

   _____

   _____

   _____

Copyright © 2009 by John Wiley & Sons, Inc.

3. "My sister heard that your dad was taking everybody to the amusement park for the day, so she wants to come too."

_____

_____

_____

Copyright © 2009 by John Wiley & Sons, Inc.

4. "Oh, no! Mary Ann brought Kelly to our cheerleading practice. Kelly can't say a nice thing about any of us. Now we have to practice in front of her."

_____

_____

_____

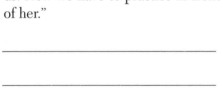

5. "There are only supposed to be ten people in the pool, but we can fit ten more in, I think."

_____

_____

_____

_____

11.12 Using a Cell Phone

Objective

When using a cell phone, students will be considerate of the time and place so as not to disturb others.

Rationale

Many children have cell phones. In most cases, it is important for the children to be able to call home for a ride, let their working parents know where they are, or give and receive information. But it is annoying when individuals have noisy personal conversations in public places and disregard their surroundings. Cell phones are part of our culture, and we must all learn to use them with consideration for others.

Thinking Questions

1. How many of you have a cell phone or can use one when you need one? *(ask for a show of hands)* What do you use them for? *(communicate with parents, talk to friends)*

2. What else can your cell phone do besides operate as a phone? *(take pictures, text, play games, do calculations)*

3. Where are some places that you should not use a cell phone? *(in class, on a plane, waiting in an office, in a library)*

4. Why do you think it disturbs people when others talk loudly on a cell phone? *(they might be trying to do something; most people don't realize how loudly they are talking!)*

5. Why do you think it might be considered rude to talk on a cell phone when you are in a public place such as a restaurant or a waiting room? *(people are having their own conversations and don't want to be interrupted by yours)*

6. Why might it be considered rude to be talking on a cell phone when you are with a friend? *(that person is ignored)*

7. Have you ever heard a cell phone go off at a quiet place, such as a movie or a house of worship? Why would that be considered rude? *(people are there to focus on something else and this is an interruption)*

8. If you were going to make up some rules for using cell phones in public, what would your rules be? *(talk softly, keep your call short, text if possible, go outside or to another room)*

Activity

Directions: What is each person doing that shows poor cell phone manners?

Answers: 1. talking too loudly   2. talking too long   3. ignoring a friend   4. not paying attention to what he is doing   5. using a phone in a public place   6. having a personal conversation   7. forgetting to turn it off

Follow-up: Role-play some of the examples so that students can actually "hear" how annoying these situations can be. They will probably find many examples of adults who are using poor cell phone manners.

11.12   # Using a Cell Phone

What is each person doing that shows poor cell phone manners?

1.

2.

Copyright © 2009 by John Wiley & Sons, Inc.

3.

4.

Copyright © 2009 by John Wiley & Sons, Inc.

11.13 Interrupting

Objective

The student will identify examples of children interrupting.

Rationale

We all speak without thinking first. Maybe we are excited with the news we have to tell; maybe we are not even listening to someone else talking, but can't wait to get our opinion expressed; or maybe we are listening but upset at what another person is saying. There are times when an interruption is permissible. For example, if there is a fire or if there is a bug crawling up my back, it is perfectly fine with me to have a conversation interrupted. But if adults are talking or if someone is expressing an opinion, it is polite to be quiet until there is a break in the conversation.

Thinking Questions

1. Most of the time when two adults are talking, what should your behavior be like? *(be quiet, don't interrupt, don't tug on their sleeves)*

2. Why is being quiet or waiting a good thing to do? *(adults might be discussing important things, you might get yelled at for interrupting)*

3. If another teacher comes into the classroom to talk to a teacher, why is it polite to let the teachers talk? *(they don't have a lot of time during school to talk to each other; they might have to talk about students and what they need)*

4. What if a parent came into the classroom to talk to your teacher? *(don't interrupt)*

5. When would be a good time to talk if two other people have already started talking? *(when both have finished speaking, when they look at you to let you know that they see you and it is your turn)*

6. What are some times when it would be okay to interrupt a conversation? *(if one of the people needed to know something right away)*

7. If you interrupt someone who is talking, how does that make the interrupted person feel? *(that you were not listening to that person, that what the person had to say was not important enough to let him or her finish)*

8. What would be a polite way to interrupt a conversation if you really have to say something? *("Excuse me. May I talk to you for a minute?")*

Activity

Directions: Which examples show someone interrupting?

Answers: 1. Yes; two adults are talking.   2. No; the girl is waiting to talk.   3. Yes; the boy is not listening to the speaker.   4. Yes; the boy is interrupting by tapping.   5. No; the girl is talking when it is her turn.   6. Yes; the boy is interrupting because he is excited but it is distracting to others.

Follow-up: Have students act out the situations showing an interruption and then how a person can wait to talk or join the conversation.

11.13   # Interrupting

Which examples show someone interrupting? Circle YES or NO after each situation. Be prepared to discuss your responses.

1.

YES   **NO**

2.

YES   **NO**

Copyright © 2009 by John Wiley & Sons, Inc.

3.

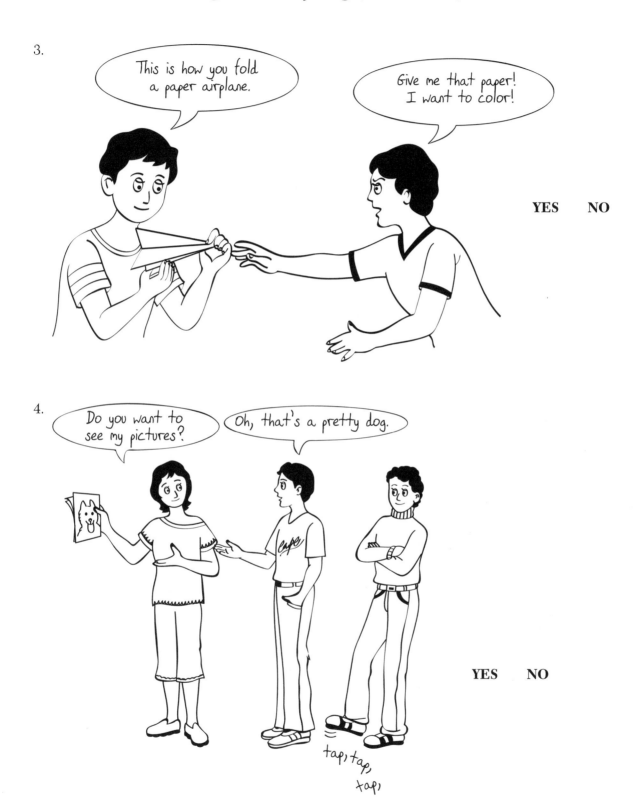

YES   NO

4.

YES   NO

Copyright © 2009 by John Wiley & Sons, Inc.

5.

YES   NO

6.

YES   NO

Copyright © 2009 by John Wiley & Sons. Inc.

11.14 Respecting Adults in the Community

Objective

The student will identify behaviors that show respect of adults in the home or community settings.

Rationale

Although some students may show respect to teachers in the classroom, they might not do so outside the building. Students should be able to generalize the idea of respect to all adults, whether or not they have a direct link to the student in terms of authority or personal relationship.

Thinking Questions

1. Who are some adults besides your parents whom you see around town or in public places? (*police officers, checkout cashiers, waitresses*)

2. What are some reasons that these people might have contact with you or tell you what to do? (*you might be buying something from them, need their services*)

3. How can you show respect toward an adult who asks you or tells you to do something? (*do it*)

4. Why should you obey someone who isn't your parent or teacher? (*they might know more about the situation than you, might be an authority figure*)

5. Are there times when you shouldn't listen to an adult? (*if it is a stranger, if the request seems wrong or odd, if it contradicts what your parents have instructed you*)

6. How does it show good manners to be respectful to an older person, especially someone who may not hear well or see well or even understand what's going on? (*older people have earned the right to be respected even though they may not be functioning well, as in the case with nursing home residents or older relatives*)

Activity

Directions: Students are to check the items on the list that are examples of showing respect to an adult in a home or community situation.

Answers: check marks by 2, 3, 5, 8, 10

Follow-up: Discuss the responses, especially how the items that were not checked show disrespect to someone, even if the person is not actually there (the owner of the car, the waitress).

11.14   # Respecting Adults in the Community

Which of these behaviors is showing respect to an adult? Put a check in front of the respectful behaviors.

❑ 1. Laughing at a woman whose hair is slightly blue because of hair rinse

❑ 2. Noticing a man planting flowers in the front of his yard and being careful to walk around them

❑ 3. Being quiet after the people in front of you in the movie theater turn around and ask you and your friends to be quiet

❑ 4. Sticking your tongue out at your mother after she tells you to clean your room and then leaves the room

❑ 5. Crossing the street where the crossing guard tells you to

❑ 6. Leaving a penny on the table at a restaurant for a tip

❑ 7. Putting a glass bottle directly in back of a tire on a car in a parking lot

❑ 8. Staying home to see your aunt and uncle and cousins even though you would rather go out with your friends

❑ 9. Saying "I don't have to listen to you" to your grandfather when he tells you to take an umbrella to school

❑ 10. Holding the door open for your neighbor who is carrying an armful of dry cleaning

Copyright © 2009 by John Wiley & Sons. Inc.

11.15 Answering Questions Appropriately

Objective

The student will identify characters who are answering questions politely and appropriately.

Rationale

Smart-aleck answers are annoying, especially when the intent is to avoid answering the question altogether. There is a time to be funny and get laughs and to give silly answers to possibly obvious questions. When someone, especially an older person or stranger, asks a question, it should be answered directly and politely.

Thinking Questions

1. What are some questions that you get asked at home? (*"Where have you been?" "Do you have any homework?" "Where are you going?"*)

2. When someone asks you a question, what kind of answer do you think you should give? (*the answer to the question*)

3. If someone asks, "Is this book yours?" and you answer, "Shut up," is that answering the question? (*no*)

4. If you said, "Yes, now shut up," is that answering the question? (*yes, but not very politely*)

5. What could be changed to make that answer more appropriate? (*leave off the "shut up"*)

6. If someone asks you a question while you are busy or thinking about something else, how could you still answer the question or person politely? (*explain that you are busy, ask the person to come back later, tell him or her that you need more time to think about it*)

Activity

Directions: Students are to read the cartoons on the worksheet and decide whether the person answering the question was polite and appropriate. They are to write YES or NO in the boxes.

Answers: 1. no   2. yes   3. yes   4. no   5. no   6. yes

Follow-up: Discuss why the characters who did not respond appropriately were impolite or did not accurately answer the question. Was the girl in number 1 paying attention to the question at all? (*based on the condition of her room, it would seem that she wasn't listening very well!*)

11.15   # Answering Questions Appropriately

Is the person in the cartoon answering the question appropriately? Write YES or NO in the box.

Copyright © 2009 by John Wiley & Sons, Inc.

11.16 Using Good Language

Objective

The student will identify or supply appropriate words to convey displeasure or excitement as an alternative to crude or vulgar comments.

Rationale

It has become sadly commonplace for people to use vulgar words, curses, or swear words without giving them a second thought. In most settings, these words and this type of language would be extremely offensive. Unfortunately, people pick up this type of language easily, and often from those at home. In this lesson, students will examine situations in which it may be tempting to use expletives or other "bad" language, but for which other words can convey the thoughts and feelings less offensively.

Thinking Questions

1. Have you ever heard anyone say, "Use good language"? *(yes)* What does that mean? *("Choose different words," "Don't say that," "Don't swear")*

2. Some people use words that are vulgar or offensive or words that are not appropriate for the time and place. Why do you think this would show bad manners? *(other people might not want to hear those words, they would find them offensive, shows disrespect if you know that and use them anyway)*

3. Why do you think some people swear or curse? *(they are angry, want to get attention, think it makes them sound tough and grown-up)*

4. Why aren't those words appropriate for being in public? *(they are offensive to other people, impolite)*

5. Some words make fun of racial or ethnic or other groups of people. How could these words hurt someone else? *(make the other person feel apart from the group, not respected, ridiculed, want to retaliate)*

6. Sometimes you might be in a situation where you can't help but listen to offensive language, such as at the movies. What are some ways to not make a big deal about the words? *(don't repeat them, don't get silly about it, recognize the words as offensive but don't start using them)*

Activity

Directions: Students are to fill in comments that they could say in each situation without using bad or offensive language.

Answer examples: 1. OWWWWW!   2. No, thank you.   3. Bad dog!   4. Oh no! Quick! I need a sponge!

Follow-up: Have students share their ideas for the worksheet characters' comments. What ideas do students have for expressing their anger or frustration besides using words?

Using Good Language

Write down what you could say in each of the following situations to express yourself using good language.

1. Hitting your hand with a hammer.

   _____

   _____

   _____

   _____

2. Looking at food you don't like.

   _____

   _____

   _____

   _____

3. Finding out that your dog ripped up your favorite poster.

   _____

   _____

   _____

   _____

4. Knocking over a glass of red soda on your mom's new carpet.

   _____

   _____

   _____

   _____

Copyright © 2009 by John Wiley & Sons, Inc.

11.17 Tattling

Objective

The student will recognize a tattling comment, and state a reason that it is tattling.

Rationale

It would be interesting to count how many instances of tattling occur in a single day. Perhaps students feel the need to report minor annoyances to feel important, to watch someone else get into trouble, or possibly because they cannot distinguish between useful information and trivial annoyances. Tattling (1) involves another person, (2) is intended to get someone in trouble or point out something negative, and (3) gives information that is not someone's business.

Thinking Questions

1. What does it mean if someone tattles? *(the person tells the teacher something about what someone else is doing)*
2. Is tattling helpful? *(no, it is usually to get someone in trouble)*
3. If someone tells me that the toilet is overflowing in the boys' bathroom, is that tattling? *(no)* Why or why not? *(it is helpful information; no one is named)*
4. If someone tells me that Boy X stuck his tongue out at Boy Z, is that tattling? *(yes; telling something to get someone else in trouble)*
5. Is it tattling if someone says that Girl Q is playing with matches on the playground? *(no; she is doing something dangerous)*
6. How can we decide if something is tattling or if it is important? *(think about how it involves other people, if it is positive or negative, or if it is not your business; if any of these factors are questionable, it is probably tattling)*

Activity

Directions: Put an OK in front of the comments that are not tattling. Put a check mark in front of the comments that are tattling. Then give at least one of the following reasons that it is tattling: 1 = involves another person; 2 = is intended to stir up trouble; 3 = not your business.

Answers: 1. OK; gives useful information   2. check mark; reasons 1, 3   3. OK; danger is involved 4. check mark; reasons 1, 2   5. check mark; reasons 1, 2, 3   6. OK; just a comment

Follow-up: Discuss why numbers 1, 3, and 6 are not tattling. Discuss what could or should be done in numbers 2, 4, and 5. Should the behavior be addressed or ignored?

11.17   **Tattling**

Put an OK in front of the comments that are not tattling. Put a check mark in front of the comments that are tattling, and write down the number of at least one reason that it is tattling.

1 = involves another person   2 = intended to stir up trouble   3 = not your business

_____ 1. "Teacher, the playground ladies said to send out only two basketballs for recess."

_____ 2. "Teacher, Mark had to stand by the wall in music class because he was goofing around."

_____ 3. "Teacher, there is a big black dog running on the playground by the swings."

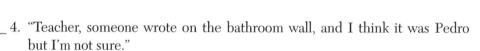

_____ 4. "Teacher, someone wrote on the bathroom wall, and I think it was Pedro but I'm not sure."

_____ 5. "Teacher, you told us to close our books, but Sarah still has hers open."

_____ 6. "Teacher, I think Mandi looks nice today."

Copyright © 2009 by John Wiley & Sons, Inc.

11.18 Thank-You Notes

Objective

The student will identify situations for which a thank-you note is appropriate.

Rationale

It isn't necessary to send written thank-you notes for many occasions, but it is a thoughtful gesture to thank someone who has spent money on you, sent a gift, or taken the time to do something special for you. Children who can be taught to send a thank-you note as a matter of course for such things will be highly esteemed by others. In this lesson, examples for such occasions are presented for discussion.

Thinking Questions

1. What is the nicest thing someone has ever done for you or given you? *(ask for examples)*
2. How did you let that person know you appreciated what he or she did for you? *(thanked them, reciprocated)*
3. What is the purpose of a thank-you note? *(to show your appreciation)*
4. How is writing a thank-you note to someone different from just telling them "thanks" and leaving it at that? *(it's lasting, takes time to write, shows that you made an effort, really appreciated their gift)*
5. When is it polite to send a written thank-you note to someone? *(if the person lives far away, if someone gave you a gift, if someone did something very special for you)*
6. What else could you say in a note besides just "thank you"? *(tell why you appreciated the gift, tell how you will use it, compliment the giver on what good taste he or she has, pass along any compliments you have received on the gift)*

Activity

Directions: Students are to examine the situations on the worksheet and decide which are good reasons to send a thank-you note to the person. They are then to write the number of the situation on the thank-you note at the bottom of the worksheet.

Answers: 1, 4, 6, 10

Follow-up: Discuss why the selected answers would warrant a thank-you note. What extra effort was shown in number 10?

11.18   **Thank-You Notes**

For which of these situations would you send a thank-you note to someone? Write the *numbers* in the thank-you note at the bottom of this worksheet.

1. A birthday gift from Aunt Zelda.

2. Someone lends you a pencil at school.

3. A friend lends you a dollar.

4. A friend's family invites you to spend a week at their lake cottage.

5. A friend's older brother takes you to the movies.

6. Your grandmother gives you fifty dollars for Christmas.

7. You go to a cookout at your neighbor's house.

8. You spend the night at your best friend's house.

9. Your sister gives you an old sweater that's too small for her.

10. A friend's dad takes you to a baseball game, buys you dinner at a very expensive restaurant, and then takes you to meet the players and get their autographs and pictures.

Copyright © 2009 by John Wiley & Sons, Inc.

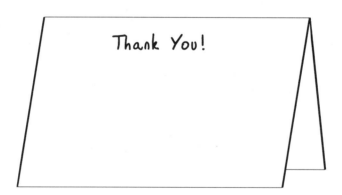

11.19 R.S.V.P.

Objective

The student will identify the abbreviation R.S.V.P. as a request to call the sender of an invitation as to whether he or she can attend the event.

Rationale

The letters R.S.V.P. are from the French expression *répondez s'il vous plaît,* which means "please reply." When an invitation is given, it is common courtesy to let the host know if you can attend, especially if R.S.V.P. is written on the invitation. In some cases, an exact head count is necessary for transporting people to another place, ordering tickets in advance, or getting enough chairs. If the courtesy of a reply is requested, it should be honored.

Thinking Questions

1. Have you ever gotten an invitation to go to something special? What? *(probably a party, picnic, sleepover)*

2. What kind of information is usually given on the invitation? *(who is giving the party, where it will be, times, other details)*

3. What does R.S.V.P. mean on an invitation? *(call the host to say whether you can come or not)*

4. Why do you think the person who sends the invitation wants you to let him or her know if you can come? *(to know how many people to prepare for)*

5. What could happen if twenty people were invited to a pizza party and nobody called to let the host know they were coming? *(they could order too many pizzas, too few, not have enough drinks)*

6. When are you supposed to call the host about the invitation? *(when you know you can or cannot make it, or by the date specified on the invitation)*

Activity

Directions: The student is given a sample invitation with questions about information on the invitation. Answers should be written on the lines below the invitation.

   Answers: 1. Roger and Frank   2. 1 o'clock   3. birthday   4. Monday, July 7   5. Roger   6. 324-5827 7. by Saturday, July 5   8. call to let them know if you can attend

   Follow-up: Have students bring in examples of invitations they or their parents have received. Look for the specific information on each invitation. Discuss how it makes the event clear to the recipient.

11.19   **R.S.V.P.**

Answer the questions below about the invitation that you just received.

It's a Birthday Party!

For: Jason Smith

At: Roger's house – 101 W. Third St.

On: Monday, July 7 From: 1:00 to 3:30

Given By: Roger and Frank

R.S.V.P. to: Roger 324–5827

by: Saturday, July 5

1. Who is giving the party? _____

2. What time does it start? _____

3. What kind of party is it? _____

4. When is the party? _____

5. Who are you supposed to call? _____

6. What is the phone number? _____

7. When are you supposed to let him know if you can come or not?

   _____

8. What does R.S.V.P. mean?

   _____

   _____

Copyright © 2009 by John Wiley & Sons, Inc.

11.20 The Golden Rule

Objective

The student will state the essence of the Golden Rule and identify examples of how people would appreciate being treated.

Rationale

No matter what one's background, religious orientation, or political affiliation is, most people would agree that the principle behind what is commonly called the Golden Rule—do unto others as you would have them do unto you or, in modern terms, treat others how you would like to be treated—reflects a good social attitude. In this final lesson, students are directed to think about how they would like to be treated by others.

Thinking Questions

1. What is meant by the Golden Rule? *(it is a famous principle to live by involving how to treat others)*
2. What are the words to the rule? *(do unto others as you would have them do unto you, treat others as you would like to be treated)*
3. What does it mean? *(just what it says—treat other people the same way you would like to be treated)*
4. Should you treat only others who are just like you—the same age, race, nationality—in this way? *(no, everyone)*
5. What would things be like if everyone treated everyone else with kindness and respect? *(it would be wonderful!)*

Activity

Directions: The student is to draw a happy face or a sad face next to the question to indicate whether he or she would like to be treated in the manner indicated.

Answers: (probably) 1. happy 2. sad 3. happy 4. happy 5. happy 6. sad 7. happy 8. happy

Follow-up: Have students discuss their own particular pet peeves as far as how they would like to be treated by others if it does not appear on the worksheet. What types of problems or disagreements are most common in their social circles? Why doesn't everyone follow the Golden Rule if it is such a good idea?

11.20   **The Golden Rule**

Draw a smiling (happy) face if you would like someone to treat you this way. Draw a frowning (sad) face if you would not like this kind of treatment.

Treat others the way you would like to be treated!

Would you like . . .

1. someone to smile at you if you were frightened in a new place?

2. someone to laugh when you made a mistake?

3. someone to invite you when everyone else in your class was invited to a party or game?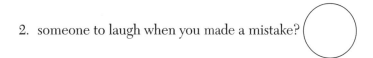

4. someone to help you if you didn't understand something?

5. someone to listen to you if you had a problem and wanted to talk about it?

6. someone to make fun of the way you walk or talk?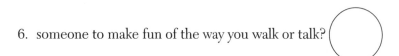

7. someone to forgive and forget if you make a mistake?

8. someone to be your friend at all times, not just when there is no one else around?

Copyright © 2009 by John Wiley & Sons, Inc.

Classroom Tips for Everyday Etiquette

- Have a class party in which guests whom the children don't already know are invited. You could engineer an activity by arranging for another class at a different school to come over to view a play, participate in a kickball tournament, or share artwork. During this time, arrange for students to systematically meet each other and practice their meeting skills.

- Allow children to bring their parents to school to read a story, share a hobby, or answer questions about some area of expertise to the class. (This could be done every Friday afternoon, for example.) Make sure students introduce their parents to the class by giving their names and telling a bit about them.

- Ask all students to have a small box of tissues to keep in their desks during cold season. Use these periods of sneezing and coughing to show students how to keep their germs to themselves.

- Challenge students to say "thank you" ten times in one day to different people. Have them keep track by using tally marks on a small piece of paper. The thank-you must be sincere to count.

- Invite a guest speaker to your class to be interviewed. This could be a person who has an interesting occupation, has traveled recently to another country, or who is willing to be interviewed. Before the speaker arrives, have students compile a list of appropriate questions to help them get to know the guest without being overly inquisitive or asking embarrassing or impolite questions.

- Many comedians get their laughs from mimicking famous people. Allow students to videotape appropriate comics from television and demonstrate why mimicking is funny in these situations. Perhaps you have an aspiring comedian in your class who would like to do some imitations of famous people.

- Get some examples of caricatures, and explain that they are cartoon representations of people with exaggerated features. If you have some good sports for volunteers, have a class artist or the art teacher draw some caricatures featuring celebrities around the school (basketball star with a ball in his hand, someone who likes to swim wearing fins).

- Invite a public official to visit your class to give a brief explanation of how your city or community is run. What public facilities are available in your town? Why is it important for everyone in the community to take pride in how the area looks? How expensive is it for graffiti to be removed? Use this opportunity to ask for suggestions for projects that the class can become involved in for showing community spirit.

- Explain the lining-up procedure for your class, and then take turns having the daily line leader go through the procedure. It can be fun to have the student speak as though he or she is a flight attendant: "Before exiting the room, please be sure to keep all hands inside your personal space. Face forward, allow adequate breathing room, and depart in a calm manner. We hope you have enjoyed your learning experience here and please visit again soon!"

- At Thanksgiving or another occasion, prepare a semiformal meal for the class to assist in and practice good table manners. With parental help, plan a menu, select jobs for the students, list materials and food items needed, and dig out the tablecloths and silverware. (You may wish to invite parents and have them work with their children to bring a table setting.) Practice each of the table manners, and use them during the meal.

- Assign students to create a restaurant by working together in small groups. Each restaurant group can make menus, set up a table for customers, and maybe even make a billboard for advertising. Have volunteer students "dine at" the restaurant, order food from a "waitress," and fill out a comment card. Throughout the entire experience, have these students practice the eating-out skills and have the nonparticipating students evaluate them.

- For an extra-credit assignment, have students sit in a public place such as a mall or supermarket and count how many people they see walking and talking on a cell phone at the same time. What conclusions do they draw?

- Bring in a local newspaper, and use it to talk to students about some of the adults in their community. Noteworthy adults might include the town librarian, a family doctor, the high school football coach, the mayor, and anyone else who might be well known in the community. If possible, invite one in for a visit.

- Explain the difference between rhetorical questions that expect no response and legitimate questions that do. Collect examples of rhetorical questions (for example, "Isn't this a nice day?" "What is the world coming to?").

- Designate a class term to express frustration, such as "oh, fudge" or "jumping jelly beans," or something equally absurd and funny.

- If you are plagued by tattling, make a "Sorry, It's Tattling" sign on a popsicle stick and hold it up when a student comes to tattle on someone. Give the child no further attention.

- Send a class thank-you note to guest speakers, parents who have sent treats or helped on field trips, and other individuals who have done something for the class. Involve all students by including signatures and brief comments on a single card.

- Have students bring in or fill out samples of invitations to events or parties, including the R.S.V.P. Students may enjoy designing invitations to attend their penthouse on the moon, breakfast with the pro football team of your region, or cruise to Europe. They can let their imaginations go!

- Design a class pin that will stand for the Golden Rule. Spray-paint the item with gold paint, and attach pins so students can wear the pin. When students have indicated that they will agree to abide by the rule, have a small ceremony in which the pins are put into place and worn for a week or two (or longer if interest is there). Remind students often what the pin stands for.